SADTU and the Struggle for Professional Unionism

SADTU and the Struggle for Professional Unionism

Edited by
Michael Cross, Logan Govender and Ahmed Essop

UNIVERSITY OF KwaZulu-Natal Press

Published in 2023 by University of KwaZulu-Natal Press
Private Bag X01
Scottsville, 3201
Pietermaritzburg
South Africa
Email: books@ukzn.ac.za
Website: www.ukznpress.co.za

© 2023 South African Democratic Teachers' Union

All rights reserved. No part of this publication may be reproduced or transmitted in any form or by electrical or mechanical means, including information storage and retrieval systems, without prior permission in writing from the publishers.

ISBN: 978 1 86914 522 4
eISBN: 978 1 86914 523 1

Managing editor: Sally Hines
Editor: Lisa Compton
Typesetter: Susan Elliott
Proofreader: Catherine Munro
Indexer: Christopher Merrett
Cover designer: Marise Bauer, M Design

Printed and bound in South Africa by Pinetown Printers

This book is dedicated to the memory of Michael Cross and Samuel Fenyane, intellectual activists in the struggle for social justice in education.

Contents

Preface and Acknowledgements	ix
Abbreviations	xi
Contributors	xv

Introduction   1
    Logan Govender and Michael Cross

1. SADTU and the Origins of Professional Unionism, 1976–1995   27
    Ihron Rensburg

2. The Influence of COSATU on the Evolution and Development of SADTU: An Insider's Perspective   69
    Khetsi Lehoko

3. Teacher Unions and Policy-Making in South Africa: Exclusion, Contestation and Collaboration   85
    Logan Govender and Michael Cross

4. Organisational Development and Efficiency: Key Ingredients for Professional Unionism   117
    Logan Govender

5. Dilemmas of Unionism and Professionalism in the Promotion of Teacher Accountability   157
    Michael Cross and Sibonokuhle Ndlovu

6. Leaders, Leadership and Change in SADTU   183
    Michael Cross and David Matsepe

7. SADTU's Future Role in the South African Education   215
   Landscape
      Ahmed Essop

Conclusion   235
   Michael Cross and Logan Govender

Index   243

Preface and Acknowledgements

This book has been long in the making. It is the outcome of conversations between Michael Cross and Samuel Fenyane, a former research officer at SADTU, and one of Michael's doctoral students. Sadly, both Michael and Samuel have left these earthly shores; Samuel in 2015 soon after initiating the project and Michael in 2021 as the final editing and revision process began. This book would not have seen the light of day had it not been for Michael's single-minded pursuit to see it through to completion. Its publication is a fitting tribute to Michael and Samuel's commitment to deepening our understanding of the complex world that is occupied by teachers, their unions and policy-makers. We hope the book contributes towards building a quality education system in South Africa and beyond.

Many people have contributed to the completion of this book. We would like to thank SADTU for supporting the project, specifically facilitating access to the organisation's archives, and we appreciate the availability of SADTU staff, members and leadership for interviews and participation at the writing retreats in the preparation of the book. Our appreciation also goes out to the book's initial copy-editor, Leatitia Romero; the publishing team at UKZN Press, particularly Debra Primo, Sally Hines; and freelance editor Lisa Compton for her insightful attention to relevant details. And, last but not least, we are grateful to our colleagues at the Ali Mazrui Centre for Higher Education Studies (AMCHES) at the University of Johannesburg, and to the university itself for providing a conducive workspace as well as administrative and logistical assistance.

Logan Govender and Ahmed Essop

Abbreviations

AATO	All Africa Teachers' Organisation
ANC	African National Congress
ATASA	African Teachers' Association of South Africa
CAPS	Curriculum Assessment Policy Statements
CEPD	Centre for Education Policy Development
CODESA	Congress for a Democratic South Africa
COSATU	Congress of South African Trade Unions
COTEP	Committee on Teacher Education Policy
CTPA	Cape Teachers' Professional Association
CTU	Ciskei Teachers' Union
CUSA	Council of Unions of South Africa
DBE	Department of Basic Education
DETU	Democratic Teachers' Union
EDASA	Education for an Aware South Africa
EI	Education International
ELRC	Education Labour Relations Council
EPU	Education Policy Unit
GEAR	Growth, Employment and Redistribution programme
IPET	Implementation Plan for Education and Training
IQMS	Integrated Quality Management System
MDM	Mass Democratic Movement
MTT	Ministerial Task Team

NALEDI	National Labour and Economic Development Institute
NAPTOSA	National Professional Teachers' Organisation of South Africa
NATU	National Teachers' Union
NECC	National Education Crisis Committee (later National Education Coordination Committee)
NECT	National Education Collaboration Trust
NEPI	National Education Policy Investigation
NETC	National Education and Training Council
NETF	National Education and Training Forum
NEUSA	National Educational Union of South Africa
NTUF	National Teacher Unity Forum
OBE	outcomes-based education
PTU	Progressive Teachers' Union
SACE	South African Council for Educators
SACP	South African Communist Party
SACTU	South African Congress of Trade Unions
SADC	Southern African Development Community
SADTU	South African Democratic Teachers' Union
SAOU	Suid-Afrikaanse Onderwysers Unie
SASA	South African Schools Act
SCNPDI	SADTU Curtis Nkondo Professional Development Institute
SGB	school governing body
TASA	Teachers' Association of South Africa
TATA	Transvaal African Teachers' Association
TFC	Teachers' Federal Council
TUC	Teacher Union Collaboration
UDF	United Democratic Front

UTASA	Union of Teachers' Associations of South Africa
WCOTP	World Confederation of Organizations of the Teaching Profession
WECTU	Western Cape Teachers' Union

Contributors

Michael Cross, who, sadly, succumbed to the Covid-19 virus in June 2021, was the founder and Director of the Ali Mazrui Centre for Higher Education Studies at the University of Johannesburg. He served as an education specialist in several national education policy initiatives in South Africa, such as the Governance Task Team of the National Commission on Higher Education and the Technical Committee on Norms and Standards for Educators. He was involved in reviews of a number of programmes across the continent, including the Tertiary Education Linkages Programme (South Africa), the Finnish Aid to Developing Countries (Finland, South Africa, Zambia, Mozambique, Bosnia, Bolivia and Nepal), quality assurance systems for postgraduate programmes in Tanzania and Mozambique, evaluation of the programmes of the Association for African Universities (AAU), and the development of the Strategic Plan for Higher Education in Rwanda. He was awarded teaching and research fellowships at several reputable institutions including Johns Hopkins University in Baltimore, Maryland, and Northwestern University in Evanston, Illinois. The Association for the Development of Education in Africa (ADEA) named him Outstanding Mentor of Educational Researchers in Africa for 2011–12. He was also a co-founder and co-editor of the book series African Higher Education: Developments and Perspectives (Brill/Sense Publishers) and the series on Higher Education Transformation (Sun Press). His most recent books include *Steering Epistemic Access in South African Higher Education* (Latin American Council for Sciences & CODESRIA, 2018) and *Knowledge and Change in African Universities: Volume 1, Current Debates* and *Volume II, Re-imagining the Terrain* (Sense Publishers, 2017).

Ahmed Essop is an independent consultant and Research Associate in higher education policy and planning at the Ali Mazrui Centre for Higher Education Studies at the University of Johannesburg. He has been involved in key policy initiatives linked to the transformation of the higher education system in South Africa, having served as the Chief Executive Officer of the Council on Higher Education (CHE) between 2010 and 2015 and as Chief Director for Higher Education Planning in the former Department of Education between 1997 and 2005. Prior to that, he served in various positions, including Deputy Director and Director at the Centre for Education Policy Development (CEPD), which coordinated the development of the education and training policy of the African National Congress in the 1990s. He holds an honours degree in Sociology from the University of Essex and a master's in International Development Education from Stanford University, Stanford, California. Aside from contributing to the writing of policy and planning documents in higher education, he has published widely in the media on key issues in higher education, including 'South African Universities Shouldn't be Playing the Global Rankings Game' (*The Conversation*, 31 October 2018); 'Decolonisation Debate is a Chance to Rethink the Role of Universities' (*The Conversation*, 16 August 2016); and 'Fees Must Fall – but Not at the Expense of Quality Higher Education' (*The Conversation*, 27 July 2016). He is also the author of two reports on aspects of higher education: *Report on the State of the Arts, Humanities and Social Sciences in South African Universities* (Mellon Foundation, December 2015) and *The Changing Size and Shape of the Higher Education System in South Africa, 2005-2017* (Ali Mazrui Centre for Higher Education Studies, University of Johannesburg, July 2020).

Logan Govender is Senior Lecturer at the Ali Mazrui Centre for Higher Education Studies at the University of Johannesburg. He was previously the Education Thematic Head of Save the Children South Africa, responsible for programming in early childhood development (ECD) and basic education. With more than 25 years' experience in the education sector, he has worked as the Undersecretary of the Teachers' Association of South Africa (TASA); an independent researcher specialising in education policy and development; and Senior Research Manager in the Education and Skills Development programme, Human Sciences Research Council, Pretoria. He earned a PhD in Education Policy and Management from the University of the Witwatersrand and an MA in Applied Linguistics from the University of Illinois–Chicago. He has a number of research-based, peer-reviewed publications to his credit, including several on teacher unions. His most recent publications include *Reimagining Basic Education in South Africa: Lessons from the Eastern Cape*, co-edited with Wendy Ngoma and Anne Mc Lennan (MISTRA and Real African Publishers, 2017), and an article co-authored with Michael Cross, 'Researching Students' Epistemic Access under Covid-19: Epistemological and Methodological Challenges' (*Critical Studies in Teaching and Learning* 10(1): 1–22 [2022]).

Khetsi Lehoko's professional career spans the education and trade union sectors. He began as a teacher in the East Rand, having completed a Primary Teachers' Certificate in 1992. He has also worked in the adult literacy and community education fields for non-governmental organisations, notably the National Literacy Cooperation (NLC) and the SACHED Trust. He joined South Africa's Department of Education in 1995 as Chief Director of Vocational and Technical Education, Adult Basic Education and Technology Enhanced Learning, and rose to the position of Deputy Director General of Quality Assurance, Further Education and Training and the Senior Certificate Examination. His trade union career included membership of the Transvaal United African Teachers' Association (TUATA), organiser for the Metal and Allied Workers' Union (1987–91), and National Education Secretary of the Congress of South African Trade Unions (COSATU). In the last capacity, he was a member of the delegation led by COSATU to the Teacher Unity Conference convened by the South African Congress of Trade Unions (SACTU) in April 1988 in Harare, Zimbabwe. He served as a member of the COSATU-led facilitating committee of the National Teacher Unity Forum (NTUF), which led to the formation of SADTU. He earned a master's degree in Education at the University of Manchester and a post-graduate diploma in School Improvement at the

University of Nottingham. Sadly, Khetsi, who was a doctoral candidate at the Ali Mazrui Centre for Higher Education Studies, was awarded his PhD in absentia, as he passed away soon after submitting his doctoral thesis in early 2020.

David Matsepe is Head of Research at the South African Democratic Teachers' Union (SADTU) and a Research Associate at the University of Johannesburg. He is the founder and Chief Editor of the journal of the South African Democratic Teachers' Union and serves as editorial board member for the *Journal of Educational Studies*, University of Venda. He holds membership in several professional organisations, including the Comparative and International Education Society (CIES), the South African Education Research Association (SAERA), the Research Committees of Education International (EI), and the Southern African Teachers' Organisation (SATO). He has several peer-reviewed publications to his credit, of which the most recent are D. Matsepe and M. Maluleke, 'The Role of Contexts in the Construction of Academic Identity in Selected South African Universities' (*International Journal of Criminology and Sociology* 10: 1509-14 [2021]), and D. Matsepe, M. Maluleke and M. Cross, 'Negotiating Successful Academic Careers in South African Higher Education Institutions' (*Gender and Behaviour* 18(4): 17022-33 [2020]).

Sibonokuhle Ndlovu is a postdoctoral research fellow at the Ali Mazrui Centre for Higher Education Studies at the University of Johannesburg. She is a recipient of the National Research Foundation Innovation Postdoctoral Fellowship, and the author of several publications on disability issues and the inclusion of students with disabilities in South African higher education. She is co-editor of two books, the first one with Phefumula Nyoni, titled *Social, Educational, and Cultural Perspectives of Disabilities in the Global South* (IGI Global, 2021), and the second, with Michael Cross, Caroline Long and Phefumula Nyoni, titled *Transformative Curricular, Pedagogies and Epistemologies: Teaching and Learning in Diverse Higher Education Contexts* (Brill, 2021). Her work is grounded on a strong diversity inclusion and social justice agenda.

Ihron Rensburg is (Interim) Ombud of the University of Cape Town; Chairperson of the UNESCO South Africa National Commission; Chairperson of the Ministerial Committee on the Review of the Higher Education, Science and Technology Landscape; Senior Advisor to the Principal, Life Fellow and Visiting Professor at King's College London; Honorary Professor at Nelson Mandela University; and an independent non-executive director of the ABSA Group. He has served as Administrator of Vaal University of Technology (2019-21), founding Vice Chancellor of the University of Johannesburg (2006-17) and Executive Committee member of Universitas 21 (U21). He was Commissioner of South Africa's first National Planning Commission (2001-5). Shortly after the end of apartheid, he was Deputy Director General of South Africa's Department of Education (1995-2001), prior to which he was General Secretary of the National Education Crisis Committee (1986-92). His recent publications are *Serving Higher Purposes: University Mergers in Post-Apartheid South Africa* (African Sun Media, 2020) and, with Shireen Motala and Michael Cross, *Transforming Universities in South Africa: Pathways to Higher Education Reform* (Brill/Sense Publishers, 2020).

Introduction

LOGAN GOVENDER AND MICHAEL CROSS

The birth of the South African Democratic Teachers' Union (SADTU) in 1990 was not just a landmark on the education landscape, but also reflected the transition dynamics of a historically divided nation moving towards a democratic political dispensation. SADTU was thus born in the throes of struggle. While the union is still seen as a product of the democratic struggle in South Africa, its post-apartheid role in education, together with that of other teacher unions, has become the centre of intense debate. As a result, SADTU today occupies a split image in the eyes of the South African public. This book explores how and why this has come about. More importantly, it attempts to reimagine the future of education in South Africa and SADTU's relevance therein.

In a global context in which education quality is constantly under scrutiny, teacher unions are often perceived to be at the centre of the downward spiral in education provision because of their propensity to engage in disruptive actions. Linda Chisholm (2019: 173), for example, observes that teacher unions are viewed 'as responsible for the poverty of learning outcomes and multitude of ills in South Africa's schooling system'. In particular, as the largest teachers' union, SADTU is frequently criticised for failing to prioritise the rights of learners and for being too 'political' in its orientation and practice. SADTU is accused of failing to transform from a classic trade union formation to a professional union capable of confronting post-liberation education challenges. A major part of the debate revolves around teacher professionalism and accountability, linked to teachers' roles in enhancing education quality. Critics refer to an earlier era when teaching was regarded as a noble calling, and teachers' dedication to the profession was unquestioned. What is often missing from the discussion is an examination of the factors underlying the seeming failure of teachers and their unions to deliver on what should be an essential part of their core business – namely, the practice and promotion of effective teaching and learning. In particular, there is a lack of understanding of the notions of 'professionalism' and 'unionism' as dynamic concepts, with various meanings and associations attached to them in different historical contexts and periods. Moreover, the ambiguous and politically charged character of teacher union-state relations globally is not always fully appreciated.

Understanding teacher union-state relations and how these impact on the work of teachers is critical to any reading of the history and role of teacher unions. As scholars in many parts of the world have shown (see, for example, Ginsburg et al. 1995; Govender 2015), while teacher unions cooperate with the state in the policy-making arena, they also resist state attempts to regulate their work and may invoke the notion of professionalism as a self-defence mechanism to protect their status as members of a professional class. Simultaneously, teacher unions may invoke their unionist identity in defence against state capture or co-optation, thereby asserting their independence in the policy arena (Govender 2008). In SADTU's case, its political alignment through its affiliation to the Congress of South African Trade Unions (COSATU) with the Tripartite Alliance led by the African National Congress (ANC) – the governing party – and including the South African Communist Party (SACP), has raised questions about the union's priorities and commitment to improving the quality of education. This is especially relevant in a country perceived to be experiencing an education crisis. Further, SADTU's affiliation to COSATU has fuelled questions around teachers' claims to professionalism by proponents who argue the incompatibility of unionism with professionalism. In this context, recent investigations and research relating to undue union influence, especially by SADTU, are reviewed.

This book traces the emergence and development of SADTU's professional unionism and explores its implications for the role of SADTU among teachers and in the education landscape in South

Africa. It does this by examining SADTU's relationship with the state, focusing on the union's struggle for recognition and its involvement in the education policy arena. Four main questions are posed: What were the context and challenges that confronted SADTU in the process of establishing itself as a professional union? What factors mediated the role of SADTU in the policy arena? What effects did SADTU's involvement in policy processes have on its members, education development and the broader South African society? What have been the main lessons for SADTU in the past 30 years, and what implications do these lessons have for SADTU's future trajectory and education development in the years ahead?

Current dynamics in South Africa's education landscape

South Africa's public education system, in particular its schooling sector, is variously characterised today as being in crisis, underperforming and in need of an overhaul. More than two decades after democracy, many schools still lack basic infrastructure and facilities, such as proper sanitation, libraries and laboratories essential to a conducive teaching and learning environment. According to the national Department of Basic Education (DBE), classroom shortages in 2018 stood at 3 487, with the highest in Gauteng (2 347) due to migration of learners from other provinces; the shortage in relation to laboratories was dire at 80.92 per cent or 19 955 schools; schools with no libraries at 74.22 per cent (14 738 schools); backlog of computer centres at 63.49 per cent (12 589 schools); 6 175 schools with furniture backlogs; and 3 898 schools with pit latrines only (described as unacceptable sanitation), the majority being in the Eastern Cape and KwaZulu-Natal provinces (Mweli 2018). Many of these deficits are to be found in historically disadvantaged schools, particularly those in black townships and the rural areas of former homelands and self-governing states (Mc Lennan 2017). Civil society organisations, such as Amnesty International, suggest that many of the shortcomings 'are in breach of not just the government's international human rights obligations but its own Minimum Norms and Standards for educational facilities', and point out that the government has failed to live up to its commitment 'to ensure that by November 2016 all schools have access to water, sanitation and electricity . . . pit latrines are replaced with safe and adequate sanitation; and schools built from inappropriate materials, such as mud and asbestos, are to be replaced' (Amnesty International 2020: 7). The prevalence of such debilitating conditions in many schools has posed particular challenges for the country's teacher professionalism project, compounded by the adoption of international curriculum, teacher accountability and assessment policies that are ill-suited to conditions in South Africa. At the same time, problems of racial exclusion and language discrimination at historically white schools, reminiscent of the apartheid era, persist. The increasing number of immigrants and refugees seeking access to education has added another layer of complexity to schooling in South Africa. To exacerbate matters, persistent poverty, high levels of crime and violence, and new challenges relating to xenophobia threaten social cohesion and undermine the very edifice of democratic life that the country is striving towards.

Stories of a failing education system in provinces such as KwaZulu-Natal and the Eastern Cape often feature in the media. As highlighted by one newspaper, a majority of schools are still without laboratories, libraries or computer centres, and 'the poorer the province, the greater the shortage in infrastructure, to the point where schools don't even have basic necessities – such as toilets and desks'.[1] Equal Education, a non-governmental organisation (NGO) which has often taken the government to task on delivery failures, undertook a five-year review on the state of education to 2019 that revealed 'critical system failures relating to data collection, the coordination and cooperation of government departments and other stakeholders, as well as severe legislative and policy gaps and implementation barriers'. These shortcomings related to such matters as the Learner Transport Policy and the need for large-scale capacity building across the schooling system for the effective provision of early childhood development (ECD) services (EELC 2019: 5–6). Negative portrayals of schooling, however, belie the reality that many schools produce excellent results; most of these are located in middle-class or rich communities, but several, against all odds, are found in poor communities as well. Nevertheless, it is clear from research that education infrastructure and performance challenges are real (Ngoma, Govender and Mc Lennan 2017).

One of the consequences of continuing inferior public education, whether real or exaggerated, is the growth in the number of affordable independent schools, now a global phenomenon, with parents from across the racial spectrum choosing to send their children to these institutions. From 2000 to 2010, learner enrolment in public schooling grew by only 1.4 per cent, compared to 75.9 per cent growth in independent school enrolments (albeit from a much smaller base). Between 2009 and 2012, 118 295 more learners entered independent schools, with Umalusi's[2] estimate of independent schools placed at 3 500 at the time (CDE 2013). As of 2021, the total number of schools in South Africa was 24 894, the majority being public schools (around 91.3 per cent or 22 740), while the total for independent schools stood at 2 154.[3] Despite the apparent decline in the number of independent schools over the last decade, the overall rise in independent schooling provision since 2010 is, arguably, partly a response to expanding black middle-class aspirations.

Many commentators point to the underachievement of learners – especially in reading and literacy, science and mathematics – as symptomatic of a failing education system. Heleen Hofmeyr (2020) notes that while there have been improvements in reading, South Africa's reading outcomes in the Foundation Phase are still poor. The 2016 Progress in International Reading Literacy Study found that 78 per cent of Grade 4 learners cannot read for meaning. Other commentators stress the challenges of coping with the rigours of independent study faced by students entering higher education institutions (Cross and Atinde 2015). More recently, concern has been raised over the high dropout rate among South African learners (Amnesty International 2020). Of the more than one million children who enter Grade 1 every year, 400 000 (about 40 per cent) will have dropped out before they reach Grade 12 (matric) (Zero Dropout 2019). In this context, policy-makers, academics and think tanks, such as the National Education Collaboration Trust (NECT) and the Mapungubwe Institute for Strategic Reflection (MISTRA), regularly propose solutions to address the situation. Strategies put forward include, among others, teacher professional development programmes; district capacity-building interventions and support for the worst-performing schools; community and parental involvement initiatives; and social cohesion programmes. Given the growth and impact of technological innovation – encapsulated today by the Fourth Industrial Revolution mantra – much emphasis is placed on e-learning, which critics argue is sometimes misplaced when schools still lack basic infrastructure and amenities. Among the many proposals for reform and change initiatives are those that focus on supporting teacher unions and the professionalisation of teachers, such as the NECT's government-business-civil-society collaboration initiative.[4]

In spite of all these efforts, in which teacher unions are heavily engaged, public criticism of teacher unions is at its peak. Media commentators such as Carol Paton have been unequivocal in their criticism that SADTU is an 'obstacle to progress' and 'has the power to block any initiative it perceives as threatening'.[5] Among academics, Jonathan Jansen (2019: 365) asserts that it is 'not only strike action that constrains education in the poorest schools but also criminal activity on the part of the union [SADTU] through the corruption of educator appointments'. Teacher unions thus find themselves at the centre of the tension between pursuing members' rights and meeting their public obligations. SADTU in particular finds itself on the cusp of managing a delicate balance between cooperation and contestation, primarily in its relations with government but also in convincing the public and media of its bona fides.

A note on methodology

This book draws on historical research, beginning with the emergence of the militant teacher unions in the 1980s, the formation of SADTU in 1990 and the organisational challenges it faced soon after its establishment. The second part of the research covers the period from 1994 to the present, when SADTU, as the largest teachers' union in the country, became involved in education policy-making in the democratic era through its participation in statutory bodies, such as the Education Labour Relations Council (ELRC), and other government-teacher union fora. The focus here is on the union's relationship with the education state (the ministry and education departments), and specifically on how the union dealt with challenges relating to alliances, organisational development and policy-making, which links to the book's overarching theme of professional unionism. As such, this book is not a comprehensive history of SADTU, much of which has been covered in the SADTU History Series Part 1[6] (available online) and in other secondary sources cited throughout the book.

The data and evidence for the telling of SADTU's story were drawn from secondary sources, including two of the authors' doctoral theses on the history of teacher unions in South Africa and their participation in policy-making in the 1980s and 1990s (Rensburg 1996 and Govender 2008, respectively), as well as recent research on education policy processes in the post-2000 era. Extensive use was made of documentary evidence from SADTU's archives, as well as interview data representing the many voices of SADTU members and officials. Significantly, as the writing of the book was commissioned by SADTU, the editors and authors had to maintain a fine balance between critique and representation of SADTU's voice. In this regard, we have drawn on Pierre Bourdieu's (1972) notion of 'epistemological break', which cautions against the dangers of reifying common-sense narratives as reflecting objective understanding or true knowledge, thereby ensuring that the lived experiences of SADTU and its members, including their voices, are balanced by intellectual rigour and theorisation of their experiences.

Two writing retreats, held in July 2018 and May 2019, as well as a workshop with the SADTU leadership in August 2019 contributed to reviewing research progress and data triangulation. Drawing on this wealth of information, the book traces the roots of SADTU, focusing on the education upheavals of the 1970s and 1980s which set South Africa on a path of political and educational transformation. In so doing, the book highlights the continuities and discontinuities in teacher trade union developments across two historical periods: from apartheid to democracy. This historical focus is important as it provides the background needed to understand current challenges relating to teacher union-state relations and the education crisis in South Africa.

Overall, the following historical markers of teacher unionism and professionalism developments in South Africa have informed the writing of this book:

- *The colonial legacy that merged with apartheid*: specifically, mission education and the colonial agenda of converting 'natives' to Christianity and 'civilised' people, which set the tone for the emergent teaching profession in South Africa (Vilardo 1996).
- *Teacher radicalisation (1940s–1950s)*: sparked by low salaries and poor conditions of service and fuelled by the emergence of African nationalism and demands for equality and social justice (Hyslop 1999).
- *Return to conservatism (1960s)*: when, with the influence of human capital theory, teachers were construed as technicians, and the role of a 'good teacher' emerged as critical to satisfying the ideological and political goals of apartheid education (Samuels 2008). In this context, teachers were not only forced into acquiescence and loyalty to the apartheid state, but were also drawn towards middle-class and professional aspirations.
- *Teacher politicisation (1980s)*: with the intensification of the political struggle for liberation in the 1980s, several militant teacher unions emerged, stressing the worker identity of teachers and the assertion of teachers' agency (Samuels 2008).
- *The entrenchment of teacher unionism (1990s)*: through the ANC government's recognition of teacher unionism as part of a democratic labour dispensation, thereby guaranteeing teachers' rights as workers. This included the establishment of the ELRC in 1993 and the passing of the Labour Relations Act in 1995.
- *Teacher accountability and policy contestation (2000–present)*: increasingly, teachers are required to take on new responsibilities, reflected in policies such as the Norms and Standards for Educators (2000) and policies which subject teachers to increased performance management and assessment regimes in pursuit of quality education.

Conceptual signposts and themes

Drawing on recent research, we use a number of conceptual markers to locate SADTU's role in education developments in South Africa. These include the contested nature of teacher union-state relations in the policy arena, and teacher professionalism, unionism and accountability debates, which provide the theoretical underpinnings of most chapters. Highlighting these conceptual markers requires an examination of SADTU's operations at three main levels: (i) relations with the state (which can be translated into collaboration, co-optation and resistance/contestation); (ii) relations with the ruling party's political alliance as the mediator of state-civil society relations; and (iii) relations with civil society, particularly other social movements articulating specific or particular interests/aspirations of sections of civil society. Flowing from the vast, although predominantly Northern, literature on these issues, SADTU's activities and policies are viewed through two dominant discourses on teacher professionalism: democratic and managerial professionalism. The changing nature of teachers' identity as workers, professionals or professional workers is also explored. Linked to these conceptual and thematic markers are the ability of teacher unions to resist state co-optation, their agency in the cultivation of policy networks and, ultimately, unions' success in embedding themselves in key organs of the education state. However, as Khetsi Lehoko suggests in Chapter 2 and Logan Govender and Michael Cross describe in Chapter 3, SADTU's close alliance with the ANC governing party and the union's entrenchment in education departments lie at the heart of the controversy around SADTU's role.

In order to deepen understanding of teacher union organisation, mobilisation and development, we also draw on social movement theory and collective action insights. As Ihron Rensburg argues in Chapter 1 on the formation of SADTU, South Africa's dramatic political and cultural change to an open polity and democratic society in the 1990s affected the tactics, programmes, membership recruitment practices and organisational structure of social movement organisations, such as teacher unions. Under apartheid, these organisations had mobilised around militant tactics such as boycotts and civil disobedience against a repressive and authoritarian state. In the context of political opportunity and democracy, however, these organisations began to change their tactics to less disruptive and non-contentious actions, including lobbying for the emerging democratic state and participating in state structures and policy-making. A related construct is social movement unionism, which draws attention to unions' focus beyond members' material interests in order to transform the social and economic structure of society. In this regard, the book interrogates the notion of how SADTU, having historically been aligned with political and civil society organisations in the struggle against apartheid, appears to have lost its way as a social movement union in the current historical conjuncture. The critical question is whether SADTU can reclaim its social movement role and how that is to be achieved, an issue that Ahmed Essop raises in Chapter 7.

We make a distinction between theory without passion and theory rooted in human experience. Borrowing from Basil le Cordeur (1985: 2), theory without passion refers to 'the absence of the human dimension' in narratives with 'an air of unreal lifelessness', or devoid of real-life experiences. Bourdieu (1972) referred to this aspect as 'theoretical theory', or theory which is removed from real-life experience and does not speak to the lives of ordinary people. We want to privilege accounts with sensitivity to the cultural and subjective dimensions of teachers' social life and human agency choices. Bourdieu saw a necessary epistemological break from this analytical practice, an idea we share in this book, and one which has informed both our methodological and theoretical approach. Thus, while recognising the real-life experiences of SADTU and its members, we have been careful to ensure robust theorisation of SADTU's professional unionism journey.

Teacher union-state relations

Teacher unions, even at the best of times, have a contested relationship with the state. While this is a commonly held view, the complexity of this relationship and how it impacts on education provision and delivery are not always understood by members of the public, including parents and the media, which purports to keep the public informed.

For example, it is easy for an emotional public, faced with the prospect of poor education quality, to forget that most teachers are accountable to the state as their largest employer (in spite of a global upsurge towards private schooling provision, though still small in South Africa); teachers also regularly clash with the state to assert their professional independence (McPherson and Raab 1988). Thus, a central feature of teacher union-state relations is its political dimension, illustrated in the experiences of a number of countries, such as the United States, Korea and Mexico, where teacher unions are seen as handmaidens of the state, serving to legitimise decisions of state elites and not the interests of teachers (Ginsburg et al. 1995; Murillo 1999). In Africa, teachers and their unions are often seen as too close to government, a situation that compromises their independence and influence in the policy arena; an example is the Uganda Teachers' Association (UTA) (Tiberondwa 1977). In Malawi, teachers reflect the state's agenda to be a modern state and are expected to advance the state's development and legitimisation project (Fuller 1991, cited in Welmond 1999). In Benin, teachers not only serve as emissaries of the education state apparatus, but they also suffer isolation from other parts of society because of the state's rupturing and deflecting of teachers' political potential (Welmond 1999).

Nevertheless, teacher unions demonstrate considerable agency in their relations with the state – for example, in the cultivation of partisan allies. In particular, political party contacts and influence are seen as crucial in shaping the outcomes of policy-making, as witnessed in Argentina, Mexico and England (Lodge and Blackstone 1985; Murillo 1999). As Marie Murillo (1999) suggests, in Argentina both union leaders and government officials have partisan identities, preferring to deal with their allies rather than with counterparts in the opposition. This is also the case with SADTU leaders and ANC-aligned officials in government, as discussed in this book, notably in Chapter 3. However, teacher unions also cultivate non-partisan alliances to win support for their views. For example, the National Professional Teachers' Organisation of South Africa (NAPTOSA), which was closely allied to the Democratic Party in the 1990s, wooed influential ANC politicians in its bid to shape the outcomes of the South African Schools Act (Govender 2015).

A related notion, state co-optation, reveals that although internal strength and resourcefulness may better place organs of civil society such as teacher unions to challenge the state, the tendency for government-aligned bodies to prosper, and for independent and autonomy-seeking ones to decline, underscores the influence of state and regime on the development of civil society (Gyimah-Boadi 1994: 125). Co-optation in this context means the 'inclusion in the network of state and regime. It also brings greater opportunities to be officially consulted or participate at one level or another in national decision making and other political processes' (Gyimah-Boadi 1994: 127).

In SADTU's case, while the union has benefited from organisational alliances/networks with political parties, policy-makers and partisan allies in civil society, such alliances do not always result in enhancing teacher unions' influence in policy-making (Govender 2008). In like vein, as Rensburg (1996: 176) has shown, leadership transfers to the political and administrative apparatuses of the emerging state to pursue the social project from within the state led to a decline in SADTU's collective action programme. Further, while SADTU may be vulnerable to state co-optation, the nature of its political alliances, particularly its affiliation to COSATU, has made it possible for the union to resist state co-optation. These themes are explored in greater detail in Chapters 1, 3 and 7.

Teacher professionalism
While SADTU emerged as part of the trade union movement in South Africa, it was inevitable that, as a teachers' union, it would have to embrace the notion of professionalism in some form or another. What does it mean to be professional? And what are its implications for a union? The concept of teacher professionalism is a complex one and has remained fluid and dynamic over the years, depending on education change developments and historical context. The growth of SADTU, as this book illustrates, constitutes an interesting, if not entirely unique, case study of teacher professionalism dynamics. In this respect, Chapter 4 by Govender focuses on organisational development and Chapter 5

by Michael Cross and Sibonokuhle Ndlovu engages with dilemmas of teacher professionalism and unionism.

Andy Hargreaves (2000: 156–66) identifies four historical phases in the evolution of teacher professionalism: the pre-professional age, the age of the autonomous professional, the age of the collegial professional, and the post-professional or postmodern age. In the pre-professional age, teaching was seen as managerially demanding but technically simple. One learned to be a teacher through practical apprenticeship. The 'good' teacher was the true teacher who devoted herself to her craft, demonstrated loyalty and gained personal reward through service. In the age of the autonomous professional, starting from the 1960s, the status and standing of teachers in many countries improved significantly in comparison with the pre-professional age. Teacher education became increasingly linked to universities, and teaching became synonymous with a graduate profession. The words 'professional' and 'autonomy' became synonymous, and over time many teachers were granted a measure of trust, material reward, the security of tenure, and professional dignity and discretion in return for satisfying the expectations of the state. In the age of the collegial professional, by the mid to late 1980s, individual teacher autonomy was becoming unsustainable as a way of responding to the increased complexities of schooling. The role of teachers expanded to embrace consultation and collaborative work with colleagues, and professional development became embedded in the life and work of the school. In the post-professional or postmodern professional age, with developments in education and society for the twenty-first century, teacher professionalism was seen to be entering a new era, driven by two forces. First was the emergence of new patterns of international economic organisation in which corporate and commercial power became extensively globalised. Second, the electronic and digital revolution in communications led to immediate, globalised availability of information and entertainment. One possible outcome of these changes and developments, Hargreaves (2000) suggests, is a new, postmodern professionalism that is broader, more flexible and more democratically inclusive of groups outside teaching and their concerns than in previous phases. This study of SADTU's development and the challenges that its members face as teachers resonates with this body of literature to varying degrees.

Despite the changing nature of the concept of professionalism, there is considerable consensus on the main features or attributes of the concept. Michael Sexton (2007) identifies three groups of attributes: the knowledge attributes, the autonomy attributes and the service attributes. These form what Terry Locke (2004) describes as the 'classical triangle' and constitute the traditional conception of professionalism that has characterised teaching in both developed and developing contexts (Govender 2008). However, the notion that teachers may be characterised as professionals in the same way as lawyers and doctors has been questioned with the passage of time. Today, to consider teachers as professionals is to enter into controversy, as there is much debate on whether teachers are indeed professionals, semi-professionals, workers or a combination of these (Bascia 2009; Govender 2015). In the South African context, given evidence questioning teachers' mastery of subject content (Spaull 2013; Taylor 2011), the case to be made for teachers as professionals becomes compromised. Moreover, the localised, context-specific nature of teachers' work makes any generalisation difficult, given the often huge gap between the urban class of professionals and rural teachers (Nelson Mandela Foundation 2005).

As employees of the state (although private employers have become increasingly significant globally), teachers are bound by state policies on the role of schools and teachers. Thus, for many teachers, as agents of the state their professional autonomy is often constrained, and the social status and prestige associated with professionals is undermined. Geoff Whitty (2008, cited in Gamble 2010: 12) notes: 'Most professionals are now employed, or at least regulated by governments. Professional status, therefore, is typically dependent on the sort of bargain an occupation has struck with the state – what is sometimes called its "professional mandate".'

Moreover, according to Hargreaves (2000), postmodern developments are releasing a set of assaults on professionalism in universities, medicine, teaching and elsewhere, whereby market principles increasingly determine government policy choices, such that schools (and other public institutions) are being rationalised, cut back, made more economically efficient, and need to compete with one another for clients. In this view, teachers and their professional organisations are seen as obstacles to, or are compelled to work within, the new trend of marketisation of education. Thus they are being restricted in the scope of their decision-making; coaxed into more temporary contracts; and experiencing a general lowering of status through discourses of derision that hold them responsible for the alleged ills of public or state education. The effect of all this is to return teaching to an amateur, deprofessionalised, almost pre-modern craft, wherein teachers have to deal with centralised curricula and testing regimes that have eroded their classroom autonomy and judgement, and subjected them to systems of administration and performance management through targets, standards and paper trails of monitoring and accountability. The issue of teacher accountability in particular is tackled in Chapter 5, which highlights the effects of teacher assessment regimes on teachers' autonomy in the classroom and their sense of professionalism generally.

Although these developments have been documented primarily in developed economies and Northern countries, similar patterns are discernible in the developing world, including many African countries. In parts of Africa, for instance, the influence of Christian mission education linked to countries' colonial experience has historically shaped teachers' professional identity, especially the notion of the 'good' or 'caring' teacher, dedicated to the needs of learners and communities (Vilardo 1996). This narrative has emerged in South Africa too, especially in the case of SADTU's relations with the education state, where questions over teacher accountability, autonomy, teachers' knowledge and professional status constitute significant areas of contestation. These areas of contestation typically play out in the policy arena and are explored in Chapter 3, specifically around the issues of curriculum and teacher assessment policies.

Teacher unionism and teacher identity
Teachers' identity has also been shaped by the idea of teacher unionism, which has given rise to the notion of teachers as workers. Unionism is

particularly prominent in the South African context and in the case of SADTU. Scholars suggest that unionism tends to prioritise labour (economic) issues, such as salaries and conditions of service, and to favour militant strategies such as strikes (see, for example, Govender 2015). As Anthony Sang (2002) observes, the trade union emphasis concentrates on teachers' economic needs and teacher protection. This focus has given rise to the perception that teacher unions are not sufficiently engaged with the professional dimension of teachers' work, a charge that has been levelled against SADTU over the years and is explored in Chapters 3 and 5. Moreover, teachers' identity has been shaped within the context of their ambiguous class location, which emphasises teachers' association with the working class and/or the middle class based on socio-economic and political factors that can shape teachers' identities and actions at particular historical moments (Hindle and Simpson 1993; Olin-Wright 1979). It is not surprising, therefore, to find teachers describing themselves as having a hybrid identity as 'professional workers' or 'worker professionals'.

Teacher professionalism discourses and revised teacher identities

Many scholars suggest that two dominant but competing discourses are currently shaping teachers' professional identity: managerial and democratic professionalism (Hargreaves and Fullan 2013; Sachs 2001; Whitty 2006), although Andrew Hargreaves and Michael Fullan use the descriptors 'business capital' and 'professional capital'. Given its global currency, managerial professionalism has emerged as the more dominant of the two discourses due to organisational change factors, accountability imperatives for teachers and the drive for more efficient systems. The values underlying managerialism – that management is inherently good, managers should have the autonomy to manage and other groups should accept their autonomy – are regarded as universal and are to be found in state education bureaucracies and schools (Sachs 2001). Echoing this efficiency and management refrain, the business capital approach, based on a market-driven education system, views teaching as technically simple. In this view, technology can replace teachers, and teaching does not require rigorous training or extensive autonomous practice in schools (Hargreaves and Fullan 2013).

Democratic professionalism, on the other hand, is viewed as an alternative to state control and emphasises the building of partnerships between teachers and excluded constituencies, such as students and community groups, on whose behalf decisions have historically been made by the professions or the state (Sachs 2001; Whitty 2006). In similar ways, the notion of 'professional capital' stresses technical knowledge, high levels of education, strong autonomous practice within schools, and continuous improvement over time that is undertaken collaboratively (social capital) and that calls for the development of wise professional judgement (decisional capital) (Hargreaves and Fullan 2013). Democratic professionalism thus seeks to go beyond traditional professionalism, which its critics regard as an outdated, romanticised view of teacher autonomy and self-regulation. In the wake of these competing discourses, according to Judyth Sachs (2001), new models of professional identity for teachers may be discerned – namely, 'entrepreneurial' and 'activist' identities.

The entrepreneurial professional typically identifies with the efficient, responsible and accountable version of service, thus feeding into the current emphasis on teacher accountability systems that utilise performance indicators and inspections for centralised control over teachers' roles (Sachs 2001: 156). Conversely, the activist professional is concerned with broader social and political agendas aimed at confronting the changing nature of teaching and teachers' roles in the era of managerialism and competition. Sachs (2001) suggests that this can be achieved largely through communities of practice, involving teachers, bureaucrats, unions, academics and others in a shared rather than an adversarial endeavour. This is reminiscent of Geoff Whitty and Martin Lawn's notions of 'professional unionism' and 'new realism' (cited in Govender 2015), and informs the collaborative instead of conflictual teacher union-state approach mooted in Chapter 5, as well as Hargreaves's notion of the post-professional or postmodern professional. Thus, what emerges in the literature is that the notion of teachers as professionals is constantly changing, leading to new and evolving forms of teacher professional identities.

A democratic professionalism seeks to demystify professional work and build alliances between teachers and other members of the school workforce, such as teaching assistants and external stakeholders, especially students, parents and members of the wider community. It encourages the development of collaborative cultures with teachers at the core, extending their responsibilities beyond the classroom to include the school, other students, the wider educational system and a broader social agenda. It thus seeks to mend the broken social contract between teachers and the state, their communities and schools, and to give new meaning to teachers' identity as professionals.

While the above discourses and concepts help to illuminate research on professionalism and unionism, their main shortcoming is their evolution in predominantly Western or Northern contexts. In particular, they assume a teacher that is competent and well qualified, which, as noted earlier, may not be entirely applicable to countries such as South Africa, given the historical inequalities in education provision. This limitation notwithstanding, they do provide a useful framework for the purposes of the book. In summary, the following conceptual signposts, historically framed, are used to inform understanding of the policies and actions of SADTU and their impact on the education landscape in South Africa:

- the contested nature of education policy-making in shaping teacher union-state relations;
- diversity of understanding and application of the notions of teacher professionalism and unionism;
- teacher unions' agency in resisting external control, including the notions of partisan alliances and collective action;
- the construct of social movement unionism, with its emphasis on socio-economic transformation;
- the constantly changing nature of teacher identity formation: professional, worker, professional worker, entrepreneurial professional and activist professional; and
- an emerging teacher accountability counterculture.

Chapter outline

Before introducing the various chapters, we give a brief account of what the book sets out to do (and not to do). First, it is not a history of teacher unions in South Africa across different time periods. Instead it examines a particular historical period, the 1980s to the present, which saw the intensification of the struggle against apartheid and the emergence of the militant teacher unions that led to the formation of SADTU, and focuses on SADTU's role in and contribution to the development of the post-apartheid education system. Second, the book is intended for a wide audience, primarily academics, researchers and policy-makers, but also students, parents, teachers and members of teacher unions, many of whom would not have had the opportunity to familiarise themselves with academic writings. Thus, the book's style varies from somewhat academic to journalistic. Third, although the individual chapters are self-standing, they cohere around the theme of professional unionism.

Chapter 1, 'SADTU and the Origins of Professional Unionism, 1976–1995', describes the social and political forces that shaped SADTU's formation from the 1980s and its role in contributing to building the post-apartheid education system. Of particular interest is the development of an alternative and democratic conception of teacher professionalism based on the recognition of the rights of teachers both as workers and as professionals. SADTU's evolution, and its conception of and struggle for professional unionism, are analysed through key shifts in the collective action strategies it pursued to establish (i) a national non-racial teachers' union and a non-racial education system within the context of a racially and ethnically based education system; (ii) a democratic and development-oriented teacher appraisal system within the context of an authoritarian evaluation system; (iii) a culture of politics of teaching that incorporates a commitment to unionism and professionalism; and (iv) a democratic restructuring and rationalisation of apartheid education. The chapter concludes with a reflection on the impact on SADTU of the transition to democracy in the early 1990s, suggesting that the union's role as a social movement union had given way to a narrower unionist focus at the expense of professionalism, which led to SADTU playing a diminished role in contributing to the development of post-apartheid education policy.

In Chapter 2, 'The Influence of COSATU on the Evolution and Development of SADTU: An Insider's Perspective', the late Khetsi Lehoko, a former COSATU national office bearer, provides a unique perspective on the federation's role and its impact on the development of SADTU. The chapter argues that SADTU's prioritisation of unionism instead of professionalism, which was the ideological dividing line between the militant teacher unions and the conservative teacher associations, was in part the result of COSATU's role in facilitating the National Teacher Unity Forum (NTUF) and the subsequent affiliation of SADTU to COSATU. It concludes with the assertion that while there is no gainsaying SADTU's achievements in the field of labour relations, particularly the parity of esteem and status between black and white teachers, SADTU still faces the challenge of simultaneously pursuing professional and policy issues to enhance the quality of schooling and address the material concerns of its members.

Chapter 3, 'Teacher Unions and Policy-making in South Africa: Exclusion, Contestation and Collaboration', examines the role of SADTU in education policy within the general context of teacher unions in the policy arena. The argument pursued in this chapter posits three main claims. First, throughout the apartheid era, teacher organisations were fragmented along racial lines and black teachers were excluded from policy decision-making. Second, with the transition to democracy, there emerged a trend towards professional unionism and increased collaboration among teacher unions; however, SADTU's political alignment with the ANC-led Tripartite Alliance has undermined its independence in the policy arena. And third, since the transition to democracy from the 1990s to the present, teacher unions' participation in policy-making has been characterised by contestation and gradually greater collaboration with education departments. The chapter concludes with the observation that the key policy challenge confronting SADTU is to deepen the professional dimension of its policy work whereby, as the largest teachers' union in the country, it is seen to lead the development of policies that benefit its key beneficiaries, the children of the poor and working class.

Chapter 4, 'Organisational Development and Efficiency: Key Ingredients for Professional Unionism', reviews the progress made by SADTU in meeting organisational growth and development challenges, and specifically the internal and external challenges it faced as it set about building the organisation, recruiting members, setting up branches, and framing its vision, mission and operational procedures. A key question that the chapter explores is whether SADTU's organisational configuration was dynamic and flexible enough to respond to societal changes and challenges, and especially whether it was able to achieve its goals with its current structure and capacity. Unions' competition for membership emerged as a fundamental challenge and is directly related to the quality of services rendered to members. The chapter argues that SADTU's biggest challenge is the development of an organisational blueprint that blends traditional unionism with what might be termed twenty-first-century unionism, giving equal attention to both industrial and professional issues. Further, SADTU needs to accelerate the upgrading of its digital and technological infrastructure to better serve its members and to be able to confront new education-sector challenges being unleashed by the Fourth Industrial Revolution.

Chapter 5, 'Dilemmas of Unionism and Professionalism in the Promotion of Teacher Accountability', assesses the role that SADTU has played in the development of teacher professionalism, teacher professional identity and teacher accountability. It argues that this role has been constrained by SADTU's approach to unionism and professionalism, and that a new strategy is needed. The new approach should be based on the concept of professional unionism, which (i) prioritises the interests of the learner as articulated by government and the public at large; and (ii) recognises that the precondition for the latter requires a cooperative rather than a conflictual relationship between different stakeholders in the education system. The authors propose that professional unionism will contribute to the strengthening of teacher professionalism and teacher identity through shared and collaborative professional development programmes. Professional unionism can also strengthen and enhance the accountability of all stakeholders through an agreed framework clearly identifying the roles and responsibilities of different stakeholders in addressing the challenges that confront the education system, including teachers' conditions of service.

Chapter 6, 'Leaders, Leadership and Change in SADTU', maps out the leadership discourse of SADTU and its leaders, and the lessons and inferences that can be extracted from its experience to inform its future as a professional teachers' union. In so doing, the chapter pays attention to five important dimensions: (i) a systematic approach to the history of SADTU; (ii) the backgrounds and the social and educational context which influenced SADTU's leaders and informed and shaped the nature of their leadership practices; (iii) the changing roles of SADTU leaders within the union and beyond; (iv) the relationship of SADTU leaders to the SADTU membership in particular, and teachers in general, and the impact of this relationship in enhancing and promoting better outcomes, not only for SADTU members, but also for the wider school communities of teachers and learners; and (v) the leadership legacy and the lessons that can be drawn to serve as a source of inspiration for the future of SADTU as a teachers' union. The main argument put forward in the chapter is that as SADTU has evolved as an organisation, it appears to have found it difficult to draw fully on the political energy, organisational discipline, value framework, and adaptability that characterised earlier generations of leaders. The chapter concludes by exhorting SADTU leaders to be more transformational in their leadership approach, assert the union's relative autonomy from external forces, engage in critical introspection and combat the organisation's negative public image.

Chapter 7, 'SADTU's Future Role in the South African Education Landscape', contends that the union's future as a key role player in education is dependent on SADTU reimagining its role and reclaiming its historical promise in contributing to the transformation of the education system. This requires rethinking SADTU's role in and understanding of six key issues: (i) reclaiming its roots as a social movement union; (ii) advocating and campaigning for education transformation; (iii) transcending the unionism versus professionalism divide; (iv) contributing to the development of education policy; (v) redefining its political role in the Tripartite Alliance; and (vi) renewing its leadership and the organisation as a whole. The chapter concludes that for continued relevance, SADTU needs to build and strengthen its alliance with civil society organisations, reset the balance between unionism and professionalism, and redefine its role in the Tripartite Alliance by insisting on its relative autonomy as an organisation.

The Conclusion summarises the main conceptual and methodological insights from the research and proposes priority programmes that both SADTU and other teacher unions should consider if they are to remain relevant in the twenty-first century. Conceptually, the notions of relative autonomy and social movement unionism emerge as critical constructs that can inform teacher union development trajectories in South Africa. However, in the present local and global conjuncture, teacher unions have to help calibrate an education system that is responsive to emerging social, economic and development imperatives. These include, among others, the national reading and literacy crisis; the deepening scourge of gender-based violence and xenophobia; climate-change effects; the Fourth Industrial Revolution; and pandemics. Teacher unionism in the twenty-first century will not only have to straddle the traditional unionism versus professionalism divide, but must also embrace these new challenges and their implications for school curricula and classroom pedagogy. Methodologically, the power of history and historical enquiry serve as an important epistemological lens for our study, while sustaining analytic objectivity in research supported by external partners remains an ongoing challenge.

Notes

1. Chris Gilili, 'The Grim Reality of Education: The Poor Get Poorer Schooling', *Mail & Guardian*, 7 February 2020, https://mg.co.za/education/2020-02-07-the-grim-reality-of-education-the-poor-get-poorer-schooling/ (accessed 5 August 2022).
2. Umalusi is the Council for Quality Assurance in General and Further Education and Training in South Africa.
3. Department of Basic Education, '2021 School Realities', https://www.education.gov.za/Portals/0/Documents/Reports/School%20Realities%202021.pdf?ver=2022-02-07-094832-243 (accessed 5 August 2022).

4. The NECT's Education Collaborative Framework (ECF) is a partnership initiative involving government and social partners aimed at increasing cooperation among stakeholders, including teacher unions, for improving education outcomes in South Africa. Details can be found at https://nect.org.za/publications/nect-and-sector-documents/education-collaboration-framework-document (accessed 5 August 2022).
5. Carol Paton, 'SA Schools under Sadtu Dominion', *Business Day*, 20 January 2016.
6. Vusumuzi 'Vusi' Khumalo and Dineo Skosana, *A History of SADTU – Part 1: An Education Giant is Born*, SADTU, 2014.

References

Amnesty International. 2020. *Broken and Unequal: The State of Education in South Africa*. London: Amnesty International.

Bascia, N. 2009. 'Teachers as Professionals: Salaries, Benefits and Unions'. In *International Handbook of Research on Teachers and Teaching*, edited by L.J. Saha and A.G. Dworkin. New York: Springer.

Bourdieu, P. 1972. *Outline of a Theory of Practice*. Cambridge: Cambridge University Press.

Centre for Development Enterprise (CDE). 2013. 'Affordable Private Schools in South Africa'. https://www.cde.org.za/affordable-private-schools-in-south-africa/ (accessed 12 September 2016).

Chisholm, L. 2019. *Teacher Preparation in South Africa: History, Policy and Future Directions*. Bingley, West Yorkshire: Emerald Publishing.

Cross, M. and V. Atinde. 2015. 'The Pedagogy of the Marginalized: Understanding How Historically Disadvantaged Students Negotiate Their Epistemic Access in a Diverse University Environment'. *Review of Education, Pedagogy, and Cultural Studies* 37(4): 308–25.

Equal Education Law Centre (EELC). 2019. 'A Report on the State of Education: Trends and Issues Characterising the Education Sector over the Last Five Years (2014–2019)'. https://eelawcentre.org.za/wp-content/uploads/a-report-on-the-state-of-education.pdf (accessed 5 August 2022).

Gamble, J. 2010. *Teacher Professionalism: A Literature Review*. Johannesburg: JET Education Services.

Ginsburg, M., S. Kamar, R. Raghu and J. Weaver. 1995. 'Educators and Politics'. In *The Politics of Educators' Work and Lives*, edited by M. Ginsburg. New York: Garland.

Govender, L.V. 2008. 'Teachers' Participation in Policy Making: The Case of the South African Schools Act'. PhD thesis, University of the Witwatersrand, Johannesburg.

———. 2015. 'Teacher Unions' Participation in Policy Making: A South African Case Study'. *Compare* 45(2): 184–205.

Gyimah-Boadi, E. 1994. 'Associational Life, Civil Society, and Democratization in Ghana'. In *Civil Society and the State in Africa*, edited by J.W. Harbeson, D. Rothchild and N. Chazan. London: Lynne Rienner Publishers.

Hargreaves, A. 2000. 'Four Ages of Professionalism and Professional Learning'. *Teachers and Teaching: Theory and Practice* 6(2): 151–82.

Hargreaves, A. and M. Fullan. 2013. 'The Power of Professional Capital'. *Journal of Sustainable Development* 34(3): 36–9.

Hindle, D. and L. Simpson. 1993. 'Teachers Don't Talk in Class! A Class Analysis of Teachers and Their Organization in South Africa'. In *Kenton-at-Broederstroom, 1992: Conference Proceedings*, edited by S. Pendlebury, L. Hudson, Y. Shalem and D. Bensusan. Johannesburg: Education Department, University of the Witwatersrand.

Hofmeyr, H. 2020. 'Revised Results Confirm Large Improvements in South Africa's Reading Outcomes, albeit from a Low Base'. RESEP Policy Brief, February. Department of Economics, University of Stellenbosch.

Hyslop, J. 1999. *The Classroom Struggle: Policy and Resistance in South Africa, 1940–1990*. Pietermaritzburg: University of Natal Press.

Jansen, J.D. 2019. 'Inequality in Education: What is to be Done?' In *South African Schooling: The Enigma of Inequality: A Study of the Present Situation and Future Possibilities*, edited by N. Spaull and J.D. Jansen. Cham, Switzerland: Springer.

Le Cordeur, B.A. 1985. 'The Reconstruction of South African History'. *South African Historical Journal* 17(1): 1–10.

Locke, T. 2004. 'Reshaping Classical Professionalism in the Aftermath of Neo-liberal Reform'. *English in Australia* 139: 113–21.

Lodge, P. and T. Blackstone. 1985. 'Pushing for Equality: The Influence of the Teachers' Unions – the NUT'. In *Policy-making in Education: The Breakdown of Consensus*, edited by I. McNay and J. Ozga. Oxford: Pergamon Press.

Mc Lennan, A. 2017. 'Policy Reform is Not System Change'. In *Reimagining Basic Education in South Africa: Lessons from the Eastern Cape*, edited by W. Ngoma, L. Govender and A. Mc Lennan. Johannesburg: MISTRA and Real African Publishers.

McPherson, A. and C.D. Raab. 1988. *Governing Education: A Sociology of Policy since 1945*. Edinburgh: Edinburgh University Press.

Murillo, M. 1999. 'Recovering Political Dynamics: Teachers' Unions and the Decentralization of Education in Argentina and Mexico'. *Journal of InterAmerican Studies and World Affairs* 41(1): 31–57.

Mweli, H.W. 2018. 'Key Priorities for the Sector'. Presentation made at the 2018 Education Indaba by the Director General of Basic Education, Pretoria. https://documents.pub/document/key-priorities-for-the-sector-elrcorgza-key-priorities-2018-education/ (accessed 6 December 2019).

Nelson Mandela Foundation. 2005. *Emerging Voices: A Report on Education in South African Rural Communities*. Cape Town: HSRC Press.

Ngoma, W., L. Govender and A. Mc Lennan (eds.). 2017. *Reimagining Basic Education in South Africa: Lessons from the Eastern Cape.* Johannesburg: MISTRA and Real African Publishers.

Olin-Wright, E. 1979. *Class Structure and Income Determination.* New York: Academic Press.

Rensburg, I.L. 1996. 'Collective Identity and Public Policy: From Resistance to Reconstruction in South Africa, 1986–1995'. PhD thesis, Stanford University, Stanford, California.

Sachs, J. 2001. 'Teacher Professional Identity: Competing Discourses, Competing Outcomes'. *Journal of Educational Policy* 16(2): 149–61.

Samuels, M. 2008. 'Accountability to Whom? For What? Teacher Identity and the Force Field Model of Teacher Development'. *Perspectives in Education* 26(2): 1–16.

Sang, A.K. 2002. 'Interest Groups in Education: Teachers' Perceptions of the Effectiveness of the Kenya National Union of Teachers'. PhD thesis, University of Cape Town.

Sexton, M. 2007. 'Evaluating Teaching as a Profession: Implications of a Research Study for the Work of the Teaching Council'. *Irish Educational Studies* 26(1): 79–105.

Spaull, N. 2013. 'South Africa's Education Crisis: The Quality of Education in South Africa 1994–2011'. Report commissioned by Centre for Development and Enterprise, Johannesburg. https://section27.org.za/wp-content/uploads/2013/10/Spaull-2013-CDE-report-South-Africas-Education-Crisis.pdf (accessed 5 August 2022).

Taylor, N. 2011. 'Priorities for Addressing South Africa's Education and Training Crisis: A Review Commissioned by the National Planning Commission'. Johannesburg: JET Education Services.

Tiberondwa, A.K. 1977. 'Professionalism and Unionism in the Teaching Service: The Development of Teachers' Organizations in Uganda'. *Utafiti* 2(1): 45–56.

Vilardo, P.J. 1996. 'The Many Faces of the Middle Class: African Teachers' Politics in South Africa, 1940–1990'. PhD thesis, Johns Hopkins University, Baltimore, Maryland.

Welmond, M. 1999. 'Teacher Identity in Africa: The Case of the Republic of Benin'. PhD thesis, School of Education, Stanford University, Stanford, California.

Whitty, G. 2006. 'Teacher Professionalism in a New Era'. Paper presented at the first General Teaching Council for Northern Ireland Annual Lecture, Belfast, March. https://www.academia.edu/16638608/Teacher_professionalism_in_a_new_era (accessed 12 September 2016).

Zero Dropout. 2019. *School Dropout: What's the Catch?* Cape Town: DG Murray Trust. https://dgmt.co.za/school-dropout-whats-the-catch-our-new-publication/ (accessed 5 August 2022).

1

SADTU and the Origins of Professional Unionism, 1976–1995

IHRON RENSBURG

The role of teachers and teacher organisations in opposing racial segregation in education in South Africa began in the late nineteenth century with the formation in 1879 of the Native Educational Association representing African teachers. In the 150 years since then, the focus of teacher organisations has shifted back and forth between professionalism and unionism. However, until the 1980s, other than brief periods of militancy linked to bread-and-butter issues such as salaries in the 1940s and opposition to the introduction of Bantu Education in the 1950s, teacher organisations were in the main characterised by a conservative approach linked to teacher professionalism. This changed in the 1980s with the emergence and proliferation of locally based militant teacher unions that defined teachers as workers and combined union-related and political issues linked to the growing anti-apartheid movement led by the United Democratic Front (UDF) and the Congress of South African Trade Unions (COSATU). The involvement of the militant teacher unions in the mass struggle against apartheid laid the platform for a deep-seated change in the politics of teaching, teacher mobilisation, collective action and organisation (Govender and Fataar 2015), which led to the formation of SADTU in 1990. Until then, collective action and the mobilisation of teachers had been limited by both the nature of their leadership – mainly conservative, non-aggressive and collaborating with the apartheid state – and the power of the apartheid state that placed heavy sanctions and disincentives on the politicisation of the teaching profession.

This chapter traces the emergence and evolution of SADTU against this protracted historical background. It highlights the evolution of SADTU through the first half of the 1990s, foregrounding sources and directions of change in organisational identity. This is done with the broader aim of tracing SADTU's struggles towards attaining professional unionism, which embraces both teachers' economic/labour concerns as well as their professional development as educators. The evolving professionalism identity of SADTU is examined through shifts in key organisational collective action frames through which social movements produce meanings, communicate, negotiate and make decisions (Fominaya 2010; Melucci 1994). The key organisational collective action frames studied and analysed include the organisation's pursuit of (i) a non-racial identity and education system within the context of a racially and ethnically based organisational trajectory and education system; (ii) a democratic and development-oriented appraisal process within the context of an authoritarian evaluation system; (iii) a culture of politics of teaching that incorporates a commitment to unionism and professionalism; and (iv) a democratic restructuring and rationalisation of apartheid education. The chapter concludes with a reflection on this early development trajectory of SADTU (1980 – early 1990s) from a social movement identity to an emergent professional union identity.

Theoretical framework

The Introduction to this book lays out the professionalism-unionism framework that underpins SADTU's evolution and development, specifically the broader social and political forces that shaped its formation as part of a social movement concerned with South Africa's liberation, and as a teachers' organisation concerned with the role of teachers in the building of a democratic education system. This chapter explains that framework through a combination of resource mobilisation theories (Edwards and Gillham 2013; Nicholls 2009), institutional theories (Powell and Colyvas 2008; Scott 2008; Suddaby 2010), and social constructivist and collective identity theories (Fominaya 2010; Melucci 1994; Scott 2008).

In particular, this chapter draws on the notion of collective beliefs and the way they are formed and transformed during protests (Klandermans 1993), as was the case with the emergence of education protests in South Africa in the 1970s–1980s. Also relevant is Edwards and Gillham's (2013) recognition of the association of resource mobilisation with a trend towards professionalisation. Further, drawing on Melucci (1994), emphasis is placed on the formation of collective identity, wherein members of the social movement have shared goals as well as shared opinions about the possibilities and limits of collective action. Importantly, however, grassroots organisations, such as teacher unions, do not exist in isolation but are embedded in a multi-organisational field with links to other organisations (Curtis and Zurcher 1973; Klandermans 1993). These links lay the foundation for organisation alliance systems or organisation conflict systems. It is within the context of a community's multi-organisational field that the social construction of protest takes place, grievances are interpreted, means and opportunities defined, opponents appointed, strategies chosen and justified, and outcomes evaluated (Klandermans 1993).

Note on methodology

This chapter draws extensively on the author's doctoral thesis, 'Collective Identity and Public Policy: From Resistance to Reconstruction in South Africa, 1986–1995' (Rensburg 1996), in which the evolution of SADTU was one of four case studies examined. Many of the primary and secondary data sources cited here are drawn from the thesis, with the exception of secondary data sources post-1996. Interviews cited from the dissertation were conducted between February and April 1995 with serving or former office bearers of SADTU, as well as with former office bearers of the National Education Union of South Africa (NEUSA) and the Western Cape Teachers' Union (WECTU), two of the founding member organisations of SADTU. (A list of interviewees is provided at the end of the chapter.) The interviews were conducted on a confidential basis, with the understanding that interviewee identities would not be revealed in the published research.

History and context of SADTU's emergence

SADTU's establishment and evolution need to be understood and located in the context of the (long) historical development of teacher organisations in South Africa. It is beyond the scope of this chapter to provide a detailed history, which can be found elsewhere (for example, Govender 1996; Hartshorne 1992; Hyslop 1986). The brief historical overview outlined below illustrates that the development of teacher unions in South Africa has mirrored broader socio-political challenges, central to which has been the ideological tension between professionalism and unionism (Govender 2004).

The first organisation to represent African teachers was the Native Educational Association established in 1879. By 1921 there were five major African teacher organisations, one in each of the four provinces and one in Transkei. White teacher organisations – under the umbrella of the Federal Council of Teachers' Associations, later to be known as the Teachers' Federal Council (TFC) – were in existence since the 1920s (Govender 1996). Coloured teachers were organised under the Coloured Teachers' Association, known as the Teachers' League of South Africa as far back as 1913 in Cape Town (Zengele 2013), while Indian teachers were organised under the Natal Indian Teachers' Society (NITS) in 1925. As Hyslop (1986) emphasises, African teacher organisations were initially more inclined to adopt 'professional' strategies of meeting with government and seeking legal recourse, rather than adopting militant 'unionist' strategies such as strikes. The same applied to organisations representing white, coloured and Indian teachers (Govender 2008). The situation would change drastically in the early 1940s, when African teachers faced huge economic hardships following the Great Depression of the 1930s. As a result, the Transvaal African Teachers' Association (TATA) launched a major campaign over salaries in 1941 under the leadership of prominent individuals such as David Bopape and A.P. Mda, who were also politically active in the African National Congress (ANC) (Hartshorne 1992). As Hyslop (1990: 95) points out, the campaign, which involved teachers, parents and pupils, 'was one of the few examples in South African history [prior to the 1990s] of teachers organising in a trade-union fashion'. More militancy was to follow when the apartheid government passed the Bantu Education Act in the early 1950s. However, this period of unionist and political militancy was short-lived, as the government reacted with repression and dismissal of TATA leaders, notably Zeph Mothopeng and Es'kia Mphahlele,[1] as well as leaders of the Cape African Teachers' Association (CATA), which had also campaigned against apartheid education (Hyslop 1986).

The crushing of teacher militancy towards the end of the 1950s ushered in a period of teacher conservatism and a focus on professionalism until the early 1980s. Simultaneously, in line with the logic of apartheid, racially based teachers' formations were established in the 1960s, although, as with African teacher organisations, their roots can be traced to the early 1900s, as outlined above. These included the African Teachers' Association of South Africa (ATASA), the Indian Teachers' Association of South Africa (TASA), the coloured Union of Teachers' Associations of South Africa (UTASA) and the white Teachers' Federal Council (TFC). These organisations espoused a traditional 'professional' approach favoured by the apartheid education authorities, relying primarily on strategies of consultation and persuasion while eschewing militant and 'political' action (Hyslop 1990; Govender 1996).

The political and educational quietism of the 1960s and early 1970s was disrupted by the mass uprising in 1976 of students in Soweto against the imposition of Afrikaans as a medium of instruction. In the aftermath of the uprising, many younger teachers in particular became increasingly dissatisfied with the racially based teacher associations' professional approach in dealing with the worsening crisis in education of the period (Hyslop 1990).[2] This dissatisfaction, together with the formation in 1983 of the UDF – a broad anti-apartheid organisation opposed to the new tricameral system of government, which excluded Africans from political decision-making, and the UDF's subsequent campaign against all aspects of apartheid (Seekings 2000) – provided the impetus for the emergence of the militant teacher unions.

In this context a sustained campaign was mounted against apartheid education, in which thousands of teachers participated and with education in black schools coming to a virtual halt. The campaign was led by the National Education Crisis (later Coordinating) Committee

(NECC), which was established in 1985 and affiliated to the UDF (Hyslop 1990: 112). The focus of the NECC and its campaign for 'people's education for people's power' resulted in the development of an alternative vision for a non-racial and democratic education system. At its first National Education Consultative Conference in 1985, the NECC emphasised the central role of teachers in people's education, specifically as agents of change, both for broader educational struggles and in respect of their professional development (Govender 2008). The progressive teacher unions (and, to some extent, ATASA) were key players in the building of this vision (Hyslop 1990: 112). As Govender (1996: 35) observes, 'the gradual influence of the UDF within black communities and renewed student protests during 1980 and especially from 1984 onwards, were to have lasting effects on the future of the teachers' movement', forcing the professional teacher associations, such as ATASA, to rethink their political and social responsibilities in black communities and also giving rise to a new, more militant crop of teacher unions. The newly emergent teacher unions aligned themselves with the struggle for a non-racial, democratic South Africa and ultimately formed the organisational core of SADTU.

Key developments in the 1980s impact on the landscape of teacher organisations

With the emergence of the UDF and the NECC, teacher mobilisation, collective action and organisation, and the politics of teaching underwent dramatic changes in the mid to late 1980s. Five overlapping and interacting developments account for these shifts. The first development was the opposition to apartheid education, as discussed above. In 1979, a militant teacher organisation, NEUSA, emerged, which, despite its later affiliation to the UDF, was seen as a fringe organisation by many teachers and teacher organisations because of its overt political character.[3] It was only with the rise of the NECC that the thrust for people's power was squarely focused on the politics of education.[4] Besides NEUSA, several smaller and militant teacher unions also emerged in the mid-1980s. These were locally based, as reflected in their names: the Mamelodi Teachers' Union (MATU); the Western Cape

Teachers' Union (WECTU); the Democratic Teachers' Union (DETU); Education for an Aware South Africa (EDASA); the East London Progressive Teachers' Union (ELPTU); the Teachers' Action Committee (TAC), which constituted teachers from Soweto who resigned during the 1976 uprising; and the Progressive Teachers' Union (PTU) (Hindle 1991; Kgari-Masondo et al. 2019). In the late 1980s into the early 1990s, a second set of militant teacher organisations emerged, including the Benoni Teachers' Union (BETU), the kwaThema Teachers' Union (KWATU) and the Northern Transvaal Teachers' Union (NOTU) (for more details, see Rensburg 1996). These unions were committed to the democratisation of school organisation and curriculum, and to the organisation of teachers as workers. Generally, their names also included the signifier 'union' to distinguish these organisations from the conservative teacher 'associations', which had traditionally shied away from politics and the organisation of teachers as workers. Some names also included the signifier 'progressive', signalling the organisation's affiliation with the surging movement for people's power and people's education (Rensburg 1996).

The second development was heightened mobilisation of the urban black population in the mid to late 1980s against apartheid political rule and authoritarian organisational practices in schools, universities, teacher training colleges, communities and factories (Alexander 2013). That mobilisation then shifted from an anti-apartheid focus to a push for the establishment of organs of people's power in various institutions. Violent clashes ensued between the apartheid state's security forces and the movement for democracy and people's power. The clashes were in response to apartheid education and rule in schools and institutions alike. This prompted the anti-apartheid movement to shift its attention to building a democratic education system and to restore people's power in education (see, for example, Gardiner 1990). As Scott (2008) observes, external factors often force social movement organisations (SMOs) to undergo institutional change. In this gathering momentum teachers had to do their work of teaching, curriculum planning, school organisation and management. The movement's focus had shifted to the nature of teacher mobilisation, collective action and organisation; the political culture of teaching; and the role of teachers in the realisation of people's power in schools and people's education.[5] Pressure was directed at teachers and their organisations to become part of the growing anti-apartheid movement.

The goal of the movement for people's power and people's education led by the NECC was clear, and teachers were seen as an irreplaceable asset in realising that goal (Kgari-Masondo et al. 2019).[6] An important part of this goal was the establishment of a single united teachers' union, comprising both the established conservative teacher organisations, such as ATASA, and the newly emergent militant unions, such as NEUSA. A united teachers' movement could be formed only by mobilising the efforts and resources of all teacher organisations in order to achieve the aims of people's power in education (following Edwards and Gillham 2013). Conservative teacher organisations that had previously collaborated with the apartheid state in realising Bantu (or 'Native') Education and had shied away from participating in the anti-apartheid political movement had to come together with the militant teacher organisations into a national movement of teachers. In contrast, the militant teacher organisations were openly engaged in political protest, opposed Bantu Education, and professed a non-racial, democratic ethic (Ballard, Habib and Valodia 2006). Thus, a united teacher movement could become the mechanism for realising people's power and people's education. By March 1986, the political movement focused its expansive socio-political project on teachers and their organisations through the conferences and mobilisation of the NECC.

The development of heightened black urban mobilisation influenced the political culture of teaching, teacher mobilisation, and collective action and organisation. The political space opened by the gathering political movement and the interventions of the NECC, while drawing in conservative teacher organisations, delegitimised their ideologies and practices. In other words, the changing political landscape (external factor) delegitimised the beliefs and practices of conservative teacher movements, making way for the formation of more militant teacher organisations (Govender 2012). Social movement organisations (SMOs) do not exist in isolation; they are linked to, and embedded within, a multi-organisational framework or network of organisations. That network may be supportive, giving rise to an alliance system which provides a resource that creates political opportunities (Curtis and Zurcher 1973; Klandermans 1993), or it may be conflictual, which drains resources and restricts political opportunities (Klandermans and Olivier 1995). It follows that the greater the network, the greater the capacity for resource mobilisation. As Nicholls (2009) has argued, networks are important in the efforts of SMOs to mobilise resources for their campaigns and programmes. The movement for people's power and people's education resembled such a network and grew stronger from its impact. The stranglehold of the conservative teacher organisations on teachers was broken, and by the end of the 1980s hundreds of militant township-based and rural teacher organisations emerged. These organisations were fully lined up behind the project of people's power and people's education (Govender 1996).

The third development in the 1970s and 1980s was the teaching profession's new cohort of more radicalised teachers, who were educated amid the mobilisation against apartheid. Thus, a militant politics made its way into the teaching profession.[7] Again, the heightened opposition to apartheid that characterised the political landscape at the time resulted in a militant politics in teaching, changing the nature of the entire movement to a militant and political one. This further pressured the conservative teacher organisations to align themselves with this movement. This state of affairs attests to Suddaby's (2010) discussion of institutional theory, in which he contends that there is no direct relationship between institutionalisation and identity formation of individuals in social movements. On its own, institutional theory fails to take full account of processes of agency and the underlying consciousness of participants, which the new radicalised teachers were able to do.

A fourth development in the mid to late 1980s was the surge of pre-emptive state actions in the education sector. Seeking to increase its loosening grip over black schools, the state launched a counter-attack, resulting in disruption of the activities of the democratic movement (Moll 1991). Educational activities were subjected to political interference on a daily basis;[8] principals were forced to fire teachers or suspend students who 'undermine lawful authority or are the cause of unrest';[9] and new authoritarian systems of panel inspection of teachers were introduced despite strong opposition from teacher organisations.[10] Teachers graduating from 'left-leaning' universities and colleges were threatened with being passed over when seeking appointments as teachers,[11] while teacher organisations that had suspended their participation in state education structures were threatened with deregistration and derecognition.[12] In addition, militant teacher organisations were banned from 'performing any act whatsoever', with executive committee members detained and some charged with contravening the bans imposed on their organisations.[13] General and executive committee meetings of some organisations were banned,[14] teaching posts were frozen, and teachers were transferred in the middle of the academic year for political reasons.[15] These state interventions were generally non-selective and were directed at both the conservative and the militant teacher organisations, prompting retaliatory and defensive campaigns from both sets of organisations. Conservative teacher associations were now drawn closer to communities from which they sought defence, and militant teacher organisations spread in the urban townships, rural villages and Bantustans.

A fifth development in this period included the declining real salaries of teachers and the difficult working conditions under which they had to perform.[16] This added to the rising militancy among the teacher population and provided the political space for the creation of a united teacher movement. Until then, militant and conservative teacher organisations had pursued unity separately. The militant teacher organisations aimed to 'unite, mobilise and politicise all teachers' on their own.[17] The conservative unions sought the creation of a unified body to be founded on the principles of a federalist teacher association within which the member organisations would maintain their own identities, assets and memberships.[18] These two streams of unity talks eventually flowed together and led to the creation of SADTU.

In sum, all five developments laid the foundation for the creation of a united teacher movement that was more political and more militant, without losing sight of teachers' professional obligations. Thus, by the late 1980s, significant momentum towards teacher unity had been achieved on the back of the intensification of the anti-apartheid struggle led by the UDF and NECC, laying the basis for formal deliberations and the influence of another key local actor – namely, COSATU.

Laying the foundation for a unitary, non-racial, democratic, non-sexist teachers' union, 1988–1990

A key factor in South Africa's teacher union formation in the late 1980s was the unity talks backed by the ANC and the World Confederation of Organizations of the Teaching Profession (WCOTP) who sought to unify the conservative and progressive teacher organisations in pursuit of the development of a non-racial, non-sexist and democratic education system. This initiative was taken forward at a conference, held on 4–8 April 1988 in Harare, which brought together the key teacher formations in South Africa and was facilitated by the South African Congress of Trade Unions (SACTU), the All Africa Teachers' Organisation (AATO) and WCOTP in close collaboration with COSATU and the host organisation, the Zimbabwe Teachers' Association (ZIMTA) (Kumalo and Skosana 2014). The aim of the conference was to facilitate unity among teacher unions in South Africa with a view to establishing a single, non-racial teacher organisation. It was attended by representatives from both the conservative teacher associations and the militant teacher unions. Highlighting the key teacher unity challenge, one former SADTU leader emphasised the need to get the progressive teacher unions talking to the established teacher associations, such as ATASA, in pursuit of teacher unity:

> I think that's where the motive for the whole meeting came about. And people just said, look, we just have to get these progressive[s]..talking to ATASA and maybe it was the first step towards this compromised reconciliation that we came up with so, I mean, we were taken up there to Harare; first instance as progressive teacher unions.[19]

Following a week of discussions, the fifteen-point Harare Accord on Teacher Unity was adopted by the participating organisations: UTASA, ATASA, TASA, NECC, NEUSA, WECTU, PTU, DETU, EDASA and the Progressive Teachers' League (PTL) (Bot 1992). Conspicuously absent were the white teacher organisations that operated under the auspices of the TFC (Govender 1996).[20] Six fundamental principles informed this accord:

- that organizations agree on the need for the national unity of teachers;
- that such an organization should be committed to a unitary, non-racial democratic South Africa, and commit itself to be part of the national mass democratic movement (MDM);[21]
- that the organization should protect and promote the rights of teachers *as workers and professionals* [emphasis added];
- that ideology shall not be a precondition for unity;
- that such an organization should commit itself to the realization of the ideals of people's education; and
- that COSATU shall convene the negotiating machinery to pursue the objective of a national, non-racial teachers' organization.[22]

This placed the teacher unity process firmly within the 1980s' thrust of maximum national unity in pursuit of a non-racial democracy, people's power and people's education. In this sense the Harare Accord represented a framework of collective action frames (following Fominaya 2010; Melucci 1994). The teacher unity process, the political culture of teaching, teacher mobilisation, collective action and school organisation were shifted outside of the political and ideological domain of the apartheid state and firmly entrenched within the socio-political project of the Mass Democratic Movement (Moll 1991). Significantly, equal weight was assigned to the rights of teachers as workers and as professionals. In this regard, the role of COSATU as facilitator of unity talks was crucial, as it underscored SADTU's eventual alignment with working-class struggles – but not before intense debate over the question of teachers' class location, as discussed in Chapter 2. It is also important to note that not only did the MDM shape the professional and ideological struggles of teachers, as the UDF did in the 1980s, but it became an important site of their day-to-day struggles where they actively participated even at school level. This active involvement and the ultimate significance of the MDM in shaping teacher unionism is reflected in comments by a female teacher, a former head of school:

> I was aware about politics because as I say that I grew up at KwaMashu, I learnt at KwaMashu. When I came back to work, the struggle was the order of the day at KwaMashu. Eeeh, I was working, when I started working as a teacher, I was staying in those meetings, we called them MDM structures. They were located in some particular schools. At KwaMashu, at night we stayed there in those meetings. It's where we discussed problems confronting the masses, about education and all problems confronting the masses politically. So when I arrived there, I was aware what was happening. Again the same time in '89, if I remember well, we would go and meet at Diakonia [Durban]. I was trying to remind myself who conscientised me.[23]

With COSATU as the facilitating organisation, and with support from international organisations such as WCOTP, the need for a sustainable teacher unity initiative backed by organisational resources was recognised, resulting in routinised and professionalised teacher unification. As social movement theorists such as Bob Edwards and Patrick Gillham (2013) have stressed, the association of resource mobilisation with a trend towards professionalisation – that is, deploying professional staff to pursue organisational goals – constitutes a key dimension in organisation building.

Following the Harare Conference, several ideological and organisational issues were debated in eleven meetings of what became the National Teacher Unity Forum (NTUF). This forum comprised representatives of the conservative teacher associations and militant teacher unions, and engaged in heated debates on five key issues: (i) whether the envisaged national organisation should be a federal or a unitary structure; (ii) whether the organisation should be purely professional in character, or be a trade union, or be reflective of both positions; (iii) the future of the assets and infrastructure of established organisations; (iv) the timetable for the dissolution of organisations; and (v) the nature of proportional representation in terms of the existing organisation.[24]

Fundamental differences over the proposed structure of SADTU, whose official launch was scheduled for October 1990, prompted COSATU to convene a special workshop on 1 September to finalise the constitution of the proposed new organisation. The final constitution resolved matters by defining the nature of the structure as a 'single national teachers' union' in the preamble; declaring as the object of the union both the advancing of collective bargaining rights (clause 6.2) as well as the maintenance of 'high standards of ethical conduct and professional integrity' (clause 6.10) on behalf of its members; and setting out the entitlement of each organisation to representatives on the Interim National Executive Committee (clause 19.2).[25] Clause 6.2 implied that both the labour rights and the professional obligations of teachers would be reflected in the programmes of the new union; clause 6.10 ensured that the leadership would comprise representatives from both the newly established and the already established organisations. Thus, the professional-unionist debate was placed at the heart of the unity process.

A number of conservative teacher associations had already withdrawn from or were less committed to the unity process. Other conservative teacher associations, such as the Transvaal United African Teachers' Association (TUATA) and the Cape Teachers' Professional Association (CTPA), were unhappy with the proposal that the new organisation be a unitary rather than federal one (Bot 1992: 6). They expressed doubts about the resolution of the questions relating to the disposal of organisational assets and were insistent that shares of the leadership be based on audited membership. They knew that it would be difficult for the militant unions to show audited membership since these unions remained unrecognised by the state and had no access to stop-order facilities. Membership audits coupled with non-recognition would have benefited the conservative teacher associations and could have resulted in a conservative leadership elected into SADTU. Resolving the issue of the distribution of resources was critical to the success of a united teachers' formation, as underlined by Walter Nicholls (2009) under the resource mobilisation theory. In 1993, three years after its launch and only after a conflict-ridden recognition campaign, SADTU acquired stop-order facilities and rapidly expanded signed-up membership to 100 000 teachers.[26] Initially, international support of SADTU accounted for a significant portion of organisational resources, but that situation changed once the organisation had obtained recognition and stop-order facilities (Kumalo and Skosana 2014). By 1993, more than 80 per cent of organisational resources were derived from membership fees. SADTU now received international support mainly in the form of management training projects. All of the militant teacher organisations dissolved prior to or soon after the launch of the new organisation, and their members took up direct membership with the new organisation.[27]

As noted above, prior to the launch of SADTU the newly emergent militant teacher unions and some of the more established teacher associations were divided on issues relating to resources and organisational form, as well as on the issues of political alignment and 'unionism versus professionalism' (Govender 2008). Consequently, the unity initiative failed, resulting in the establishment of two major teachers' formations: SADTU and the National Professional Teachers' Organisation of South Africa (NAPTOSA). NAPTOSA was formally launched in August 1991, a year after SADTU's formation. NAPTOSA constituted itself as a federal alliance comprising the racially based conservative teacher organisations that had emerged under apartheid. Among them were ATASA, which enjoyed the recognition of the Department of Education and Training (overseeing black African education), and the TFC, which had the recognition of the Department of Education, House of Assembly (which oversaw white education).[28] As Logan Govender (2008: 327) asserts, 'NAPTOSA had set itself in direct opposition to SADTU – by privileging teacher professionalism, not teacher unionism, and by espousing the principle of political non-alignment, which meant that although its members supported certain political parties, the teachers' federation itself would not be formally allied to a party or movement.'

The establishment of SADTU, merging unionist with professional associations, had broader ramifications at the international level.[29] SADTU leaders held that it was their resolution of the professionalism-unionism debate (elaborated below) that had encouraged the unification of the two dominant international teacher organisations, the WCOTP and the International Federation of Free Teachers' Unions (IFFTU). Until their merger, these organisations espoused separate identities of professionalism and unionism, mirroring the culture of politics of teaching and the dynamics of teacher organisation in South Africa until the establishment of SADTU.

In the sections that follow, SADTU's evolving professional-unionism identity is examined through shifts in several key organisational collective action frames through which social movements realise their goals (Fominaya 2010; Melucci 1994). These include SADTU and the transformation of the politics of teaching, organisation and collective action; non-racialism, recognition and collective bargaining; non-racialism and the campaign for a single school calendar; teacher evaluation, defiance and the transition to democracy; settling the professionalism versus unionism debate; and the four R's: restructuring, rationalisation, retrenchment and remuneration in the context of professional unionism. In essence, the issues that will be highlighted speak to the union's commitment to unionism and professionalism; a non-racial identity and education system within the context of a racially and ethnically based education system; a democratic and development-oriented appraisal system within the context of an authoritarian evaluation system; and a democratic restructuring and rationalisation of apartheid education.

SADTU and the transformation of the politics of teaching, organisation and collective action, 1990–1995

Following SADTU's launch in October 1990, the organisation adopted a radical transformation project and militant strategy to end apartheid education.[30] Transforming the culture of the politics of teaching, teacher mobilisation, collective action and organisation was tackled with even greater energy by the organisation and its largely youthful leadership.[31] The resolution adopted at the launching congress signalled the beginning of a new era in the politics of teacher mobilisation and organisation, including the right of every teacher to be informed, to be politically active and to have freedom of expression. Other resolutions focused on democratically elected parent-teacher-student associations; favourable teacher-to-pupil ratios; the important role of early childhood education; the abolition of the apartheid 'own affairs' education system and its replacement by a single democratic Ministry of Education; implementation of a common school calendar; ending discrimination against female teachers; and official recognition of SADTU by the Ministry of National Education.[32] As can be seen, the footprint of the UDF and the NECC was writ large in SADTU's founding resolutions.

The push of the anti-apartheid movement in the 1980s to one of people's power and people's education dominated the emergence and early development of SADTU (Kumalo and Skosana 2014). This was demonstrated in at least two ways. First, the concern for maximum unity of the oppressed in the struggle against the apartheid state had direct implications for the political culture, mobilisation, collective action and organisation of teachers, as well as the capacity to attain professionalism. Teachers had to be united in a militant movement that would aggressively enter into combat against apartheid education and education departments in order to advance the project of people's power, thus appealing to SADTU's unionist inclinations. Second, the gathering movement for people's power and people's education called for the defiance of apartheid education authorities and the institutionalisation of democratically elected organs of people's power in their stead. That concern for unity and commitment continued into the early development of SADTU. In this regard, SADTU's emerging identity in the early 1990s resonates with Cristina Fominaya's (2010) collective identity theory, specifically in terms of how social movements promote and retain commitment and unity between their members. The stakes had changed from ungovernability and armed insurrection to a negotiated sharing of power, national unity and nation building. This project later dominated the identity of SADTU, particularly with regard to its political alliances (discussed in Chapter 3). Simultaneously, the democratic project breathed new life into professionalism, which helped to revitalise conservative teacher associations that were delegitimised in the 1980s.

SADTU's own organisational identity as a social movement changed through new recruitment strategies, services, and shifts in organisational approaches founded on an ethos of teacher professionalism (Powell and Colyvas 2008; Scott 2008). Thus, the evolution and collective identity of SADTU are closely tied to the organisation's project to transform the political culture of teaching, teacher mobilisation and schooling within a context of striving to professionalise.

Non-racialism, recognition and collective bargaining

As part of the UDF and NECC legacy, SADTU was founded on the principle of non-racialism and was thus committed to the achievement of a non-racial education system. The organisation was determined to change the nature of the political stakes of the education system along with its associated educational practices. In the early 1990s, two interconnected campaign strategies were adopted in the pursuit of non-racialism: a campaign to achieve recognition from the minister of national education as the only teachers' union representing teachers on a non-racial, national basis, to be followed by a national campaign to implement a single, uniform school calendar in all the racially and ethnically based education departments (Rensburg 1996).

The organisation of apartheid education was complex, convoluted and fragmented. South Africa's 1983 constitution distinguished between 'general' and 'own' affairs. African education was a general affair under the responsibility of a white minister. Coloured, white and Indian education was an own affair under the responsibility of racially segregated departments, against which the UDF and other anti-apartheid organisations had campaigned in the 1980s. The Department of National Education (DNE) determined the general policy across all racial groups for formal and informal education. This policy informed the norms and standards for funding education, salaries, conditions of service and teacher registration, as well as norms and standards for the curriculum. There were an additional four racially exclusive ministries alongside the DNE, each of which had control over the education of a designated population group. These were further fragmented with a further ten Bantustan ministries, ultimately resulting in nineteen operating departments under fourteen cabinets, all of which implemented their own negotiations for the appointment of teachers (NEPI 1992).

SADTU sought to confront this racially and ethnically fragmented system.[33] Until then, the conservative teacher associations had received recognition from the racially and ethnically based departments of education, reflecting the apartheid state's favourable disposition towards 'professional' associations and its non-recognition of teacher unions. But SADTU had membership from across these departments and, as a signal of its commitment to a single ministry of education and to non-racialism, it sought recognition from the DNE.[34] However, the attendant difficulties in gaining recognition as a non-racial union from the racially fragmented departments forced SADTU to seek recognition as a staff association.[35] Key among these difficulties was SADTU's realisation that it did not have the necessary resources to collect membership fees, provide membership services and maintain the organisation.

Confronted by this reality, SADTU adopted a multi-pronged strategy.[36] It would negotiate for interim recognition agreements with the various education departments, which would run parallel to the broader process of negotiating the implementation of a single department of education and a national collective bargaining mechanism. The interim agreements would include access to educational sites, stop-order facilities, the right to be consulted on all matters concerning members' interests, clearly defined dispute and grievance procedures, and, critically, that SADTU would be recognised as the collective bargaining representative of its members. SADTU's ability to subsequently access and mobilise resources to implement its strategy for recognition as a professional union was a determining factor in its organisational maturing (see, for example, Edwards and Gillham 2013).

Prompted by the slow responses to its call for negotiations, the organisation launched a national day of action on 8 August 1991 in support of its modified recognition campaign.[37] By the end of the first quarter of 1992, four education departments – the Department of Education and Training, the Department of Education, and the departments responsible for coloured and Indian education – had entered into negotiations on recognition agreements with SADTU.[38] The apartheid state, however, set its own terms for recognition: SADTU had to formulate a code of conduct in which it undertook not to participate in strikes, provide its membership lists to prove its support base, and accept rules of conduct in negotiations with the department.[39]

Unmoved by the state's position and informed by organisational learning from COSATU, SADTU would over the following two years engage in and win collective bargaining rights and the institutionalisation of mediation and conciliation mechanisms for the teaching sector. Moreover, the apartheid state's insistence on a code of conduct, combined with the conservative teacher associations' campaign for professionalism, prompted SADTU to speed up discussions on and adopt its own Teachers' Code of Conduct.[40] Later the organisation also adopted a Bill of Rights for Teachers as well as a document on Disciplinary Procedures. The first draft of the Teachers' Code of Conduct, a cornerstone of professionalism, was presented for discussion at the organisation's First National Congress in 1991 and, together with the Bill of Rights for Teachers and the document on Disciplinary Procedures, was adopted at the organisation's Second National Congress in 1993. In essence, SADTU was giving effect to its obligation to the 'professionalism' dimension in its early struggle to attain professional unionism.

In pursuit of its goal to establish a collective bargaining mechanism for all teachers, an essential union mechanism, SADTU was joined by ideological adversaries UTASA and NAPTOSA in negotiations with the DNE. SADTU's campaign for recognition was also extended to include negotiations on collective bargaining of teachers with those of the broader public sector such as other public sector and health workers.[41] As Cristina Fominaya (2010) asserts, collective action is socially constructed and shaped through interaction. Ultimately, on the back of its campaigns, SADTU, together with other teacher organisations, would succeed in helping draft the Education Labour Relations Act of 1993, which provided for the 'regulation of labour relations in education, including collective bargaining, the establishment of an Education Labour Relations Council, the registration of certain organisations in the teaching profession, their admission to the said Council, and the prevention and settlement of disputes'.[42] This was a significant early step in SADTU's struggle towards professional unionism.

The preceding account illustrates how SADTU's struggles for a non-racial education system and society came to life in its campaign for recognition as a non-racial teachers' union (Amoako 2014). The account of that event cycle also shows how organisational social projects become revised, partly influenced by dominant exogenous organisational determinants – here the organisation of apartheid education into a system of racially and ethnically based departments – and partly influenced by the need to maintain organisation and to recruit and defend members' interests through the institutionalisation of collective bargaining rights and mediation and conciliation mechanisms for the teaching profession (Rensburg 1996). The account also illustrates how new policy questions arose as an organisational strategy and, in turn, how organisational programs and identity were revised. The pursuit of a collective bargaining mechanism for all teachers and the goal of combining all public servants' negotiations into a single mechanism reflect the shift from an initial sole concern for organisational recognition to an understanding of SADTU's place within the wider public service. At the same time, the adoption of the Teachers' Code of Conduct, the Bill of Rights for Teachers and the Disciplinary Procedures document brought SADTU in line with some of the requirements imposed by the apartheid state. These measures, combined with negotiations with the apartheid state, facilitated the routinisation and increasing professionalisation of SADTU (Rensburg 1996).

Non-racialism and the campaign for a single school calendar

SADTU's campaign to implement a single school calendar in all education departments as a first step towards the creation of a single education system was announced in the heat and excitement of the organisation's launch in 1990. However, once again SADTU ran headlong into the complex organisation of apartheid education and into bureaucratic and political resistance mounted by the government.[43] SADTU's First National Congress 'mandated the National Executive Committee to pursue the matter of the *Uniform* School Calendar further with education allies "taking into account that the school holidays were Christian orientated" [emphasis added]'.[44] The matter was taken off SADTU's list of short-term objectives, as research results had raised doubts about the feasibility of a single school calendar. This shifted the campaign to one of a uniform calendar with the possibility of a geographic rather than non-racial structure.[45] The dawn of a democratically elected government finally resolved the matter. The Government of National Unity organised the newly created nine provincial education departments into four geographic clusters for purposes of creating a uniform non-racial school calendar.

Thus, the campaign for a common calendar, embedded in a wider social project of the creation of a single education system, reveals how SADTU's organisational strategy in its implementation phase underwent change from a call for a single school calendar to that of a uniform calendar as it confronted exogenous organisational determinants (following Fominaya 2010), shown here to be the organisation of apartheid education and bureaucratic and political resistance. As with SADTU's campaign for recognition as a non-racial teachers' union, the event cycle of the school calendar campaign reveals how existing conditions and relations mediate organisational social constructions.

Teacher evaluation, defiance and the transition to democracy

Implicit in the push for people's power and people's education was the rejection of apartheid authorities. The militant teacher unions were the means through which that socio-political project was carried into the arenas of teaching, teacher mobilisation, collective action, curriculum and schooling (Amoako 2014). For teaching and curriculum, this strategy implied the defiance of the authority of the inspectors and evaluators of teachers, and was formalised by the NTUF at its Bloemfontein meeting on 18–19 August 1990 as follows: 'no classroom visits [may] be done by inspectors or subject advisers for the purpose of evaluation but ... inspectors may visit schools for the completion of certain administrative functions'.[46] That socio-political project was transferred into the emerging identity of SADTU through the continuing collective action of its organisational branches nationwide.[47] Defiance of educational authorities had clear and direct implications for teaching and evaluation. Refusing inspectors and subject advisers access to schools had implications for the evaluation of quality education. Branches of SADTU argued that the prevailing evaluation system was outdated and served political victimisation.[48] Critiques by teachers were wide-ranging and specific and included the following: the prevalence of political bias in the system; unchecked powers wielded by inspectors; victimisation on the basis of organisational affiliations; extended probation periods for new teachers; incompetent inspectors; sexual harassment and discrimination of female candidates for promotion; irrelevant evaluation criteria; the practice of 'one-off' visits which inspectors relied on for appraisal was flawed, as was the arbitrariness of scores given; the process was clouded in secrecy; it was difficult to challenge inspectors' assessments; contextual factors, such as high pupil and teaching loads in black schools, were absent in the appraisal; the process was open to patronage; and 'merit awards' offered as incentives to improve teacher performance were subject to abuse.[49]

The defiance campaign led to disciplinary action being taken against a number of teachers, prompting affected SADTU branches to threaten mass action in their defence (Amoako 2014). The sporadic nature of the campaign continued and took a particularly adversarial tone in the self-governing Bantustans of Venda, Lebowa, Gazankulu and Ciskei, as well as in the Southern Transvaal region of the Department of Education and Training.[50] The nature of the stakes was well summarised by one SADTU leader:

> SADTU has declared a moratorium on inspection until a fair and democratic system of inspection has been found. Such a

system shall be a product of negotiation and intense discussions and consultation with all relevant education components. We accordingly call on our members to continue resisting inspection by undemocratic and witch-hunting inspectors. We also warn the affected bantustans to refrain from harassing and intimidating those of our members who refuse to be inspected.[51]

A forthright approach to the combined policy questions of defiance and evaluation was adopted at SADTU's Second National Congress in 1993. In its resolutions on evaluation, the organisation proposed that there should be joint planning, control and ownership of the process of teacher evaluation/appraisal with the following objectives:

(i) to link teacher evaluation/appraisal to issues such as conditions of service, school governance, etc.; (ii) to deal with immediate issues through the Department of National Education, while putting broader issues on the agenda of the National Education and Training Forum; (iii) to coordinate the activities of various task groups of SADTU dealing with evaluation/appraisal; (iv) to produce interim guidelines on appraisal for distribution to membership; (v) to prepare in whatever way necessary for the discussion with the DNE [on] interim guidelines and long term restructuring of [the] system of evaluation/appraisal; and (vi) to declare a moratorium on evaluation/appraisal pending the outcome of the ongoing negotiations.[52]

SADTU also suggested that the broad principles and guidelines prepared by the Education Policy Unit at the University of the Witwatersrand be used as a basis for developing an alternative system for evaluation/appraisal. These principles were subsequently included in SADTU's 'principles of performance appraisal', which formed the basis upon which the organisation led discussions and negotiations with education departments and other teacher associations.[53]

In this manner, SADTU sought to shape the nature of the stakes and the politics of teacher appraisal by shifting the process from one that was inspector based and bureaucracy oriented to one that was developmentally oriented, participatory, transparent, context dependent and reproducible (Govender, Hoffmann and Sayed 2016). SADTU also sought to move its own trajectory and identity from one dominated by defiance to one in which it provided leadership in the transformation of the actual reality faced by teachers. That is, it sought to refocus teachers on professional policy matters, notably teacher performance, curriculum development, teaching practice, school organisation and management.

Settling the professionalism versus unionism debate

Until the emergence of the NTUF in the late 1980s, the prevailing view of professionalism was shaped by the mainly uncontested domination of the culture of teaching by the apartheid state exercised in various degrees through the several racially and ethnically based education departments. That view of professionalism was a particularly narrow one within which

> teachers were expected to be well-dressed, civil and reasonable, and had to refrain at all times from actions which could lead to confrontation between themselves and their employer ... Teachers were expected to teach under bad conditions in schools, and apply a racist curriculum in class. And when teachers would dare raise their voices against these problems, they would be victimized.[54]

As we have seen, this politically laden professional culture was contested by emergent militant teacher organisations in their identification with the UDF and NECC's calls for an alternative education system.[55] Buoyed by militant mass action in their communities and the push of people's power and people's education, these organisations inserted into the debate the notion of teacher unionism as a counter to a narrow professionalism. For them, initially the weight lay powerfully in favour of the notion of teachers as workers. They were influenced both by their youthful members and by the emergence and eventual dominance of worker mobilisation, organisation and collective action by COSATU and its leadership role in the unification of teachers through the NTUF. The tenacious struggles of the conservative teacher associations – carriers of the narrow notion of professionalism – influenced the emergent perspectives of militant teacher unions.

The response of the conservative teacher associations was significant. They contended that 'professionals' put the child first, while 'unionists' neglect the child to advance their own interests. Remarkable about this counter-strategy was that the conservative teacher associations now took the struggle over meaning(s) to parents, political leaders and the broader community by placing full-page paid advertisements in the print media.[56] This strategy encouraged the unionists to take a comprehensive stand on what was fast becoming a debate that pitted professionalism and professionals against unionism and unionists. The ad hoc, sporadic, militant mass actions of the emergent teacher unions, the NTUF and, later, SADTU – which were dominated by broader political concerns, struggles for organisational recognition, conditions of service, defence of members and salary disputes, all of which contributed to the disruption of schooling – added credibility to the claims of those advocating a narrow professionalism and anti-unionism. In these struggles over meaning(s), the public seemed more receptive to the claims of the conservative teacher unions.

The substantive response of SADTU to this challenge came at its First National Congress in 1991. In a document appropriately titled 'Unionize for Democratic Professionalism', the congress tackled this vital ideological debate and process of meaning construction.[57] SADTU's response asserted that 'the trade union and professionalism aspects [are] two sides of the same coin',[58] and the organisation mounted its own campaign of meaning construction. This response echoes similar arguments made by scholars such as Geoff Whitty and Martin Lawn (cited in Govender 2015) who maintain that teachers can exhibit traits of both professionalism and unionism, without the one undermining the other.

Powerfully influenced by its environment, the dominant social constructions of professionalism, a resurgence of conservative teacher associations and an increasingly hostile public, but also by its history and social project, SADTU worked to shift from favouring unionism to advancing both unionism and professionalism. Thus SADTU was transforming the politics of teaching, teacher mobilisation, collective action and organisation. Collective bargaining was now viewed as the dominant basis for the construction of a relationship with teachers as both educators and employees.[59] Institutional frameworks soon replaced ad hoc talks and consultations that were dominated and determined by the apartheid state. The Education Labour Relations Act and the Education Labour Relations Council became the formal channels for the regulation of conflict, collective bargaining, mediation and conciliation. Even the conservative teacher associations were pulled into the orbit of collective bargaining. As SADTU's collective identity was shaped by its environment, so SADTU shaped that environment, resulting in the successful incorporation of its social change goals and interests in the transformation of the apartheid state, and establishing a professional union ethos that would unravel in all its complexity post-1999 (see subsequent chapters in this book).

The four R's: restructuring, rationalisation, retrenchment and remuneration in the context of professional unionism

As discussed above, SADTU's first two years of existence and identity were dominated by the ideological and policy questions of non-racialism and education, recognition, and professionalism versus unionism. However, the year 1993 saw contestation over four new ideological and policy questions: the unilateral restructuring of education by the apartheid state in its last days; rationalisation of apartheid education; retrenchment of educators; and a salary dispute. Discussions at the SADTU's Second National Congress were dominated by these interlinked questions that now brought the organisation face to face with the politics of macro-education planning and reform as part of the broader struggle to fuse professionalism with unionism.[60]

By the end of 1992, teachers managed by the department responsible for coloured education were informed that 3 200 teachers were 'surplus', prompting SADTU to advise its membership that an additional 8 000 temporary teachers could also lose their jobs. The organisation, together with political allies, threatened retaliatory strike action.[61] Later, it was announced that the same education department also planned to freeze 6 000 teaching posts.[62] Schools in the same department were running without stationery for the first time,[63] and the crisis then spread to the DET, responsible for the education of black pupils, following its retrenchment of teachers.[64] It was clear that the state now found the maintenance of apartheid education unsustainable. These plans and actions were taken without the participation of those concerned or their organisational representatives.

Trouble also began to emerge with negotiations on teacher salaries, which opened in late November 1992. The state had made an initial bid of a 5 per cent salary increase in response to SADTU's call for a 25 per cent increase. However, on 15 January 1993, the state president announced that the government could only afford a 5 per cent increase.[65] A meeting between SADTU and the state president on 15 March failed to resolve the issue and the SADTU membership decided to embark on strike action.

Simultaneously, SADTU demanded that the state halt its unilateral restructuring and rationalisation program; demonstrate practically its intention to stop retrenchments, implementation of former white Model C schools and privatisation of education; and consult with all relevant role players and establish a forum to negotiate interim arrangements for the restructuring of education.[66] A high-level intervention on the eve of the strike by Nelson Mandela, president of the ANC, persuaded the state president to accede to SADTU's demands.[67] After discussions with the DNE, an agreement was reached that the Joint Salary Negotiation Forum would meet within four weeks to attend to the reopening of salary negotiations.[68]

Plans were also made to urgently convene the National Education and Training Forum (NETF), an initiative of the MDM, to discuss rationalisation and retrenchments in the education sector.[69] But trouble erupted within SADTU on the calling off of the salary strike.

Preparations for the strike had already reached a crescendo in a number of branches and regions of the organisation. Mass meetings in which teachers displayed unprecedented militancy, the holding of strike ballots, alliance formation with other teacher organisations and social movement organisations, and the mobilisation of support from students and parents had all been completed.[70] With the strike called off by the organisation's National Executive Committee at the last minute, following the state's commitment to reopen negotiations on the salary increase, disagreements erupted relating to the problems of communication and consultation between head office, regions and branches (Vadi 1993: 75).

Various SADTU branches vowed to continue the strike in defiance of the union's call for the action to be suspended.[71] The state launched its own counteraction against those who had continued with the strike. Money was deducted from teachers' salaries, resulting in teachers retaliating against both SADTU leadership and the state. Some demanded the immediate cancellation of their monthly union subscriptions.[72] School principals were barred from schools, members in one of the largest SADTU branches threatened to withhold promotion reports of pupils from departmental officials, and departmental offices were picketed.[73] The salary negotiations with the state did not materialise, prompting SADTU to re-initiate mobilisation for a national strike.[74] Only in late July 1993 did talks resume between the state and 44 public servants' employee organisations in the Joint Salary Negotiation Forum.[75]

SADTU's Second National Congress in July 1993 was dominated by the leadership's handling of the aborted strike and the failure of the state to meet its obligations. When a social movement organisation is in conflict, there is an opportunity for it to strengthen its group solidarity (Fominaya 2010). This was the case when SADTU abruptly abandoned the strike, resulting in disagreements about communication between head office, regions and branches. As a result, SADTU devised a comprehensive set of demands for the new wage talks with the state. These included (i) an across-the-board increase of 30 per cent 'which could be staggered in order to give lower paid teachers a bigger salary increase than the "highly paid" category'; (ii) housing subsidies to be paid to all teachers; (iii) opposition to increased taxation, which 'will nullify the salary increase'; (iv) 'equal pay for equal work' as a new basis for compensation of teachers; and (v) a thirteenth cheque (service bonus). The congress also set a deadline of 22–23 July for the finalisation of salary negotiations, failing which a national strike would be called.[76] It should be noted that SADTU's confidence in making such huge demands so early in its development would not have been possible without the support of COSATU, the ANC and other alliance partners, which underpinned the social movement collective identity and group solidarity arguments.

With the deadline to conclude salary negotiations approaching, SADTU modified its salary demand to a 15 per cent,[77] and later a 12.5 per cent, salary rise.[78] In return, the state offered 5.6 per cent.[79] In the face of this offer, SADTU committed to a national strike. Accompanied by a large-scale and unprecedented mobilisation of teachers,[80] more than 100 000 of an estimated 280 000 teachers embarked on strike action that included demands for an immediate halt to all unilateral rationalisation and cutback measures, including salaries, retrenchment of human and material resources, and withdrawal of service benefits. With wage talks deadlocked, SADTU accused the state of trying to crush the union with its threats to withdraw the union's recognition agreement.[81] The crippling national teachers' strike[82] ended on 20 August 1993, ten schooldays after it had started, following a bargaining breakthrough with a new state offer to increase salaries. For SADTU, this was a breakthrough. Having forced the state to reopen negotiations, SADTU claimed victory.[83]

The strike by members and supporters of SADTU represented the first successful attempt ever by South African teachers to stage a national strike.[84] Despite intra-organisational differences, especially those that emanated from the aborted strike, SADTU emerged strengthened from these national actions. With the organisation's skilful management of the strike, new membership increased significantly from 60 000 to 90 000 signed-up members. Importantly, the national actions reduced the costs associated with local collective action by teachers. SADTU united teachers across the fragments of apartheid education, making possible a national, non-racial collective action by teachers, including both so-called unionists and professionals. As a result, SADTU's claims to being a professional union were strengthened.

Union leadership and identity in the transition, 1994/1995

Following its successes in the education labour relations arena, SADTU's focus shifted to the country's first democratic elections and their implications for the union. In this regard, SADTU recognised the need to build organisational capacity to contribute effectively to the establishment of a new democratic order and education system. In particular, the union prioritised leadership training, especially in negotiation skills; management training for school principals and heads of departments; and implementation of organisational projects in areas varying from teacher evaluation to curriculum development and training.[85] Attention was directed at improving organisational efficiency, services, recruitment and income generation. New departments for national organisation, education, media, paralegal services, research, accounts and dispatch were created; a resource centre was established; and organisational calendars and a journal dealing with professional issues were added to the organisation's existing newsletter (see Chapter 4 for more details).

With the country's first national elections dawning, SADTU directed its attention to participation in this historic event. Having refrained until then from openly aligning with the ANC, SADTU elected to support the party in its efforts to win the elections. Several organisational leaders were nominated to ANC election lists, prominently within the Department of Education at both national and provincial levels. This development, which saw the organisation release several of its most experienced, skilled and prominent leaders (such as its national president and general secretary) to the political and administrative arms of the new state, opened up a new phase in SADTU's development trajectory.[86]

This development sheds significant light on the dynamics of social movement organisations in transitional societies (see, for example,

Melucci 1994; Snow and Benford 1992). Having campaigned for a long period against apartheid, skilled leaders were needed to continue the transformation process. Yet the effects of leadership haemorrhage on social movement organisations can be devastating. Releasing skilled, experienced and prominent leaders also has implications for wider political-cultural processes, including democratisation, and the relationship between and roles of the emergent state and civil society. Leadership losses have formed a significant part of SADTU's organisational transformation, and subsequently its identity as an organisation. As discussed in later chapters, SADTU's claims to professional unionism would become the subject of intense scrutiny in light of its political alignment policies, and in the context of South Africa's 'education crisis'.

Conclusion

This chapter has traced the roots and evolution of SADTU from its early beginnings as part of the anti-apartheid protests of the 1980s led by the UDF and ANC. It has also illustrated its changing organisational identity and the broader struggles for professionalism that emerged as the sum of its social project, goals, strategies, programs and collective action. Collective identities are interwoven with existing realities. Two aspects are worth highlighting in this regard. First, the complex and racially and ethnically fragmented nature of apartheid education influenced the mobilisation, collective action and organisation of teachers on a non-racial basis in campaigns for non-racial recognition and a single school calendar. Second, shaping SADTU's organisational identity were the prevailing social constructions of professionalism with its roots in the apartheid era and emergent unionism through militant teachers' identification with the broader labour movement led by COSATU and union rights won in the early 1990s.

Demographic shifts in social movement organisations influence the possibilities and opportunities for mobilisation, collective action and organisation, especially when those shifts are accompanied by the rise of dominant political movements and new cultures of politics, mobilisation, collective action and organisation. Changes in the political regime dramatically impacted on the evolution of SADTU's organisational identity through losses of skilled, experienced and prominent leaders to the emergent state's political and administrative apparatuses. Consequently, these factors have influenced the broader struggle for professional unionism, as elaborated in Chapters 4 and 6.

This chapter has also shown how dominant social constructions that frame public policy domains and policies are themselves confronted by emergent, alternative social constructions, as was the case with a conservative reading of professionalism against the broader notion of professional unionism. The establishment of SADTU in 1990, and its subsequent struggles for non-racialism and recognition, embodied this ideological shift. Ultimately, this chapter has shown how a social movement organisation can be a vital participant in the processes of meaning construction, contestation of dominant social constructions, and the transformation of public policy domains and public policy. The emergence of SADTU within the policy domain, especially from 1990 onwards, thus signalled the entry of a critical actor. Of vital importance for transitional societies, as well as for public policy debate and for the success and sustainability of processes of democratisation, is the survival of these social movement organisations, a theme addressed in Chapter 7.

Important theoretical insights can be extracted from the experience of SADTU in its early days. This chapter has shown that five changes in the organisation's environment and internal organisational structure induced shifts in organisational identity. These were the wider societal transition from conflict and the push for people's power in the 1980s to negotiated power-sharing and nation building; SADTU's successful mobilisation of membership; its successful campaigns for recognition; its success at institutionalising collective bargaining rights of teachers; and its successful organisation of national collective action against the fragmented system of apartheid education in the 1990s.

Many of these sources of change in organisational identity pre-dated the transition to an open polity and democratic society – significant in this regard was the emergence of the smaller militant teacher unions which identified with the UDF, NECC and COSATU. The different sources of change outlined had lasting impacts on the organisation's identity. The effects by the different sources of change included the scope of original organisational goals, objectives and demands, such as those for recognition, a single school calendar, unionism and teacher evaluation. Moreover, during the transition period SADTU experienced organisational routinisation and professionalisation as it embarked on both combat against and negotiations with the apartheid state. SADTU's shift to a routinised and professionalised structure and culture was prompted by (i) the leading role COSATU played in facilitating teacher unity; (ii) SADTU's successful mobilisation of teachers who required formal representation in matters such as salary negotiations and dispute resolution, which imposed on the organisation a culture and structure of effective, efficient and reproducible leadership and representation; and (iii) SADTU's negotiations with the apartheid state and participation in collective bargaining structures, which imposed its own discipline on organisational culture and structure.

The transition to an open polity and democratic society impacted on the later evolution of SADTU. With leadership transfers to the political and administrative apparatuses of the emerging state, the organisation experienced a decline in collective action. SADTU entered the twenty-first century and the transition to democracy in South Africa as a participant in the country's political and social reconstruction through its involvement in the reconstruction of the identity of the state. The organisation has since shed several of those leaders to the emergent democratic state at national and provincial levels of government (elaborated in Chapters 4 and 6). It remains to be seen whether SADTU, in the wake of these losses, can continue to play a leading and dynamic role in the transformation of public policy domains and public policy, an issue taken up in Chapters 3 and 7. More importantly, in the context of a deepening education crisis and a weakened economy, SADTU will be hard-pressed to live up to its claims as a professional union. This and related challenges are explored in various chapters of this book.

Notes
1. Zeph Mothopeng was a political activist and would become president of the Pan Africanist Congress (PAC); Es'kia Mphahlele was a South African writer and educationist.

2. See Nkomo (1990) for a succinct analysis of the education crisis and the responses of key actors such as teachers, students and the broader community.
3. Interview C6.
4. Interviews C1 and C5. For an analysis focusing on the impact of school boycotts and the mobilisation and politicisation of township communities on the politics of the conservative teacher organisations, see Moll (1991).
5. Interview C6.
6. Soweto Parents Crisis Committee, 'Report on National Consultative Conference on the Crisis in Education', 28–29 December 1985, Johannesburg; National Consultative Conference on the Crisis in Education, 'Resolutions' and 'Keynote Address', 19 March 1986, Durban; Obery (1986); Campbell (1986). See also *Cape Times*, 23 June 1988; *Sunday Times*, 16 August 1987; *Sunday Times Extra*, 6 December 1987; *South*, 26 November 1987 and 22 June 1989; *The Sunday Star*, 14 August 1988; *Natal Post*, 30 May and 7 June 1989.
7. Interview C6.
8. Alleged by the Teachers' Association of South Africa, 5 April 1989. See *Business Day*, 9 May 1989; *Natal Post*, 2 May 1989; *The Leader*, 2 October 1987; *Weekly Mail*, 22 November 1985; *Die Burger*, 4 July 1987 and 18 April 1988; *Rapport Extra*, 1 May 1988.
9. *Natal Post*, 26 June 1988; *The Star*, 10 April 1984; *Sunday Tribune*, 6 October 1984.
10. *Natal Mercury*, 7 September 1987.
11. *Cape Times*, 6 August 1987.
12. *Natal Witness*, 4 April 1989; *Natal Post*, 4 April 1989; *Sunday Times Extra*, 26 June 1988.
13. *Cape Times*, 25 February 1989; *The Star*, 4 January and 14 February 1989; *Weekly Mail*, 27 January 1989.
14. *Argus*, 27 May 1988; *Cape Times*, 11 November 1988; *Citizen*, 27 May and 15 June 1988; *Eastern Province Herald*, 23 November 1988; *Rapport Extra*, 4 December 1988.
15. *Sowetan*, 12 October 1988.
16. No data are available on declining real salaries in the 1980s, but cuts in teacher service bonuses from 8.3 per cent to 5.5 per cent of annual salary opened a new front in the battle with government in 1985. *The Star*, 11 March 1985; *Sunday Tribune and Mirror*, 12 December 1984. Earlier, teacher organisations had reached a deadlock with government over a pay rise in 1984. *Sunday Express*, 17 June 1984; interview C6.
17. Interview C1.
18. *The Star*, 12 April 1988; see also Moll (1991).
19. Interview with Duncan Hindle, former SADTU president, 28 July 2014.
20. The white teacher organisations in 1989 included the Transvaal Teachers' Association, Transvaalonderwysersvereneging, the South African Teachers' Association, Suid-Afrikaanse Onderwysersunie, the Natal Teachers' Society,

Natalse Onderwysersunie, the Association of Orange Free State Teachers and the South African Association for Technical and Vocational Education (Govender 1996).
21. The Mass Democratic Movement (MDM) evolved in the early 1990s and is generally regarded as the successor to the UDF.
22. SADTU (1991: 10); see also Moll (1991: 196-7). For a media account, see *New Nation*, 23 February 1989.
23. Interview with female head of school, KwaMashu, 1 October 2014.
24. Interviews C1, C2, C5 and C6; SADTU (1991: 10).
25. SADTU (1991: 10-110); see also the constitution booklet issued by SADTU.
26. Interviews C1 and C2.
27. DETU, WECTU and NEUSA all dissolved immediately after the launch of SADTU in 1990 (SADTU 1991: 12).
28. Of the remaining teacher formations, UTASA, which enjoyed the recognition of the Department of Administration, House of Representatives (overseeing coloured education), chose to remain unaffiliated until it was able to resolve outstanding organisational and policy issues. Eventually UTASA joined the federation in November 1994. TASA, which had been recognised by the Department of Education and Culture, House of Delegates (Indian education), had disbanded in 1992 and encouraged its members to join SADTU.
29. Interviews C2, C4 and C5.
30. *Argus*, 5 October 1990; *Cape Times*, 4 October 1990; *Leader*, 5 October 1990; *New Nation*, 5 October 1990; *South*, 4 October 1990; *Sowetan*, 4 October 1990; *The Star*, 2 and 5 October 1990; *Sunday Star*, 7 October 1990; *Sunday Times Extra*, 7 October 1990; *Sunday Tribune*, 7 October 1990; *Volksblad*, 4 October 1990; *Weekly Mail*, 5 October 1990.
31. Only one of the conservative teacher associations later remained within the fold of SADTU, the 10 000-member TASA, which drew its membership from the authoritarian Indian education department as well as by its membership of the NTUF. Membership of SADTU and of the emerging coalition of conservative teacher associations (later named NAPTOSA) was split equally in 1993, with SADTU and NAPTOSA each claiming membership of 100 000 teachers. Interviews C1, C4 and C10.
32. *Natal Post*, 17 October 1990; SADTU (1991: 5-8).
33. For a summary of SADTU's recognition campaign, see 'The Campaign for the Recognition of SADTU', *New Nation*, 27 March 1992, p. 15.
34. Interviews C3, C5, C7, C8 and C9; SADTU (1991: 7).
35. SADTU (1991: 14-15). See also *Sowetan*, 29 November 1990.
36. Interview C8; SADTU (1991: 14). See also *Natal Mercury*, 15 October 1991.
37. SADTU (1991: 15). See also *Argus*, 8 August 1991; *Business Day*, 1 and 8 August 1991; *Beeld*, 1 and 7 August 1991; *Cape Times*, 8 August 1991; *Citizen*, 8 August 1991; *City Press*, 11 August 1991; *Daily Dispatch*, 8 August 1991; *Leader*, 9 August 1991; *New Nation*, 2 and 16 August 1991; *Pretoria News*, 6 August

1991; *Rapport Extra*, 28 July and 4 August 1991; *South*, 1 August 1991; *Sowetan*, 29 July and 5 and 8 August 1991; *Volksblad*, 27 July 1991; *Evening Post*, 7 August 1991.
38. *Cape Times*, 19 September 1991; *City Press*, 22 February 1992; *Learning Roots*, September 1991; *Natal Post*, 13 November and 4 December 1991; *New African*, 28 November 1991; *New Nation*, 27 September and 4 October 1991 and 17 January 1992; *Rapport*, 23 March 1991.
39. *Die Burger*, 20 September 1991.
40. Interview C8; SADTU (1991: 38-9; 1993a: 36-42).
41. SADTU (1991: 15; 1993a: 11).
42. Republic of South Africa, *Government Gazette* 340 (15181), 20 October 1993.
43. Interview C8; SADTU (1991: 6).
44. SADTU (1993a: 13).
45. Interview C8; SADTU (1991: 26-7).
46. SADTU (1991: 26-7).
47. Interview C8; SADTU (1991: 26-7).
48. *Beeld*, 24 January 1991; *Daily Dispatch*, 22 June 1991; *Natal Witness*, 24 January 1991; *Sowetan*, 1 February 1991; *Natal Mercury*, 22 November 1991.
49. Interviews C3 and C10. See also Chetty et al. (1993: 3).
50. *Daily Dispatch*, 9 July 1992; *New Nation*, 8 May 1992; *Sowetan*, 18 and 25 June and 20 July 1992.
51. Northern Transvaal regional chairperson of SADTU, quoted in *New Nation*, 8 May 1992.
52. Northern Transvaal regional chairperson of SADTU, quoted in *New Nation*, 8 May 1992.
53. SADTU (1993b: 7-8).
54. 'South African Democratic Teachers Union (SADTU): Professionalism and Unionism', *New Nation*, 3-9 April 1992, p. 18.
55. Interviews C4, C5 and C8.
56. See, for example, the advertisements placed by the Cape Teachers' Professional Association (CTPA): 'The CTPA position with respect to the temporary teachers' campaign' (*South*, 28 February – 6 March 1991) and 'The CTPA position with respect to inspectors of education and subject advisers' (*South*, 21-27 February 1991); by UTASA: 'Press Statement' (*Sunday Times*, 26 July 1992); and by TUATA: 'TUATA. Against defamation and disruption' (*City Press*, 20 May 1990, and *Sowetan*, 21 May 1990), 'TUATA. Students! The new South Africa needs you to learn' (*City Press*, 3 June 1990, and *Sowetan*, 5 June 1990), 'TUATA. And what of our children's future?' (*Sowetan*, 30 July 1990), 'TUATA poses questions to SADTU' (*Sowetan*, 1 October 1990), 'TUATA. There must be a new beginning' (*New Nation*, 29 November 1991), 'TUATA. An appeal to parents' (*New Nation*, 13 March 1992) and 'TUATA. An appeal to the community' (*City Press*, 19 July 1992).

57. Interview C2; SADTU (1991). See also *New Nation*, 4 October 1991; *Weekly Mail*, 13 September 1991.
58. 'South African Democratic Teachers Union (SADTU): Professionalism and Unionism', *New Nation*, 3-9 April 1992, p. 18; interview C2. See also Hindle and Simpson (1993).
59. For a summary of the organisation's collective bargaining strategy and campaign, see 'SADTU and Collective Bargaining', *New Nation*, 10-16 April 1992.
60. *South*, 26 June 1993; *Sowetan*, 9 July 1993; *Weekly Mail*, 9 July 1993.
61. *Cape Times*, 18 February 1993; *South*, 19 October 1992; *Sowetan*, 11 and 12 January 1993; *Weekly Mail*, 29 January and 19 February 1993.
62. *The Star*, 25 November 1992.
63. *New Nation*, 29 January 1993.
64. *Sowetan*, 26 February 1993; *Weekly Mail*, 5 March 1993.
65. *Sowetan*, 26 February 1993; *Weekly Mail*, 5 March 1993.
66. *Sowetan*, 26 February 1993; *Weekly Mail*, 5 March 1993.
67. *Citizen*, 22 March and 24 April 1993.
68. *Citizen*, 22 March and 24 April 1993.
69. *Business Day*, 2 June 1993.
70. *Beeld*, 13 May 1993; *South*, 8 May 1993; *Sowetan*, 13 May 1993; *Sunday Tribune*, 16 May 1993; *Weekly Mail*, 7 May 1993.
71. *Beeld*, 21 May 1993; *Cape Times*, 26 May 1993; *Sowetan*, 25 May 1993.
72. *The Star*, 5 September 1993.
73. *Business Day*, 29 September and 13 October 1993; *Citizen*, 21 October 1993; *New Nation*, 7 July 1993; *Sowetan*, 21 July, 1 September, and 6 and 7 October 1993; *The Star*, 25 September, 8 October, 18 and 29 November, and 6 December 1993.
74. *Citizen*, 18 August 1993.
75. *The Star*, 23 July 1993.
76. *The Star*, 23 July 1993. Also interview C2; Vadi (1993).
77. *Beeld*, 20 August 1993.
78. *Citizen*, 30 November 1993.
79. *Citizen*, 30 November 1993.
80. *Beeld*, 20 August 1993; *Cape Times*, 23 August 1993; *South*, 20 August 1993.
81. *Beeld*, 20 August 1993; *Business Day*, 20 August 1993; *Sowetan*, 27 August 1993; *The Star*, 20 August 1993.
82. The teacher strike and protests had cost the Department of Education and Training alone at least R240 million in staff expenses during the 1993/94 financial year, according to a report tabled by the auditor general in the National Assembly. Strikes and stay-aways by teachers had lost nearly 450 000 man-days, while actions by pupils and other organisations against the increased matriculation examination fee had sapped another 524 399 man-days, according to the report (*Sowetan*, 30 March 1995).

83. 'SADTU's Strike Victory', pamphlet issued by SADTU head office, June 1994.
84. Interviews C7 and C9.
85. Interviews C2, C3, C10 and C11.
86. Interviews C2 and C6.

References

Alexander, N. 2013. *Education and the Struggle for National Liberation in South Africa: Essays and Speeches by Neville Alexander (1985–1989)*. 2nd ed. Sea Point: The Estate of Neville Edward Alexander.

Amoako, S. 2014. 'Teacher Unions in Political Transitions: The South African Democratic Teachers' Union (SADTU) and the Dying Days of Apartheid, 1990–1993'. *Journal of Asian and African Studies* 49(2): 148–63.

Ballard, R., A. Habib and I. Valodia. 2006. 'Social Movements in South Africa: Promoting Crisis or Creating Stability?' In *The Development Decade: Economic and Social Change in South Africa, 1994–2004*, edited by V. Padayachee. Cape Town: HSRC Press.

Bot, M. 1992. 'The Politics of Teacher Unity'. *South African Institute of Race Relations Spotlight* 1(92): 1–23.

Campbell, J. 1986. 'The NECC: Doing Battle with the DET'. *Work in Progress* 45(November/December): 17–19.

Chetty, D., L. Chisholm, M. Gardiner, N. Magau and P. Vinjevold. 1993. 'Rethinking Teacher Appraisal in South Africa: Policy Options and Strategies'. Johannesburg: Education Policy Unit, University of the Witwatersrand/NECC.

Cross, M., R. Mungadi and S. Rouhani. 2002. 'From Policy to Practice: Curriculum Reform in South African Education'. *Comparative Education* 38(2): 171–87.

Curtis, R. and L. Zurcher. 1973. 'Stable Resources or Protest Movements: The Multi-organisational Field'. *Social Forces* 52(1): 53–61.

Edwards, B. and P.F. Gillham. 2013. 'Resource Mobilization Theory'. In *The Wiley-Blackwell Encyclopaedia of Social and Political Movements*, edited by G. Ritzer and J. Goodwin. Oxford: Blackwell Publishing.

Fominaya, C.F. 2010. 'Collective Identity in Social Movements: Central Concepts and Debates'. *Sociology Compass* 4(6): 393–404.

Gardiner, M. 1990. 'Efforts at Creating Alternative Curricula: Conceptual and Practical Considerations'. In *Pedagogy of Domination: Towards a Democratic Education in South Africa*, edited by M. Nkomo. Trenton, New Jersey: Africa World Press.

Govender, L. 1996. 'When the "Chalks are Down": A Historical, Political and Social Interpretation of Teacher Militancy in South Africa'. Pretoria: HSRC.

———. 2004. 'Teacher Unions, Policy Struggles and Educational Change, 1994–2004'. In *Changing Class: Education and Social Change in Post-apartheid South Africa*, edited by L. Chisholm. Cape Town: HSRC Press.

―――. 2008. 'Teachers' Participation in Policy Making: The Case of the South African Schools Act'. PhD thesis, University of the Witwatersrand, Johannesburg.

―――. 2012. 'The Mediation of Teacher Unions' Participation in Policy Making: A South African Case Study'. Paper presented at the SACHES Conference on Education and Societal Dynamics: Possibilities for Educational Change in the Southern African Region, Port Elizabeth, 29 October – 1 November.

―――. 2015. 'Teacher Unions' Participation in Policy Making: A South African Case Study'. *Compare* 45(2): 184–205.

Govender, L., N. Hoffmann and Y. Sayed. 2016. 'Teacher Professionalism and Accountability'. Working Paper 2016/01. Cape Town: Centre for International Teacher Education, Cape Peninsula University of Technology.

Govender, S. and A. Fataar. 2015. 'Historical Continuities in the Education Policy Discourses of the African National Congress, 1912–1992'. *South African Journal of Education* 35(1): 1–8.

Hartshorne, K. 1992. *Crisis and Challenge: Black Education 1910–1990*. Cape Town: Oxford University Press.

Herman, T. 1993. 'From Uni-dimensionality to Multi-dimensionality: Some Observations on the Dynamics of Social Movements'. *Research in Social Movements, Conflict and Change* 15: 181–201.

Heywood, M. 2015. 'The Treatment Action Campaign's Quest for Equality in HIV and Health: Learning from and Lessons for the Trade Union Movement'. *Global Labour Journal* 6(3): 314–35.

Hindle, D. 1991. 'Blackboard Power: The New Teacher Politics'. *Indicator South Africa* 9(1): 71–4.

Hindle, D. and L. Simpson. 1993. 'Teachers Don't Talk in Class! A Class Analysis of Teachers and Their Organisation in South Africa'. In *Kenton-at-Broederstroom, 1992: Conference Proceedings*, edited by S. Pendlebury, L. Hudson, Y. Shalem and D. Bensusan. Johannesburg: Education Department, University of the Witwatersrand.

Hyslop, J. 1986. 'Teachers and Trade Unions'. *South African Labour Bulletin* 11(6): 90–7.

―――. 1990. 'Social Conflicts over African Education in South Africa from the 1940s to 1976'. PhD thesis, University of the Witwatersrand, Johannesburg.

Kgari-Masondo, M.C., S.T. Masondo, D. Mosina, D. Mncube and B. Mpanza. 2019. *Demythologising SADTU: Historical Significance of SADTU as an Educational Vehicle of Change and Continuity*. Pietermaritzburg: Shuter and Shooter.

Klandermans, B. 1993. 'A Theoretical Framework for Comparisons of Social Movement Participation'. *Sociological Forum* 8(3): 383–402.

Klandermans, B. and J. Olivier. 1995. 'Social Movements in South Africa: An Interdisciplinary Research Programme'. Pretoria: HSRC and KLI.

Kumalo, V. and D. Skosana. 2014. *A History of the South African Democratic Teachers' Union (SADTU)*. Johannesburg: SADTU.

Melucci, A. 1994. 'The Process of Collective Identity'. In *Social Movements and Culture*, edited by H. Johnston and B. Klandermans. Minneapolis: University of Minnesota Press.
Moll, I. 1991. 'The South African Democratic Teachers' Union and the Politics of Teacher Unity in South Africa, 1985-1990'. In *Apartheid Education and Popular Struggles*, edited by E. Unterhalter, H. Wolpe, T. Botha, S. Badat, T. Dlamini and B. Khotseng. Johannesburg: Ravan Press.
National Education Policy Investigation (NEPI). 1992. 'Governance and Administration: Report of the NEPI Governance and Administration Research Group'. Cape Town: Oxford University Press and NECC.
Nicholls, W. 2009. 'Place, Networks, Space: Theorising the Geographies of Social Movements'. *Transactions of the Institute of British Geographers* 34(1): 78-93.
Nkomo, M. 1990. *Pedagogy of Domination: Towards a Democratic Education in South Africa*. Trenton, New Jersey: Africa World Press.
Obery, I. 1986. 'People's Education: Creating a Democratic Future'. *Work in Progress* 42(May): 8-13.
Olivier, P. 1989. 'Bringing the Crowd Back In: The Nonorganizational Elements of Social Movements'. *Research in Social Movements, Conflict and Change* 11: 1-30.
Powell, W.W. and J.A. Colyvas. 2008. 'Microfoundations of Institutional Theory'. In *The Sage Handbook of Organizational Institutionalism*, edited by R. Greenwood, C. Oliver, K. Sahlin and R. Suddaby. Thousand Oaks, California: Sage.
Rensburg, I.L. 1996. 'Collective Identity and Public Policy: From Resistance to Reconstruction in South Africa, 1986-1995'. PhD thesis, Stanford University, Stanford, California.
Scott, W.R. 2008. 'Approaching Adulthood: The Maturing of Institutional Theory'. *Theory and Society* 37(5): 427.
Seekings, J. 2000. *The UDF: A History of the United Democratic Front in South Africa 1983-1991*. Cape Town: David Philip.
Snow, D. and R. Benford. 1992. 'Master Frames and Cycles of Protest'. In *Frontiers in Social Movement Theory*, edited by A. Morris and C. Mueller. New Haven: Yale University Press.
South African Democratic Teachers' Union (SADTU). 1991. 'Secretariat Report'. First National Congress, 10-12 October, Nasrec, Johannesburg. SADTU National Archives, Matthew Goniwe House, Johannesburg.
———. 1993a. 'Secretariat Report'. Second National Congress, July. SADTU National Archives, Matthew Goniwe House, Johannesburg.
———. 1993b. 'Secretariat Report to the SADTU NEC Meeting', 7 August.
Suddaby, R. 2010. 'Challenges for Institutional Theory'. *Journal of Management Inquiry* 19(1): 14-20.
Vadi, I 1993. 'SADTU Teachers Strike Back'. *South African Labour Bulletin* 17(3): 70-5.
Zengele, T. 2013. 'The Unionization of the Teaching Profession and Its Effects on the South African Education System: Teacher Unionism in South Africa'. *Journal of Social Science* 35(3): 231-9.

Interviews

C1 Former NEUSA office bearer, 2 February 1995.
C2 Former CTPA office bearer, 4 March 1995.
C3 Former WECTU office bearer, 1 February 1995.
C4 Former CTPA office bearer, 16 February 1995.
C5 Former NEUSA office bearer, 2 February 1995.
C6 Former WECTU office bearer, 1 February 1995.
C7 Former NEUSA office bearer, 4 April 1995.
C8 Former NUESA office bearer, 5 April 1995.
C9 Former TASA office bearer, 4 April 1995.
C10 Former TASA office bearer, 4 April 1995.
C11 Former NEUSA office bearer, 5 April 1995.

2

The Influence of COSATU on the Evolution and Development of SADTU

An Insider's Perspective

KHETSI LEHOKO

The Congress of South African Trade Unions (COSATU) played a critical role in the establishment of SADTU, which partly explains SADTU's strong unionist identity, and in facilitating the national teacher unity process. As discussed in Chapter 1, the establishment of SADTU as a national non-racial teachers' organisation in 1990 was preceded by a lengthy process, beginning in 1988, to establish a *single* national, non-racial trade union organisation. This process was spearheaded by the National Teacher Unity Forum (NTUF), and its impetus was the intensification of the mass struggle against apartheid in the early 1980s, which gained momentum following the 1976 revolt of school students in Soweto against apartheid education. The main goal of the NTUF was to assert the hegemony of the Mass Democratic Movement (MDM) in education by bringing together the old established conservative teacher associations, such as the African Teachers' Association of South Africa (ATASA), which had remained outside the struggle, and the new militant teacher unions that emerged in the 1980s and were an integral part of the anti-apartheid struggle. This goal was based on the recognition by the National Education Crisis Committee (NECC), which coordinated the struggle against apartheid education, that teachers were central to achieving the vision of a non-racial and democratic education system, which would open the doors of learning to all, as envisaged in the Freedom Charter, which was adopted by the Congress Alliance[1] in June

1955 and provides the guiding vision for the establishment of a non-racial, non-sexist and democratic South Africa.

The centrality of teachers required that the conservative teacher associations, which were numerically strong given the closed shop agreements they enjoyed under apartheid, be brought into the fold of the MDM. This sentiment informed the process of the teacher unity talks and was succinctly captured in a speech delivered by Jay Naidoo, COSATU general secretary, at the Conference of the Cape Teachers' Professional Association (CTPA) in 1988:

> The mass struggle by millions of our people and students has found teachers not leading but following the example being set. The choice is now yours. You have a choice of involving yourselves in the struggle for a new society in which the nightmare of racism and exploitation is banished or you can be ensnared by the material benefits the system now offers you in the form of house loans, pensions, promotions etc. The latter choice will undoubtedly alienate you from the mass struggle of our people for a new society (Naidoo 1988: 10).

This chapter expands on COSATU's role, impact and influence on the evolution and development of SADTU. It argues that SADTU's focus on, and prioritisation of, unionism instead of professionalism, which was the ideological dividing line between the conservative teacher associations and the militant teacher unions, was in part the result of COSATU's role in facilitating the NTUF and SADTU's subsequent affiliation to COSATU. The chapter is informed by the author's role and participation in the NTUF as a member of the COSATU facilitating team. The facilitating team comprised the following COSATU officials: Jay Naidoo, general secretary; Chris Seoposengwe, shop steward, National Union of Mineworkers, and chairperson, National Education Committee; and myself, Khetsi Lehoko, national education secretary.[2]

The emergence of COSATU

The formation of the United Democratic Front (UDF) in 1983 and COSATU in 1985 were two key events in the intensifying struggle against apartheid in the 1980s (Kgari-Masondo et al. 2019: 30). As elaborated in Chapter 1, the formation of both the UDF and COSATU constituted an important backdrop to the emergence of the smaller militant teacher unions and, ultimately, the push for teacher unity in South Africa in the lead-up to the establishment of SADTU in 1990.

COSATU was formed on 30 November 1985, after years of negotiations between, among others, the Council of Unions of South Africa (CUSA), the Federation of South African Trade Unions (FOSATU), the Azanian Confederation of Trade Unions (AZACTU) and the South African Workers' Union (SAWU) (Twala and Kompi 2012: 174). Unions that were aligned to the Black Consciousness Movement – namely, CUSA and AZACTU – did not join the new federation because it adopted the Freedom Charter, which signalled alignment with the African National Congress (ANC) (Kgari-Masondo et al. 2019: 31). CUSA and AZACTU would eventually merge into the National Council of Trade Unions (NACTU), while FOSATU, formed in 1979, would eventually become part of COSATU, in spite of differences over involvement in political struggle.

The main aim of COSATU was to organise workers to fight for the improvement of their material conditions, and to ensure workers' involvement in the national democratic struggle. At the same time, it fiercely asserted its independent role within the liberation movement. The adoption of the Freedom Charter by COSATU and many of its affiliates in 1987, however, moved the union closer to the ANC. Eventually COSATU became part of the Tripartite Alliance with the ANC and the South African Communist Party (SACP) in the 1990s (Twala and Kompi 2012: 174-5).

In the late 1980s, the UDF, COSATU and other like-minded structures formed the MDM. The MDM continued with mass mobilisation for the rest of 1989, including a number of marches and rallies (Kgari-Masondo et al. 2019: 32-3). It was in this context that the national teacher unity initiative was launched.

The NTUF and the question of coordination

The first step in the process leading to the NTUF was a conference on teacher unity, which was convened by the South African Congress of

Trade Unions (SACTU) and international teacher bodies in April 1988 in Harare, Zimbabwe. The details of the conference are not repeated here, as they are discussed in Chapter 1. However, it is important to highlight that both the conservative teacher associations (except for the Teachers' Federal Council [TFC], which represented white teachers) and the militant teacher unions were in attendance, led by Sydney Mufamadi, who was then the assistant general secretary of COSATU.

Although there was agreement on the need to pursue teacher unity, the key question to be answered was who would coordinate the unity talks. Two options were put on the table. The option put forward by the militant teacher unions was that the talks should be coordinated by the NECC, given its role in coordinating the struggle for the establishment of a non-racial and democratic education system as part of the UDF and the fact that it comprised national formations representing students, teachers, parent associations and academics. This option was ruled out for two reasons. First, the NECC could not fulfil this role as it had been rendered ineffective by the then prevailing state of emergency, with its leadership either in hiding or in detention. Second, its role as a neutral arbiter was compromised by the fact that the militant teacher unions were part of the NECC; consequently, it would have been both a player and a referee in the process.

The second option, which was put forward by the convenors of the conference and which was ultimately adopted, was to ask COSATU to facilitate the unity talks. This was supported for four reasons. First, although individual members of COSATU and its leadership were targeted by the state security forces, its organisational infrastructure remained relatively intact and functional despite the state of emergency. Second, it had experience in facilitating unity talks given the processes that culminated in the formation of COSATU in December 1985. Third, following its establishment, it had successfully facilitated the merger of 33 unions that initially formed COSATU into fifteen industrial unions. Fourth, and importantly, although part of the MDM, which was aligned to the ANC, COSATU was committed to maintaining the independence and autonomy of trade unions from political parties during this period. This commitment was based on the recognition that large numbers of workers who were members of COSATU-affiliated trade unions belonged to different political parties. Hence, the conservative teacher associations regarded COSATU as a neutral arbiter between them and the militant teacher unions.

Although COSATU agreed to facilitate the unity talks, it is important to note that despite its accumulated experience and expertise, it was a relatively young organisation in 1988 – no more than three years old. COSATU was thus preoccupied with ensuring that its own centre as an organisation held, especially given the changing political context and the tentative steps towards national negotiations for a new democratic constitutional dispensation.

What did COSATU represent and stand for?

To understand and appreciate how COSATU influenced the nature and direction of SADTU, the principles and key organisational pillars that held COSATU together need to be recognised. COSATU itself was the outcome of protracted unity talks that spanned nearly five years and brought together worker organisations that held very different views on the role of a trade union, in terms of both its obligations to its members on the factory floor and its role in the broader society. In this context, COSATU adopted the following founding principles to build consensus and facilitate unity:

- the independence of the trade union movement from any external control;
- the participation of the membership in decision-making;
- one country, one federation, one industry, one union: the unity of workers at national level and within defined industrial sectors was paramount in advancing the material conditions of the membership;
- worker control: leadership of the federation at each level should have workers in the majority in order to provide the voice of the rank and file;

- proportional representation: participation in decision-making structures to be determined by the numerical strength of the membership of individual unions; and
- non-racialism.

Negotiating principles and framework for the NTUF

The founding principles of COSATU informed its facilitation of the unity talks and its approach to the nature and form of a united teachers' organisation. At the outset, the principle of non-racialism was unanimously adopted as one of the founding principles of the new organisation. However, after several meetings, four issues emerged as areas of contestation and disagreement. The first issue related to the principle of proportional representation. The conservative teacher associations were numerically stronger than the newly formed militant teacher unions. However, the militant teacher unions insisted that all participating organisations must be equally represented in the new organisation. On this point, COSATU was not willing to brook any compromise, as proportional representation was a key pillar of its internal democracy and organisational structure.

The second issue, which was linked to the first, was about fair distribution of assets and resources brought by the different organisations into the newly formed organisation. This was of particular importance to the conservative teacher associations, who were financially strong and had accumulated assets over a long period of time. The facilitating committee argued that this was not an ideological issue and was therefore not an insurmountable problem. Indeed, it was an issue that COSATU had to confront in the merger talks that brought together different unions to form industrial unions.

The third issue was whether the newly formed organisation should be structured on federal or unitary lines. The conservative teacher associations, which were federally based, were reluctant to dispense with their regional autonomy and authority. They argued that their ability to maintain control at the local and regional level would be seriously eroded by a unitary structure. Conversely, the militant teacher unions supported a unitary and democratic structure. They argued that a federally based organisation would entrench existing racial and ethnic identities and divisions that defined the conservative teacher associations, including dispersing power and authority to semi-autonomous regional structures. This was contrary to and would undermine the intention to create a single national, non-racial and democratic teachers' organisation, which would be led by democratically elected leadership that is at all times accountable to and controlled by its members. This, the militant unions argued, was more than the question of organisational structure. It was about internal democracy consistent with a founding principle of COSATU – namely, one industry, one union – which was non-negotiable in the merging of the different unions in the federation. Indeed, the facilitating team was clear that its mandate was to create a single national, non-racial teachers' organisation. However, this fundamental difference was not subject to the hurly-burly of negotiations to reach a compromise, as it was subsumed by an even more fundamental divide regarding the character of the new organisation.

This was the fourth issue, which was the divide between, and the ideological contestation over, unionism and professionalism. On the one hand, the insistence of the militant teacher unions on foregrounding unionism and pursuing unionist goals was due to the apartheid state's proletarianisation and deprofessionalisation of black teachers, who were un- and underqualified, and the resultant lack of parity between black and white teachers in relation to salaries and conditions of service. The conservative teacher associations, on the other hand, insisted on maintaining their status as professionals, even though this had been undermined by the apartheid state.

The facilitating committee took a middle path, arguing that unionism and professionalism were not mutually exclusive, and that the need to promote the professional identity and status of teachers went hand in hand with the need to advance their economic and worker interests. However, this argument did not find traction among the contending organisations. The divide between unionism and professionalism broke the camel's back and precluded the establishment of a *single* national, non-racial teachers' organisation. The conservative teacher associations, except for the Teachers' Association of South Africa (TASA), withdrew from the NTUF and in 1991 formed a new organisation, the National Professional Teachers' Organisation of South Africa (NAPTOSA), which grew to become the second-largest teachers' organisation in South Africa. And SADTU – which was launched in October 1990 on the back of the militant teacher unions, with its ideological foundations firmly rooted in unionism and focused on the economic interests of its members (namely, wages, working conditions, fringe benefits and job security) – grew to become the largest teachers' union in South Africa.

The facilitating committee may not have realised the full significance of the ideological division between unionism and professionalism and, as a result, may not have paid sufficient attention to addressing it. This is understandable given that COSATU's mandate was to facilitate the creation of a single national, non-racial teachers' organisation. Its mandate did not include the character of the new organisation in terms of its trajectory, policies and ideological orientation, which were matters to be developed as part of the evolution of the organisation over time. In this sense, the debate about unionism and professionalism in the NTUF was premature. Furthermore, COSATU did not have experience or an understanding of professionalism, which speaks to the development of professional identities and characteristics in terms of values and behaviours, far removed from the identity and struggles of workers on the factory floor. And neither did COSATU understand that the pursuit of professionalism is central to the transformation and development of a quality education system.

The unionism versus professionalism divide might have been transcended if the NECC had facilitated the unity talks. The NECC would have been better placed to make the connections between unionism and professionalism, given its focus on developing an alternative vision for the creation of a non-racial and democratic education system informed by the concept of people's education for people's power, as discussed in Chapter 1.

Affiliation to COSATU

Once SADTU was established in 1990, the next and logical step, given its strong leaning towards unionism, was to find an organisational and political home among the existing trade union federations. COSATU, which served as its midwife, was the obvious choice for three reasons. First, there was political and ideological affinity given COSATU's role in the MDM and the struggle against apartheid, in which the militant teacher unions had participated prior to the formation of SADTU. Second, COSATU would provide the newly formed union with the institutional infrastructure, expertise and legitimacy necessary to enable it to grow and consolidate its presence in schools. Third, an association with COSATU would reinforce its unionist image and leanings, which were intended to protect its members and improve their salaries and working conditions.

SADTU's application for affiliation, which was tabled at a meeting of COSATU's Central Executive Committee, was met with mixed reactions that were in part a reflection of long-standing ideological differences that divided the unions within the federation into two groupings. The first group believed that unions should focus not only on shop-floor issues in the workplace but also on issues that affected workers in the wider society. This perspective was informed by an understanding that black workers were not only exploited as workers on the factory floor, but were also oppressed and discriminated against in the wider society in the same manner as the general black population. On the basis of this duality, this group advocated for the central and critical role of the union movement in the National Democratic Revolution (NDR), led by the ANC, to establish a non-racial democracy free of exploitation and oppression. They viewed the affiliation of SADTU to COSATU as a strategic victory, as it would enhance the capacity of the MDM to challenge the ideological and organisational hegemony of apartheid in the education system. Thus, they welcomed SADTU into the ranks of the workers' movement.

The ideology of the second group was rooted in the notion of the autonomy of the labour movement and its decision-making processes, independent of any external influences, including political parties (Theron 2016). This position can be traced to the political tradition of the FOSATU, which emphasised the building of democratic shop-floor structures around the principles of worker control and accountability (Barrett and Mullins 1990: 25). While this group recognised the importance of establishing a national, non-racial teachers' organisation, they did not believe that COSATU was an appropriate home for SADTU. They advanced three arguments in opposing the affiliation of SADTU. First, teachers, by virtue of their (middle-)class position, were conservative and would dilute the militancy of the union movement. Second, the conflictual nature of shop-floor struggles in the workplace was not appropriate in the educational context, as it would lead to the disruption of schooling, which was not in the interests of learners. Third, teachers, unlike workers who can negotiate shop-floor recognition agreements, wage increases and improved working conditions independently from the union, cannot do the same at a school level. This is due to fundamental differences between the nature of the employer in the private and public sectors. In the public sector, the employer is national, and negotiations on salaries and conditions of service take place and are governed by rules and regulations agreed at the national level in the Education Labour Relations Council (ELRC), established in 1993. In the private sector, however, the nature of the employer-employee relationship differs based on the character of the company – that is, whether it is national, regional or local. And even when a company is national, workers are able to negotiate issues specific to the factory in which they are employed. Thus, worker representatives on the factory floor are engaged with the employer on issues affecting workers on a daily basis. In the main, this is not the case with teachers, which results in conflicts with school management, who implement policies designed at the national level, leaving little room for school site-based negotiations.

Thus, this second group favoured SADTU remaining an independent organisation that could negotiate with government at a national level and reach agreement on a social contract aimed at addressing all professional matters, including salaries and working conditions that affected teachers. After a lengthy debate, the position of the grouping that supported SADTU's affiliation prevailed, and SADTU was accepted into the ranks of COSATU in 1993.

Affiliation: pros and cons

The affiliation to COSATU had both positive and negative implications for SADTU. On the positive side, it gave SADTU access and exposure to the knowledge, expertise and experience that resided in COSATU, which would be invaluable in relation to building a strong union, as well as in its negotiations with the education authorities to improve the working conditions of its members. COSATU had developed within its ranks a large number of worker leaders and officials who had accumulated knowledge and expertise in organising workers, negotiating with employers and facilitating internal democracy. This expertise was forged and shaped during the hard-fought battles that were won and lost since the re-emergence of the trade union movement in the early 1970s. The art of negotiating agreements was gained through practical experience in engaging employers. The practice of seeking mandates and reporting back to members during negotiations was ingrained into the culture of the federation and its affiliates. As Steven Friedman (1987) argues, a mere commitment to democracy is not sufficient and does not automatically ensure worker participation in decision-making. Building democratic grassroots unionism requires the establishment of deliberate structures and practices.

These traditions and practices were shaped in struggle. No amount of training and workshops without actual practice and direct engagement with employers can prepare unions and their leadership to engage in a meaningful and constructive manner in the interest of their membership. It was these practices and traditions that would benefit the newly formed SADTU. In addition, affiliation to COSATU provided a home for SADTU and a sense of support and solidarity in the event of victimisation of its members. However, this positive aspect of its affiliation was not fully realised. This was in large part due, as indicated above, to fundamental differences between the private and public sectors. In the former, negotiations occur at different levels, including the shop floor, while in the latter, negotiations are limited to the national level. Thus, SADTU's membership did not have the exposure or opportunity to negotiate at the school level, which would have enhanced their understanding of the intricate and complex processes of engaging authority. This may go some way in explaining the lack of participation by SADTU members in organisational activities, as discussed in Chapter 4. Furthermore, the moment that SADTU joined COSATU coincided with the onset of preparations for negotiations over a new democratic political dispensation, which became the main focus of the seasoned and senior leadership of COSATU. Thus, building the organisational, leadership and membership capacity of its new affiliate was not top of COSATU's agenda. SADTU's limited opportunities were compounded soon thereafter by the departure of senior leaders from the labour movement, including SADTU, into new positions in government post-1994 (discussed in Chapters 4 and 6). These factors deprived SADTU of the opportunity to learn and draw from COSATU's experience in organisational strategies for building democratic unions and the rules of engagement in the context of labour relations and educational transformation. This lost opportunity partly diminished SADTU's ability to engage the new democratic government in fulfilling the vision of providing a quality education for all learners.

On the negative side, affiliation to COSATU reinforced SADTU's emphasis and narrow focus on unionism. Although industrial unions occasionally engaged in policy issues relating to their economic sector, they focused mainly on bread-and-butter issues affecting workers, particularly annual negotiations on wages and working conditions. The intensity and protracted nature of these negotiations meant that in practice there was little time or energy to devote to broader policy issues. As discussed in Chapters 1 and 3, labour issues dominated SADTU's agenda and activities in its early years, leaving little opportunity to engage with professional and policy issues regarding the professional development of its members and improving the quality of education.

COSATU's participation in the Tripartite Political Alliance, together with the ANC and the SACP, has also negatively impacted on SADTU. As an affiliate of COSATU, SADTU has become embroiled in the political and ideological battles of the Alliance, especially in the post-2010 period (see Chapter 3 for more details). This has distracted SADTU from developing and driving the transformation agenda in the schooling system, which has dented its image and status within the broader community. In addition, SADTU's proximity to the ANC, and by extension to government, through its affiliation to COSATU has resulted in a reluctance on the part of the education authorities to engage openly and robustly with SADTU on its role in facilitating or impeding progress in the transformation of the schooling system. There is thus no consensus on the strategic priorities necessary to enhance the quality of schooling and on the role and responsibilities of both government and teacher unions in achieving this goal.

The negative impact of COSATU and its participation in the Tripartite Alliance should not be interpreted to suggest that SADTU should disaffiliate from COSATU and/or that it should not align itself politically with the ANC. However, this alignment should take place in an open and transparent manner, and as long as its members are persuaded that it is strategic to do so, both in advancing their material interests and in influencing the transformation of the education system. The key issue that confronts SADTU today is ensuring that – both within COSATU and in the Tripartite Alliance – it maintains its relative autonomy and positions itself in such a way that it does not compromise its role in providing honest and robust input on the way forward in transforming education in South Africa.

Conclusion: what did the formation of SADTU represent?

Despite its shortcomings, the formation of SADTU as a progressive teachers' union represented significant gains in the history of organising teachers in South Africa. First, it provided the first opportunity for teachers to belong to a national and non-racial organisation, which defied the old racial categorisation of teachers under apartheid and forced the government to deal with a single union that represented the interests of all teachers regardless of race. Second, SADTU's formation provided teachers with the opportunity to voluntarily join an organisation of their choice in line with the democratic principle of the right to freedom of association, thus challenging the long-standing closed shop agreements that were enjoyed by the old racially based teacher associations. This was a significant step in the democratisation of schools. Third, the formation created an alternative teachers' voice in the public discourse on matters of education.

There were also great expectations that SADTU, given its origins in the struggle against apartheid in general and Bantu Education in particular, would play a central role in contributing to the transformation of the schooling system and rebuilding the culture of learning and teaching in a democratic South Africa. These expectations were premised on the assumption that the old struggles against apartheid would be replaced by a new struggle in which SADTU would become a key change agent for shaping education policy and enhancing the quality of learning and teaching in the classroom.

However, SADTU has fallen short of meeting these expectations. This is largely due to its prioritisation of unionism over professionalism. There is no gainsaying SADTU's achievements in the field of labour relations – in particular, the parity of esteem and status between black and white teachers. Yet, as South Africa celebrates more than 25 years of democracy, the key question that SADTU needs to address if it is to regain public confidence is whether it can pursue professional and policy issues simultaneously to enhance the quality of schooling and address the material concerns of its members. There are encouraging signs that this is happening, as discussed elsewhere in this book. However, only time will tell whether the convergence of union and professional interests will be successful in transforming the schooling system.

Notes

1. The Congress Alliance, a joint anti-apartheid front led by the African National Congress, included the South African Indian Congress, the Coloured People's Congress and the (white) Congress of Democrats.
2. This chapter is a personal insider perspective by a senior COSATU official who was involved in the teacher unity process and is not an official COSATU view. The author, who, sadly, passed away soon after submitting this contribution, was unable to access documents relating to the teacher unity talks as these could not be found in the COSATU archives.

References

Barrett, J.T. and A.F. Mullins. 1990. 'South African Trade Unions: A Historical Account, 1970-90'. *Monthly Labor Review* 113(10): 25-31.

Friedman, S. 1987. *Building Tomorrow Today*. Johannesburg: Raven Press.

Kgari-Masondo, M.C., S.T. Masondo, D. Mosina, D. Mncube and B. Mpanza. 2019. *Demythologising SADTU: Historical Significance of SADTU as an Educational Vehicle of Change and Continuity*. Pietermaritzburg: Shuter and Shooter.

Naidoo, J. 1988. 'Teacher Unity in the Context of the Broader Community Struggle'. Address to the Conference of the Cape Teachers' Professional Association, 23 June, Cape Town.

Theron, J. 2016. *Solidarity Road: The Story of a Trade Union in the Ending of Apartheid*. Auckland Park: Jacana Media.

Twala, C. and B. Kompi. 2012. 'The Congress of South African Trade Unions (COSATU) and the Tripartite Alliance: A Marriage of (In)Convenience?' *Journal of Contemporary History* 37(1): 171-90.

3

Teacher Unions and Policy-Making in South Africa
Exclusion, Contestation and Collaboration

LOGAN GOVENDER AND MICHAEL CROSS

Teacher union-government relationships occur in a reform context focused on improving educational outcomes at a time of increased competition amongst nation-states as well as economic austerity. Teachers are the objects of most of these reforms, and teacher unions are pressed to advocate on their behalf. In many countries, unions focus their energies on influencing policy development; when they are able to strike up a working relationship with government, teacher unions must balance maintaining these relationships with advocacy work on the part of their members. Teacher unions attempt to achieve this balance by identifying issues that are simultaneously of interest to teachers and government, by augmenting or extending reforms initiated by government, or by engaging in parallel play with government developing and implementing reforms of their own (Bascia and Osmond 2013: 6).

This chapter examines the role of SADTU in education policy in the context of the role of teacher unions in the policy arena in general. It addresses four questions: (i) What was the historical background that framed the participation of teacher organisations in education policy in South Africa? (ii) What role did SADTU play in the education policy process at its launch in 1990 and subsequently? (iii) What policies has

SADTU initiated and engaged with and what outcomes have been achieved? (iv) What were the enabling and constraining factors that have impacted on SADTU's participation in this process?

The chapter argues that, under apartheid, black teachers and teacher organisations were excluded from participation in policy development processes. However, this changed in the 1980s with the emergence of militant teacher unions aligned to the struggle for democracy (detailed in Chapter 1). They challenged the previous hegemony of the conservative teacher associations, which emphasised professionalism and political non-alignment, and actively participated in the contestation over and search for alternatives to apartheid education. This culminated in the demand for 'people's education for people's power' led by the National Education Crisis Committee (NECC). At a more formal level, after its launch in 1990, SADTU, both directly and indirectly through its members, made a mark in the various policy development processes initiated by the Mass Democratic Movement (MDM) to prepare for the transition to democracy.

The legitimation of teacher unions under a democratic dispensation post-1994, including their participation in policy-making, impacted on the nature and content of teacher union-state relations. This shifted gradually from contestation to increased collaboration with the state, and also resulted in increased collaboration between the different teacher organisations, notwithstanding differences in approach and emphasis. For example, unlike SADTU, the National Professional Teachers' Organisation of South Africa (NAPTOSA), the second-largest teacher organisation, prioritises professionalism over unionism (Govender 2015; see also Chapter 1 in this book). The significance of teacher unions' participation in policy-making is not limited to the hope that it would enable teachers to influence policy outcomes. It is also about social and policy learning and its implications for teachers' daily practice, including their organisational development.

However, the nature and impact of teacher union-state relations are also influenced by external factors linked to the broader political environment. In this regard, the key factor is SADTU's alignment with, and participation in, the political Tripartite Alliance led by the African National Congress (ANC) and including the Congress of South

African Trade Unions (COSATU) and the South African Communist Party (SACP). This has undermined the union's independence in the policy arena, except with regard to issues that advance the workplace or economic interests of its members (Govender 2008), highlighting the need for SADTU to assert its relative autonomy and independence in the context of its participation in the Alliance.

The chapter begins with an exploration of key theoretical and conceptual underpinnings relating to teacher union-state relations and the participation of teacher unions in policy processes. It then provides a brief overview of the role of teachers in policy processes under apartheid, including the response of black teachers, in particular, in the 1980s when resistance to apartheid intensified, and the impact of the latter on the dynamics of participation in education policy processes in the transition to democracy. Against this background, the chapter reviews SADTU's participation in and engagement with education policy development processes, focusing on key policy moments and how these shaped the organisation's participation across three periods: the transition to democracy, 1990–1994; the democratic era, 1994–1996; and 1996 to the present. These policy moments include the rise of teacher unionism and SADTU's role in the development of policies leading to the institutionalisation of labour relations in education; SADTU's engagement with and contribution to the development of policy as part of the ANC Education Alliance (which replaced the NECC); SADTU's recognition of the need to assert its independence and relative autonomy from the Tripartite Alliance in education policy matters; and, finally, SADTU's gradual inclination towards teacher professionalism in the face of increasing public criticism over its unionist character and perceptions that pursuing the narrow self-interest of its members trumped the interests of learners and education quality.

Teachers' participation in policy-making: conceptual and theoretical parameters

This chapter builds on the assumption that conceptions of policy and the participation of civil society organisations in public policy processes depend on the nature of the relationship between civil society and the state. In this regard, drawing on Antonio Gramsci's (1971) concept of hegemony, we argue that the role in the policy process played by SADTU, as a social movement deeply rooted in civil society, was shaped by its changing relationship to both the apartheid and the democratic state. More specifically, when the state lacks hegemony and rules by force or repression, civil society responses in the policy process assume the form of contestation and/or a search for alternatives. This is what characterised the role of teachers in the policy process under apartheid. On the other hand, Gramsci 'sees the identical relationship between civil society and the state as a manifestation or projection of civil society to the state power; in other words, as an elevation of the civil society to the state power: as an hegemony formed within and around the base of society to be elevated to the political hegemony of law, representation and force, etc.' (Gundogan 2008: 52). Thus, civil society organisations, such as teacher unions, could become embedded within the state, representing broad state interests that are ultimately reflected in legislation and policy outcomes. This is characteristic of the South African democratic state and is evident in the close relations SADTU has often had with the governing party and government (Govender 2004). However, the very same political/ideological nature of this relationship has constrained and mediated SADTU's ability to influence and shape education policy.

An important factor in exploring teacher union-state relations is the contending ideological conceptions – professionalism and unionism – that have historically shaped teachers' agency. For many decades prior to the 1980s, the two ideologies were regarded as incompatible and contradictory, founded as they were on diverging understandings of teachers as workers and teachers as professionals (Ozga and Lawn 1981). Teachers who embrace professionalism, which has historically been associated with the ideal of service and has become synonymous with strategies of persuasion and reason rather than force (Adhikari 1993), believe that the organisational form best suited for the pursuit of their professional goals is the professional association. This has given rise to the perception that teachers who embrace unionism and establish teacher unions as the organisational form to pursue their material interests, including enhanced conditions of service, are not concerned with the professional dimension of teachers' work. When the issue of political power and contestation for control of policy-making is placed at the forefront of their agendas, teacher unions are inclined to clash with state policy-makers and professional teacher associations, as was the case in South Africa pre-1994 (Govender 1996).

The traditional view of perceiving professionalism and unionism as contrasting and mutually exclusive ideologies has been the subject of much criticism. Jenny Ozga and Martin Lawn (1981) argue for a more flexible approach and assert that unionism is an expression of professionalism. Similarly, pointing out that the distinction between economic and professional issues in education is false, Kenyan teachers have argued that if students are to have optimal conditions for learning, then teachers must have optimal conditions for teaching (Sang 2002). The critique of the conservative view of teacher professionalism has been further refined and has given rise to notions of 'new realism' and 'professional unionism', which advocate the complementarity of both professionalism and unionism, and emphasise collaboration rather than confrontation in teacher union-state relations (Torres et al. 2000). The notion of new realism (attributed to Martin Lawn and Geoff Whitty [1992], cited in Torres et al. 2000) emphasises providing better service to members, regaining professional status and leadership in the educational debate, and developing a long-term vision on educational reform. In like vein, professional unionism, while retaining the traditional features of unionism and professionalism, goes further and recognises the need for teacher unions to address issues of school productivity and efficiency, as well as mechanisms for performance management, discipline and dealing with incompetence (Kerchner and Mitchell 1988). In this chapter, we argue that while SADTU's ideological positioning has historically oscillated between unionism and professionalism, SADTU became more inclined towards a professional unionism approach in its relations with state education organs in the 1990s, as evidenced in its active participation in policy decision-making processes. However, professional unionism's potential is yet to be fully realised, as SADTU members, faced with accountability and performance challenges, tend to revert to their traditional ideological roots of defiance in their relations with the state. Moreover, SADTU's location within the Tripartite Alliance has emerged as a key mediating factor, constraining its independence and influence in the policy arena (as discussed in Chapter 4 and elsewhere in this book).

Teacher-state relations under apartheid: exclusion and resistance

Under apartheid, the unequal status of black and white teachers was based on the racist ideological underpinnings of the state. White teachers were privileged and enjoyed a symbiotic relationship with the state based on a common ideological and political orientation. Although black teachers, along with the black population as a whole, were regarded as second-class citizens and excluded from participation in education policy processes, they actively opposed the introduction of apartheid education policies, specifically the Bantu Education Act of 1953. In fact, many black teachers left the profession given their in-principle opposition to apartheid in general and Bantu Education in particular. However, the intensification of state repression in the late 1950s and early 1960s curtailed teachers' resistance. Black teacher organisations, which were organised along racial and ethnic lines, were politically docile in this period. These organisations included the African Teachers' Association of South Africa (ATASA); the Teachers' Association of South Africa (TASA), which represented Indian teachers; and the United Teachers' Association of South Africa (UTASA), which represented coloured teachers. They defined their role in terms of 'non-involvement in politics and dedication to "professional" life as the best path for the teacher' (Hyslop 1999: 112). This was reflected in their approach to dealing with the apartheid education authorities, which relied primarily on strategies of consultation and persuasion while eschewing militant and political action (Hyslop 1990). However, their voices were systematically excluded from the policy domain. As such, teacher organisations during this period came to be seen as part of the hegemonic apartheid state (drawing on Gramsci 1971).

The militant teacher unions, which emerged in the 1980s, regarded the established black teacher associations as handmaidens of the apartheid state rather than the custodians of their members' interests or the interests of the broader community. They identified with and participated in the anti-apartheid struggle, arguing that the struggle against apartheid education and for the rights of teachers as workers could not be separated from the broader struggle for democracy. And as the struggle against apartheid intensified, the militant teacher unions played a critical role in the movement for people's education for people's power, which was spearheaded by the NECC. Among other things, these unions campaigned against subject inspectors (who were seen as agents imposing apartheid-based bureaucratic controls on, rather than supporting, the professional development of teachers) and undertook a project to develop alternative pedagogies and subject curricula (Govender 2004; Nkomo 1990). Thus, the 1980s saw the authoritarian, racist and technocratic model of policy-making come under serious threat, with strident cries for a more inclusive and participatory education policy process.

An important outcome of the teacher militancy of the 1980s was the national teacher unity initiative, which led to the formation of SADTU and its rival NAPTOSA in the early 1990s, the former adopting a strong unionist approach to policy engagements. NAPTOSA adopted a more professional approach, paying greater attention to teacher development, while SADTU continued to prioritise militancy, although not as much as its predecessor organisations – the other militant teacher unions – had in the 1980s. An important campaign that SADTU pursued in the post-apartheid era was its opposition to the role and functions of the inspectorate, and it worked to implement a more transparent and developmental teacher performance management system.

SADTU's role in education policy: the transition to democracy, 1990–1994

The launch of SADTU in October 1990 came on the heels of dramatic political changes earlier that year with the unbanning of the ANC and other political organisations. The way was paved for negotiations towards a new political dispensation embodied in the Congress for a Democratic South Africa (CODESA) talks and the adoption of the Interim Constitution, which heralded the dawn of democracy in April 1994. In parallel with the preparatory talks between the ANC and the apartheid state on the framework for negotiations, the MDM initiated a wide-ranging policy development process to prepare to govern, which covered the economy and various social sectors such as education, health and welfare. In education, the first steps in this process were taken by the NECC, which established the National Education Policy Investigation (NEPI) to explore education policy options within a value framework based on the ideals of the democratic movement (Gerwel 1992). NEPI yielded twelve research reports that covered the full spectrum of the education system from early childhood education to higher education,[1] representing the democratic movement's ideas on a future education system. Subsequently, the MDM consolidated its education policy in anticipation of a new ANC-led government through the development of the ANC's Policy Framework for Education and Training (which came to be known as the Yellow Book) and its Implementation Plan for Education and Training (IPET) in 1994.

SADTU was an active participant in these policy processes. As an affiliate of the NECC and in line with the NEPI principle that parents, students and teachers must participate in the development of educational policies (Sayed 1995), SADTU was represented on the NEPI Executive Committee, research groups and consultative fora (SADTU 1993). Similarly, it participated in the various task teams established by the ANC to develop the Yellow Book and its Implementation Plan. However, in this period SADTU's participation was as a junior partner, rather than as an independent teacher union contributing in its own right, as it had not yet developed substantive education policies as an organisation. This limited role has been interpreted by some analysts as a sign of the weakening of SADTU, which had become inward-looking and concentrated largely on building its own organisation and campaigning around salaries and working conditions (see, for example, Deacon and Parker 1998). The focus on organisation building in this period can hardly be a sign of weakness, especially given the embryonic nature of SADTU structures and the struggles the organisation had to wage to seek recognition as a national non-racial teacher union from the apartheid state. In reflecting on the challenges faced by the union during this period, former SADTU president Duncan Hindle recalls:

> There were financial constraints in the union. It was early days and we were still doing battle with [the National Party] government around issues of stop orders and recognition; so there were some difficulties, including being able to facilitate the necessary consultative processes within the union to formalise policy positions.[2]

This prioritisation of union-related issues over broad education policy was consistent with SADTU's development trajectory at the time (as discussed in Chapter 4). Further, there is no gainsaying the fact that SADTU was not only successful in achieving recognition. It also played a key role in the institutionalisation of labour relations and collective bargaining in education through its role in the processes leading to the promulgation of the Education Labour Relations Act in October 1993 and the subsequent establishment of the Education Labour Relations Council (ELRC) in 1994 (as discussed in Chapter 1).

Another important development that not only captures the professionalism-unionism debate within SADTU during this period, but also shaped the organisation's influence in the policy arena, was the decision to affiliate to COSATU. Former SADTU official Rej Brijraj recollects:

> There were many that thought there was no need for a teachers' organisation to become part of a workers' federation. There were those that felt that teachers are professionals and they should have a different orientation rather than becoming part of COSATU. However, when the dynamics of the transformation and the reasons for becoming part of the federation were explained, namely, that you would not lose your professionalism but rather you would gain 'a thing' regarded as a worker as

well – a professional worker. So that joining SADTU does not compromise your professionalism; moreover, you will also have all the rights of workers and it is important for you to associate with the workers so that you have greater bargaining power.[3]

Overall, given SADTU's focus during this period on building the organisation and its involvement in policy work as a relative newcomer, coupled with the decision to affiliate to COSATU and remain a part of the Tripartite Alliance, the union was arguably in the early stages of becoming embedded in the hegemony of the evolving post-apartheid state; likewise, its identity as a professional union was very much in its infancy. Nevertheless, a critical question for SADTU in the current conjuncture is whether its affiliation to COSATU, specifically, lies at the heart of persistent criticism of its neglect of professional matters.

SADTU's role in education policy: the democratic era, 1994–1996

In the period immediately following the establishment of the Government of National Unity led by the ANC, SADTU continued to prioritise its union-related focus. This is not surprising; despite the significant gains made on the labour front in the period before 1994, the apartheid-era inequalities in the conditions of service between black and white teachers remained in place. Moreover, redress was constrained by the introduction of the Growth, Employment and Redistribution (GEAR) programme, a home-grown structural adjustment programme introduced by the democratic government to address the fact that the state coffers were empty as a result of the apartheid state's mismanagement of the economy. Thus, despite an ANC-led government, it took a protracted struggle, including strikes, marches and rallies by teachers across the political and ideological spectrum, to achieve parity in salaries and conditions of service between black and white teachers, as well as agreements on salary increases, post-provisioning norms and teacher retrenchment (NAPTOSA 1998; SADTU 1995).

In relation to education policy in this early period, SADTU continued to participate in policy processes as part of the ANC-led Education

Alliance rather than contribute by developing its own positions on systemic policies. This was due in part to confidence that the ANC-led government, which included many senior ex-SADTU officials in both the legislature and the bureaucracy, would implement the education policies of the MDM. As Hindle explains:

> To a certain extent, there was a huge optimism, we'd just elected a democratic government, it was our government, we were relatively confident with the kind of legislation that was coming out of certain processes and in the interests of certainly the membership of the union, so I think it wasn't based on an expectation or suspicion of government at that stage and that's why we were able not to get involved fully in every aspect of it [policy-making] (cited in Govender 2008: 291).

The Education Alliance, which replaced the NECC that had disbanded in 1994, comprised the ANC, the SACP, COSATU, and the student and teacher organisations that were previously affiliated to the NECC. To coordinate its activities, it established a Working Committee chaired by the SACP's Blade Nzimande, who was also the chairperson of the multiparty Education Portfolio Committee in parliament. SADTU was represented in the Alliance Working Committee by Assistant General Secretary Mxolisi Nkosi. The link between the ANC in government and the ANC outside of government – represented by the Education Alliance – was provided by the ANC Education Study Group in parliament, which, in addition to the Education Alliance, consisted of the ANC members of parliament on the Education Portfolio Committee. It provided a forum for the ANC and its allies to engage with policy and legislative issues prior to these being debated in the Education Portfolio Committee, and to overcome the growing sense of alienation experienced by them from legislative and policy processes more generally. As Blade Nzimande and Susan Mathieson (2003) suggest, the ANC Education Study Group played a significant role in education policy development by making strategic interventions into the policy and legislative process. In some respects, these developments represent SADTU's early incorporation into the emerging democratic state hegemony, but, as will be discussed, it was a highly contested process, which became enmeshed with SADTU's struggle for professional unionism and autonomy. This was evident in the contestation over the 1996 South African Schools Act (SASA), the purpose of which was to transform the governance, funding and organisation of schooling (Govender 2008). SASA would emerge as the most significant school education policy initiative of government post-1994, and given its implications for teacher unions and their members, SADTU's positioning in relation to the SASA policy formation process is an important chapter in the union's development.

The South African Schools Act, 1996

It was apparent from the outset that the transformation of the school system would be highly contested, pitting the progressive forces represented by the Education Alliance against the conservative forces representing the white community that was bent on protecting their erstwhile privileges. In broad terms there were two main dividing lines. The first centred on school funding: free education versus the charging of user fees. The second division was over governance: the powers, functions and composition of school governing bodies (SGBs) – in particular, equal representation versus representation based on a parental majority.

The contestation over school transformation also played itself out within the Education Alliance and among education stakeholders more broadly. In February 1996, the Ministry of Education released a White Paper on Organisation, Funding and Governance of Schools based on the recommendations of an investigation undertaken by a Review Committee on which all stakeholders, including SADTU, were represented. However, SADTU was highly critical of the Review Committee process, as observed by senior SADTU officials:

> You see it looked very tempting, enticing to be appointed to the Review Committee, but to a certain extent the Review Committee was set up very much as a listening agency, it was meant to solicit the views of a wide range of the public as it were

... and therefore one has to ask the question whether it was strategic even to be on that Review Committee, whether in fact the voice of the union was not marginalised by being there in that we were unable to essentially make comments from our side because we were part of the process.[4]

The voice of transformation had been watered down because of the technical/expert inputs by conservative unions [e.g. NAPTOSA] and their allies ... it was a very technical exercise as if the [Review] Committee was not grappling with the aspirations of the majority of the people. Progressive forces had to win over conservative forces in the committee so that progressive changes could be included.[5]

Thus, the development of SASA was to be mediated by issues of consensus and legal and fiscal realities; moreover, in spite of SADTU's political alliances, the union's views would not be privileged.

Following the Review Committee process, the draft South African Schools Bill was released, whereupon the subject of negotiations with the SGBs of affected schools, as required by section 247 of the Interim Constitution, became a major issue. The negotiations resulted in a revised Bill tabled in parliament in which the Ministry of Education had compromised on a range of issues that were not in line with the policies of the Education Alliance. This pitted the ANC in government against the ANC and its Education Alliance partners outside government. Although the ministry, through the ANC Study Group, accommodated some of the concerns of the Education Alliance, it was not willing to compromise on two key issues: the charging of user fees and the principle that parents would constitute the majority on SGBs. SADTU lost the battle within the Education Alliance and was forced to accept the compromises. The heated debates within the Education Alliance also pointed to inconsistencies in SADTU's opposition to a parental majority. As Thami Mseleku, an ex-SADTU official who had joined the bureaucracy, recalls:

> I remember that the chairperson of the Study Group – Comrade Blade [Nzimande] – pulling the carpet under SADTU's feet by saying, 'There are very serious contradictions here because the parents are the workers, the working class of this country who must actually be leading the reconstruction of education and development. I don't understand why we, who . . . are actually a teachers' union and part of the working class, can argue that the working class is ignorant and therefore shouldn't be given the power and the authority' (cited in Govender 2008: 309).

More importantly, the perception was created within the Education Alliance that SADTU prioritised the sectoral (or private) interests of its members against the national (or public) interests, which constitutes the kernel of SADTU's struggle towards professional unionism – that is, striking an appropriate balance between professionalism (towards the public good) and unionism (enhancing teachers' labour/economic interests). And it is in this regard today that SADTU has been urged by various interest groups, including civil society, to prioritise the professional interests of teachers over their unionist/labour needs, if it is to transcend its history of being too narrowly focused.

During this period, SADTU members also enjoyed the opportunity to participate in the development of the new teacher education policy through their involvement in the establishment of the South African Council of Educators (SACE) in 1995. Responsible for the regulation of the teaching profession, SACE aims to enhance the status of the profession through the registration and professional development of teachers, including inculcation of a code of ethics to guide teacher behaviour. SADTU also influenced the new teacher education policy in 1997–1998 through representation on the Committee on Teacher Education Policy (COTEP).[6] COTEP provided advice on teacher education to the Department of Education and the Technical Committee on the Revision of Norms and Standards for Educators, which conducted consultative workshops in all provinces, thus providing teachers, including SADTU members, with the opportunity to engage in a key issue affecting them.

However, it was SADTU's engagement in the policy-making process of SASA that became a defining policy moment for the union during this period. On the one hand, its policy strength and influence derived from its close relationship with and participation in the ANC Education Alliance; on the other hand, developing policy positions as part of a collective undermined its independence as a union. This was especially the case when SADTU's policies, which were consistent with those of the Education Alliance, came into conflict with policy shifts of the dominant partner in the Alliance, the ANC, which was also the governing party. Moreover, the fact that many of SADTU's senior leaders had moved into the legislature and bureaucracy made no difference as they had to operate within the policy framework of the governing party. They were unable to 'introduce new ways of thinking and operating within the state policy cycle (from formation to implementation to review) by the often static weight of institutional tradition and values' (NALEDI 2006: 18). These bureaucratic and political features of the transition had a significant impact on SADTU's ability to influence policy processes (Govender 2008).

SADTU's experience in this period was a salutary lesson for the union, which came to the realisation that it had to develop and fight for its own independent policy positions. There were other lessons as well. First, SADTU recognised that making individual organisational submissions in the parliamentary process would have a greater impact than joint submissions as part of the Education Alliance (Govender 2008). Second, SADTU had failed to utilise the 'power of repetition' effectively in public presentations in parliament by sending several representatives to reinforce key arguments as some constituencies had done; instead SADTU sent 'one representative to articulate the concerns of thousands of teachers'.[7] Third, the union learned that changing positions and making concessions were an integral 'part of the politics of negotiations', a legacy of the CODESA talks that characterised South Africa's transition (Govender 2008). Fourth, SADTU realised that, politics aside, influencing policy required well-researched technical inputs, as demonstrated by its main rival, NAPTOSA. Arguably, one of the main reasons for NAPTOSA's strength in this regard was its claim to professionalism, including the fact that it had highly experienced former educationists and bureaucrats, as well as lawyers with expertise in education law and policy, among its senior officials. Fifth, unlike its experience with the social movements that constituted the MDM during the struggle against apartheid, SADTU could not rely on other civil society organisations allied to the governing party to advance its agenda, which revealed the changing nature of state-civil society relations (Govender 2008).

In summary, SADTU's involvement in policy-making during this early democratic period was very much focused on enhancing the labour conditions of its members, while the union simultaneously grappled with the implications of its political alliance with the ruling party, specifically its influence and independence in the policy arena. It paid little attention to the professional dimension of educators' development during this time. These issues would force SADTU to examine more closely its claims to professional unionism post-1996.

SADTU's role in education policy: the democratic era, 1996 to the present

In the post-1996 period, SADTU continued to focus on addressing the unionist/economic needs of its members. Issues relating to post-provisioning norms and the status of temporary teachers would resurface post-2000 as the country's economy faltered amid widespread government corruption and allegations of state capture. These developments constrained government's ability to adequately address school infrastructure needs and provide quality access to education, especially in rural provinces such as KwaZulu-Natal and the Eastern Cape. Simultaneously, teacher unions' struggles, led by SADTU, extended beyond shop-floor concerns to embrace broader policy issues, such as cutbacks in education spending and rationalisation policies in the mid to late 1990s (Vally and Tleane 2001).

However, the policies that SADTU and other teacher unions, such as NAPTOSA, would become most engaged with were those related to curriculum reform, teacher accountability and professional development, given government's and unions' recognition of the importance of these policies in the delivery of quality basic education. In the process, SADTU came to understand that while its limited influence could be ascribed to the politics of policy-making and constraints on its independence, it was compounded by capacity constraints and the narrow preoccupation with organisational development and labour-related issues. SADTU recognised that it needed to raise its *professional* profile if it was to meet and influence the numerous education policy challenges of the day. As a result, from the mid-1990s onwards, SADTU began paying more attention to building its in-house policy capacity through the appointment of education specialists and researchers, and by strengthening links with progressive academics and education policy units both within and outside the universities (discussed further in Chapter 4).[8] This enabled SADTU to intervene in and respond more effectively to policy issues based on its own organisational interests and perspectives. This assertion of its relative autonomy from the governing party also resulted in a shift in its relations with the state on education policy matters, from collaboration – the forced compromises of SASA – to contestation and collaboration, especially with regard to curriculum, teacher accountability and professional development. This shift also signalled SADTU's attempts to move towards professional unionism so that the union could respond to both the economic and broader educational interests of its members and society at large. Whether SADTU succeeded in these endeavours is questionable.

Curriculum policy
In February 1997, the minister of education launched Curriculum 2005 (C2005), which was a fundamental revision of the school curriculum based on the principles of outcomes-based education (OBE) (Lungu 2001). Policy-makers hoped that the envisaged curriculum reform would lead to improved quality of teaching and learning outcomes. At the centre of C2005, which introduced eight new learning areas, was a major change in the culture and pedagogy of schools, requiring teachers to shift from a didactic approach to learning to a learner-centred approach (Welton 2001). Its implications for teachers and classroom practices were enormous and required, among other things, the retraining of teachers –

the large majority of whom were poorly trained and un- or underqualified – and administrators; new materials, different from traditional content-based texts; and new relationships between administrators, teachers, learners, parents and employers. Understandably and unsurprisingly, there was contestation over the launch of C2005. SADTU, as part of the ANC-led Tripartite Alliance, did not oppose OBE in principle, while the other teacher organisations cautiously welcomed the new curriculum, in spite of the fact that teachers had not been party to the decision to adopt OBE (Kruss 1998). However, SADTU, together with other teacher organisations and stakeholders, was concerned that the implementation time frames were unrealistic given the need for the large-scale training of teachers and the lack of basic infrastructure and resources to launch C2005.

Mounting public pressure, combined with the concerns of the teacher organisations, led the government to institute a review of C2005 through the appointment of a Ministerial Review Committee in 2000. Surprisingly, teacher organisations were not officially represented on the Review Committee, which led to sharp reactions, especially from SADTU. While NAPTOSA and the Suid Afrikaanse Onderwysers Unie (SAOU)[9] were generally more sympathetic to the review process, SADTU was concerned about a perceived detraction from official OBE policy, which it highlighted in its detailed response to the Review Committee's report:

> The overall findings appear to imply that teachers are really the cause for the failure of the new system. The material conditions under which they teach, the lack of support, learning materials and inadequate training have not been given sufficient attention as primary factors for the barriers experienced with implementation. Instead, there is emphasis on the teachers' lack of understanding of complex language, confusion with assessment, failure to transfer learning into classroom practice etc. for the failure of C2005. Outcomes-Based Education is relatively resource-based and as long as inequalities persist this would create major barriers to the implementation of C2005.

The report does not make a clear distinction between OBE and Curriculum 2005. It is therefore open to the interpretation that OBE has also failed. Although SADTU has endorsed the new approach we still feel the need to re-open critical dialogue to ensure a common understanding of Outcomes-Based Education among all stakeholders (SADTU 2000: 3).

Subsequently, teacher organisations were involved in the development of the Revised National Curriculum Statement (RNCS) for General Education and Training (GET) in April 2002, which replaced C2005. SADTU's participation in the revision process ensured that the curriculum not only remained outcomes-based but was more workable, secular and responsive to poorer constituencies. This underlines SADTU's concern for learners from poor and working-class communities, where the majority of its members are employed (perhaps a lesson learned from Nzimande's earlier criticism of SADTU for not prioritising working-class interests during deliberations on the Schools Act). As a result, the RNCS was more user-friendly, showed greater alignment with assessment, and embraced values of social justice, equity and human rights (SADTU 2002). In a study focusing on the RNCS process, the small size of the Mathematics subject committee (six members with only one secondary school teacher) in a curriculum process with short timelines was found to have lent to a fast-paced formulation process that encouraged 'borrowing' of foreign curricula, with 'relatively limited feedback from practicing primary school teachers' (Addy 2012: 190). Nii Addy's 2012 research findings further underscore the exclusion of teachers from South Africa's curriculum process, reminiscent of policy-making pre-1994.

Overall, experience in the curriculum policy development process led to SADTU's growing realisation that it could not rely on its allies in government to advance its policy concerns or to prioritise the interests of its members. This was all the more so given the exclusion of teacher organisations as key stakeholders from the Review Committee (although they were subsequently included in the revision process) (Chisholm

2005), which was symptomatic of a growing tendency within government not to fully engage in participatory policy processes (Govender 2004). In later years, such exclusion would lead to a serious rift between SADTU and education authorities, as reflected in the 2012 call for the resignation of the director general of basic education Bobby Soobrayan, who was seen to be driving a strongly unilateral and exclusive education policy agenda and undermining ELRC collective agreements.

Teacher accountability

Perhaps the biggest and most drawn-out policy contestation between teacher organisations led by SADTU and government in the post-apartheid era has been in the area of teacher performance appraisal. Teacher appraisal and evaluation policy underpinned by an authoritarian approach was hugely contested as part of the struggle against apartheid education in the 1980s and has continued to be contested as part of teachers' struggles for a democratic appraisal system post-1994 (Chisholm 1999). As Michael Samuel (2005: 5) suggests, this is due to the escalating demands on teachers flowing from new school governance arrangements and new policies, and 'reflects back to an earlier era in which teachers were being framed to become technicians of the State agenda, albeit in a new State with a new transformatory agenda'. Internationally, market dictates are increasingly shaping government policy choices, leading to rationalisation of schools and making them more economically efficient. The effect of this is to intensify the deprofessionalisation of teaching by eroding teachers' autonomy and subjecting them to stringent and time-consuming performance management and accountability systems (Hargreaves 2000). Similarly, in South Africa, teachers are being co-opted to develop accountability for their employer. This has emerged in two key areas – namely, teacher appraisal and assessment policies.

SADTU has been the leader among teacher organisations in the development of an alternative democratic teacher appraisal system. In fact, its first proactive involvement in policy dates back to 1992, when it commissioned the Education Policy Unit (EPU) at the University of the Witwatersrand to research alternative appraisal models, which would

inform SADTU's negotiations with the state. The outcome, which was based on a participatory research method, was a Developmental Appraisal System (DAS) that was piloted in 1996-97 in 93 schools in eight provinces. Subsequently, with the support of other teacher organisations such as NAPTOSA, it was adopted by the ELRC in 1998 (Chisholm 1999). The appraisal system comprised two main elements:
- democratisation of the process of evaluation by the inclusion of the appraisee, a peer nominated by appraisee, a union representative and a senior management person; and
- emphasis on positive, process-oriented assessment focused on improving practice.

The new system reflected a shift from bureaucratic to professional control of the appraisal process, and as Shireen Motala (2003: 519) asserts, 'the story of this appraisal system is thus also a story about the role of the South African Democratic Teachers' Union in promoting professionalization of teaching practices both inside and outside government'.[10]

However, implementation of the new appraisal system ran into serious challenges in the following years. Critics argued that it was too ambitious, complex and time-consuming, and bureaucrats felt that the DAS was a way of escaping monitoring by rendering teachers as competent professionals. This led to the introduction of Whole School Evaluation (WSE) by the Department of Education in 2001, which focused on the performance of the school as a whole rather than simply on individuals, an approach that SADTU and other teacher organisations embraced. The attempts to combine the two systems into an Integrated Quality Management System (IQMS) that focuses on both the development and the performance appraisal of educators have been less successful, giving rise to confusion over the status of teacher evaluation policies (Sayed and Kanjee 2013). SADTU's main objection to the IQMS was that teacher development should precede performance appraisal and evaluation, and the latter should not be linked to pay progression. Teachers also perceive IQMS as an attempt to blame them for the shortcomings of the education system. Therefore, to this day teacher appraisal and evaluation policy, which is central to teacher accountability measures, remains obfuscated and an area of ongoing contestation between teacher unions and the government. Significantly, it lies at the heart of SADTU and other unions' struggles for professional unionism, as teacher accountability and performance are seen as synonymous with teachers' identity as professionals (see, for example, Hargreaves and Fullan 2013; Sachs 2001) and critical to their mandate to deliver quality education services in the interests of the broader public good.

Teacher accountability is also an issue in the context of the learner assessment policy pathway, which emerged initially with the 2007 Assessment Policy and again with the release of the education department's Action Plan 2014 (Kanjee and Sayed 2013). The proposed assessment policy, by favouring formal testing over informal assessment, lends itself to promoting a discourse of reporting and recording as opposed to a discourse of assessment for improving learning and teaching (Kanjee and Sayed 2013). It thus potentially feeds into the discourse of managerial professionalism (Hargreaves and Fullan 2013; Sachs 2001) as teachers will be required to maintain portfolios of work on their assessment practices. In 2015, teacher unions united in opposing the administration of the Annual National Assessments (ANA), and the contestation around ANA continues as teacher unions and the department try to forge a new assessment dispensation to replace them. School assessment policies thus represent another site of contestation between teacher organisations and government, with potential future challenges for teachers' professional growth. Today, teachers are being exhorted by government and education stakeholders to assume traditional professional roles that emphasise service and loyalty, and which simultaneously subject teachers to increased performance management and assessment regimes in pursuit of quality education. Teacher unions, not just in South Africa but globally, see this as an attack on teachers' autonomy as professionals, and tackling the increasing bureaucratisation of assessment regimes is a critical policy component of SADTU's struggle for professional unionism.

In summary, in the post-1996 era and leading up to the present, SADTU has been and continues to be confronted by curriculum modifications and related changes affecting the professional status of its members. However, this has not deterred SADTU and other teacher unions from forging a new, more collaborative relationship with policy-makers.

From contestation to collaboration

More recently, since 2010, there is increasing evidence that the contestation around policies is giving way to greater collaboration, without necessarily compromising the independence of teacher organisations, including SADTU. This is reflected in the range of initiatives that SADTU, either on its own or together with other teacher organisations, has been involved in, including the following:

- The successful campaign to make History compulsory in the school curriculum. This was underlined by the minister of basic education's approval of the recommendation of the History Ministerial Task Team to make History a compulsory subject for students beyond Grade 9 to include Grades 10 to 12 from 2023 onwards (DBE 2018).
- The gains in systemic evaluation and assessment through participation in the National Curriculum Assessment Task Team, which is reviewing Curriculum Assessment Policy Statements (CAPS) with the aim of reducing assessment tasks to a more manageable number. This represents SADTU's ongoing efforts to advocate for assessment *for* learning as opposed to assessment *of* learning.
- The development of ELRC policies to improve the status and conditions of service of Grade R practitioners to improve the quality of early education.
- The review of the ELRC policy on post-provisioning norms to ensure an adequate supply of educators.
- The establishment of the *Teachers' Journal*.

Arguably, the most important collaborative initiative is the activities of the SADTU Curtis Nkondo Professional Development Institute (SCNPDI), which was established in 2013 to facilitate the professional development of SADTU members and other teachers. Linda Chisholm (2019) underscores that such developments are linked to the collaborative work between South African teacher unions and Education International[11] in their global quest for the achievement of quality education:

> Together with the state, all teacher unions – including SADTU, the National Professional Teachers' Organisation of South Africa (NAPTOSA) and the Suid Afrikaanse Onderwysersunie (SAOU) – have supported and participated in new initiatives to promote teacher development: whether in the form of participation in the development of strategic frameworks for policy, the roll-out of pilots by the South African Council of Educators to test new models of continuous professional development or indeed the formation of their own institute for professional development (Chisholm 2019: 173).

As such, significant progress has been made in the delivery of teacher professional development programmes. The programmes have been funded by the Teacher Union Collaboration (TUC) in partnership with the Department of Basic Education (DBE),[12] and by the Education, Training and Development Practices Sector Education and Training Authority (ETDP SETA). The teacher unions engaged through the TUC include SADTU, the Professional Educators' Union (PEU), the National Teachers' Union (NATU),[13] SAOU and NAPTOSA. During 2011, the collaboration between the DBE and teacher unions developed programmes aligned to the DBE's Action Plan and the Integrated Strategic Planning Framework for Teacher Education and Development in South Africa (ISPFTED). The main objectives of the TUC programme are:

- to address teacher development issues;
- to ensure ongoing professional development of teachers in South Africa;
- to strengthen delivery capacity in the education system for teacher development; and

- to support teacher unions in their agenda to professionalise their unions.

The primary beneficiaries are school leaders (principals, senior management teams), practising teachers, mentors/lead professional teachers, special needs teachers, and un- or underqualified teachers. Priority is also given to provinces, geographical areas/districts and subjects that have been identified as being in urgent need of support. All training programmes include an assessment of baseline skills where practically possible, as well as a post-training assessment as the first indication of training benefit. Provincial education departments may request unions to conduct specific programmes to meet their needs (SADTU 2013).

Since the introduction of the TUC initiative in 2011, more than 50 000 teachers were reached by training programmes between 2011 and 2013. The programmes include CAPS Foundation Phase Resource Development (SADTU members were involved in developing the training manual); Intermediate Phase Training for teachers; Assessment for Learning; Senior Management Training; and District-Based Professional Development Initiatives (SADTU 2013). Between 2014 and 2021, more than 10 500 teachers were trained by the SCNPDI in a range of topics, including professional learning communities; school management training (Governance, Policy and Leadership); Intermediate Phase Mathematics Training; Primary School Reading Improvement Plan Training; and robotics and coding training for 15 500 teachers in 2022,[14] no doubt influenced by the turn to online learning in the wake of Covid-19. However, teacher union strikes and other disruptive activities, as well as the lack of a professional ethos among some teachers and officials associated with SADTU, can easily undermine the positive effects of teacher professional development at the classroom level (see Chapter 5). Thus, a key challenge for the union is managing the tension between its unionist/labour interests and its professional obligations.

In addition, SADTU's commitment to collaboration is reflected in the launch of the *Teachers' Journal*, an independent, multidisciplinary peer-reviewed journal published in conjunction with academics and specialists in the education sector. It aims to accommodate papers from a wide variety of sectors within the field of education, particularly those that reflect fundamental teaching ethics and teaching pedagogy. SADTU also plans to hold an annual conference on issues concerning teachers and teaching and learning from 2023 onwards. The journal was approved by the National General Council (NGC) of SADTU at their national conference in October 2017.

Thus, in the current period, SADTU, in collaboration with other teacher unions, is making concerted efforts to enhance the quality of education services, in particular by focusing on teacher professional development, in addition to improving teachers' conditions of service. Increased collaboration between teacher unions and government, as well as among teacher unions themselves, is symptomatic of progress towards achievement of a stronger professional-unionist orientation in education policy practices in South Africa.

Conclusion

Political and ideological forces have historically shaped teachers' and unions' participation in education policy-making in South Africa. While these forces have sometimes led to the exclusion of teacher associations and unions from policy processes, especially during the apartheid era, teacher unions have continued to fight for a stake in policy-making throughout the country's history. Today, as the largest teacher union, SADTU is at the forefront of this contest. At the same time, SADTU's role in policy-making has been questioned and often criticised for being too narrowly focused on unionist/labour concerns. In short, it needs to expand the professional dimension of its policy work.

Overall, from the 1990s onwards, there was a gradual improvement in teacher union-state relations in South Africa. This was due in large part to the new ANC-led government's favourable labour relations policy, as well as teacher unions' ability to adapt to the changed political and economic conditions that shaped the country's political transition. Both professionalism- and unionism-oriented teacher unions took advantage of the more open and inclusive education policy environment to assert their ideological and organisational identities. Although this did not always translate into direct influence on policy outcomes (for example, SADTU in relation to the Schools Act), teacher unions have been able to leave their mark on key policies, both economic and education-related.

In the pre-1994 period, SADTU contributed to education policy development as part of the MDM, but its focus was very much on building the organisation and gaining union recognition. Immediately after 1994, SADTU relied on the collective strength of the ANC Education Alliance, including its affiliation to COSATU, and the ANC Education Study Group to impact policy change. This period was short-lived as the union had to compromise on some of its own policy positions – for example, in relation to the Schools Act and curriculum policy. In Gramsci's state hegemony conception (Gundogan 2008), SADTU may be seen to have become embedded within the state, representing broad state interests ultimately reflected in legislation and policy outcomes. However, being a member of the broader ruling political alliance also came with benefits, leading the union to pursue a proactive, relatively autonomous role in policy-making. Nevertheless, SADTU's continued affiliation to COSATU and the Tripartite Alliance remains an albatross around its neck, and the union should examine more carefully whether a more independent positioning in relation to the broader labour movement and the ruling party would serve its members, and learners, more effectively.

More recently, especially post-2010, SADTU and other teacher unions, recognising their important role in education development work, have cultivated strong working relations with the education departments in key areas such as teacher professional development to contribute to improved education quality. This has led to fewer disruptions in education through strikes and mass protests, which had characterised South Africa's education landscape for many years. In spite of these collaborative initiatives, contestation remains in key policy areas. This includes policies on teacher assessment, systemic education assessments (ANA) and, for SADTU, differences with the department/government over the privatisation of education and rural education policies. There is little doubt that SADTU's role in policy-making would be greatly enhanced if it were to reach agreement with the state in the critical areas of teacher accountability and teacher performance. This would not only boost SADTU's claim to professional unionism but would also go a long way to quelling criticism that the union is not concerned with the quality of teaching and learning.

Today, while embracing an ideological approach based on professional unionism, teacher unions in South Africa continue to reflect their traditional ideological roots in their relations with the state. SADTU's location within the Tripartite Alliance, which offers SADTU political leverage in its relations with the state, is significant. While SADTU has vastly improved its organisational policy expertise and professional profile, its policies and actions continue to be shaped primarily by a unionist ethos. Moreover, it is in the nature of teacher union-government relations that there will be contestation around education policy and labour issues, notably salaries and teachers' working conditions.

Teacher unions continue to play an important role in South Africa's policy-making landscape. The current period of increasing collaboration between teacher unions and government is a positive development. And as long as collaboration trumps disruptive contestation in the sector – the debilitating effects of a global pandemic, a worsening economic crisis and corrupt governance practices notwithstanding – the quality of education provision in South Africa will receive a much-needed boost. However, the key policy challenge that confronts SADTU is to deepen the professional dimension of its policy work whereby, as the largest teacher union in the country, it is seen to lead the development of policies that benefit its key beneficiaries, the children of the poor and working class. As such, the union should be championing campaigns that address school infrastructure shortages in rural communities and deepening its professional development programmes to improve teacher quality. In this context, SADTU can make an immense contribution as it continues its struggle towards professional unionism.

Notes

1. The areas covered were adult basic education, adult education, curriculum, education planning systems and structure, governance and administration, human resources development, language, library and information services, post-secondary education, support services and teacher education.
2. Interview with Duncan Hindle, former SADTU president, 14 December 2004.
3. Interview with Rej Brijraj, former SADTU vice-president of media, 13 December 2004.
4. Interview with Duncan Hindle, former SADTU president, 14 December 2004.
5. Interview with Rej Brijraj, former SADTU vice-president of media, 13 December 2004.
6. COTEP was a sub-committee of the Committee of Heads of Education Departments (HEDCOM), which comprised the national and provincial heads of education.
7. Interview with Glen Abrahams, former SADTU vice-president of education, 8 May 2003.
8. The main link was with the Education Policy Unit (EPU) at the University of the Witwatersrand and the Centre for Education Policy Development (CEPD), a policy NGO established to coordinate the development of the ANC's education policy in the early 1990s.
9. SAOU represents white Afrikaans-speaking teachers.
10. Interestingly, the senior bureaucrat in the Department of Education at the time was former SADTU president Duncan Hindle, who, together with the union's secretary general, Thulas Nxesi, had previously promoted alternatives to the old system within SADTU.
11. Education International is a global union federation of teachers and other education employees representing more than 32 million teachers and education support personnel in 178 countries.
12. In 2009, the then Department of Education was split, with the Department of Basic Education (DBE) responsible for school education and the Department of Higher Education and Training (DHET) responsible for post-school education, including workplace-based training.
13. PEU and NATU are the other two national teacher unions recognised by the ELRC, in addition to SADTU, NAPTOSA and SAOU.
14. Email communication from Renny Somnath, SADTU education officer, 19 October 2022.

References

Addy, N.A. 2012. 'Teachers' Roles in the Institutional Work of Curriculum Reforms: Comparing Cases from Botswana and South Africa'. PhD thesis, Stanford University, California.

Adhikari, M. 1993. *'Let us Live for Our Children': The Teachers' League of South Africa, 1913–1940*. Cape Town: UCT Press.
Bascia, N. and P. Osmond. 2013. *Teacher Union Governmental Relations in the Context of Educational Reform*. Brussels: Education International.
Chisholm, L. 1999. 'The Democratisation of Schools and the Politics of Teachers' Work in South Africa'. *Compare* 29(2): 111–26.
———. 2005. 'The Politics of Curriculum Review and Revision in South Africa in Regional Context'. *Compare* 35(1): 79–100.
———. 2019. *Teacher Preparation in South Africa: History, Policy and Future Directions*. Bingley, West Yorkshire: Emerald Publishing.
Deacon, R. and B. Parker. 1998. 'Education, Development and Democracy in South Africa'. In *South Africa in Transition: New Theoretical Perspectives*, edited by D.R. Howarth and A.J. Norval. London: Macmillan.
Department of Basic Education (DBE). 2018. 'Media Release: History Curriculum on the Way to Complete Overhaul in Basic Education', 18 December. https://www.education.gov.za/Newsroom/MediaReleases/English1/tabid/2311/ctl/Details/mid/8469/ItemID/6565/Default.aspx (accessed 27 March 2020).
Gerwel, J. 1992. Foreword to *National Education Policy Investigation: The Framework Report*. Johannesburg: Oxford University Press/NECC.
Govender, L. 1996. *When the 'Chalks are Down': A Historical, Political and Social Interpretation of Teacher Militancy in South Africa*. Pretoria: HSRC.
———. 2004. 'Teacher Unions, Policy Struggles and Educational Change, 1994–2004'. In *Changing Class: Education and Social Change in Post-apartheid South Africa*, edited by L. Chisholm. Cape Town: HSRC Press.
———. 2008. 'Teachers' Participation in Policy Making: The Case of the South African Schools Act'. PhD thesis, University of the Witwatersrand, Johannesburg.
———. 2015. 'Teacher Unions' Participation in Policy Making: A South African Case Study'. *Compare* 45(2): 184–205.
Gramsci, A. 1971. *Selections from the Prison Notebooks*. New York: International Publishers.
Gundogan, E. 2008. 'Conceptions of Hegemony in Antonio Gramsci's Southern Question and the Prison Notebooks'. *New Proposals: Journal of Marxism and Interdisciplinary Inquiry* 2(1): 45–60.
Hargreaves, A. 2000. 'Four Ages of Professionalism and Professional Learning'. *Teachers and Teaching: Theory and Practice* 6(2): 151–82.
Hargreaves, A. and M. Fullan. 2013. 'The Power of Professional Capital'. *Journal of Sustainable Development* 34(3): 36–9.
Hyslop, J. 1990. 'Teacher Resistance in African Education from the 1940s to the 1980s'. In *Pedagogy of Domination: Towards a Democratic Education in South Africa*, edited by M. Nkomo. Trenton, New Jersey: Africa World Press.
———. 1999. *The Classroom Struggle: Policy and Resistance in South Africa: 1940–1990*. Pietermaritzburg: University of Natal Press.

Kanjee, A. and Y. Sayed. 2013. 'Assessment Policy in Post-apartheid South Africa: Challenges for Improving Education Quality and Learning'. *Assessment in Education: Principles, Policies and Practice* 20(4): 442-69.

Kerchner, K.T. and D.E. Mitchell. 1988. *The Changing Idea of a Teachers' Union*. London: Falmer Press.

Kruss, G. 1998. 'Teachers, Curriculum 2005 and the Education Policy-Making Process'. In *Vision and Reality: Changing Education and Training in South Africa*, edited by W. Morrow and K. King. Cape Town: UCT Press.

Lungu, G.F. 2001. 'The Educational Policy Process in Post-apartheid South Africa: An Analysis of Structures'. In *Implementing Education Policies: The South African Experience*, edited by Y. Sayed and J. Jansen. Cape Town: UCT Press.

Motala, S. 2003. 'Reviewing Education Policy and Practice: Constraints and Responses'. In *South African Education Policy Review*, edited by L. Chisholm, S. Motala and S. Vally. Sandton: Heinemann Publishers.

National Labour and Economic Development Institute (NALEDI). 2006. *Assessing the Impact of SADTU on Education Policy in South Africa*. Johannesburg: NALEDI.

National Professional Teachers' Organisation of South Africa (NAPTOSA). 1998. 'Report on the Period 11 November 1994 to 28 October 1998'. NAPTOSA National Archives, Pretoria.

Nkomo, M. (ed.). 1990. *Pedagogy of Domination: Towards a Democratic Education in South Africa*. Trenton, New Jersey: Africa World Press.

Nzimande, B. and S. Mathieson. 2003. 'Transforming South African Education: The Role of the ANC Education Study Group, 1994 to 1999'. Occasional Paper No. 3, Centre for Education Policy Development, Johannesburg.

Ozga, J. and M. Lawn. 1981. *Teachers, Professionalism and Class: A Study of Organised Teachers*. London: Falmer Press.

Sachs, J. 2001. 'Teacher Professional Identity: Competing Discourses, Competing Outcomes'. *Journal of Educational Policy* 16(2): 149-61.

Samuel, M. 2005. 'Accountability to Whom? For What? Teacher Identity and the Force Field Model of Teacher Development'. Keynote Address at the 50th International Council on Education for Teaching (ICET) World Assembly 2005, Pretoria.

Sang, A.K. 2002. 'Interest Groups in Education: Teachers' Perceptions of the Effectiveness of the Kenya National Union of Teachers'. PhD thesis, University of Cape Town.

Sayed, Y. 1995. 'Educational Policy Developments in South Africa, 1990-1994: A Critical Examination of the Policy of Educational Decentralisation with Specific Reference to the Concepts of Decentralisation, Participation and Power'. PhD thesis, University of Bristol.

Sayed, Y. and A. Kanjee. 2013. 'An Overview of Education Policy Change in Post-apartheid South Africa'. In *The Search for Quality Education in Post-apartheid South Africa: Interventions to Improve Learning and Teaching*, edited by Y. Sayed, A. Kanjee and M. Nkomo. Pretoria: HSRC.

South African Democratic Teachers' Union (SADTU). 1993. 'Secretariat Report'. Second National Congress, July. SADTU National Archives, Matthew Goniwe House, Johannesburg.

———. 1995. 'Secretariat Report'. Third National Congress, August. SADTU National Archives, Matthew Goniwe House, Johannesburg.

———. 2000. 'SADTU Response to the Report of the Review Committee on Curriculum 2005'. Internal organisational report. SADTU National Archives, Matthew Goniwe House, Johannesburg.

———. 2002. 'Secretariat Report'. Fifth National Congress, September. SADTU National Archives, Matthew Goniwe House, Johannesburg.

———. 2013. 'Co-ordinating the Professional Development of Teachers'. *Infinity* (1): 12–15.

Torres, C.A., S. Cho, J. Kachur, A. Loyo, M. Mollis, A. Nagao and J. Thompson. 2000. 'Political Capital, Teachers' Unions and the State: Value Conflicts and Collaborative Strategies in Educational Reform in the United States, Canada, Japan, Korea, Mexico and Argentina'. Latin American Center, University of California, Los Angeles. www.isop.ucla.educ/lac/cat/fpriart.htm (accessed June 2003).

Vally, S. and C. Tleane. 2001. 'The Rationalization of Teachers and the Quest for Social Justice in Education in an Age of Fiscal Austerity'. In *Education and Equity: The Impact of State Policies on South African Education*, edited by E. Motala and J. Pampallis. Sandton: Heinemann.

Welton, J. 2001. 'Building Capacity to Deliver Education in South Africa?' In *Implementing Education Policies: The South African Experience*, edited by Y. Sayed and J. Jansen. Cape Town: UCT Press.

4

Organisational Development and Efficiency
Key Ingredients for Professional Unionism

LOGAN GOVENDER

This chapter posits the view that a strong organisational base is a prerequisite for a teacher union seeking to strike the right balance between professionalism and unionism. An organisational presence across the country, covering urban and rural, rich and poor communities, provides the springboard for harnessing the diverse needs of teachers. These include teachers' economic needs, such as decent salaries, as well as their professional growth needs, for all of which a well-oiled organisational machinery is essential. Thus, the building of branches, membership growth, financial security, effective communication, quality of membership services and internal stability are necessary for teacher union efficiency in the conduct of its day-to-day operations. In practice, however, this is easier said than done. As discussed in Chapter 1, SADTU was launched in October 1990 after a long and protracted process – lasting some three years – under the auspices of the National Teacher Unity Forum (NTUF). In the early years following its launch, SADTU faced a two-fold task, which concentrated its focus and determined its priorities. It had to build and consolidate its organisational structures and seek recognition as a national non-racial teacher union from the apartheid state that was hostile to both non-racialism and teacher unionism. Moreover, as the prospect of the first democratic elections in South Africa drew closer, SADTU needed to define its role in and relationship to the new, democratic government, whose birth it had contributed to through its participation in the anti-apartheid struggle.

SADTU therefore had to balance its strong unionist orientation with an equally strong emphasis on teacher professionalism.

The changing political environment thus posed new challenges for SADTU. These were summarised by Tom Bediako of the All Africa Teachers' Organisation (AATO) and Education International (EI)[1] at SADTU's Third National Congress in August 1995:

- consolidate your political, social, professional and economic gains;
- develop new relations with the Government of National Unity – maintaining your independence but at the same time ensuring that the aspirations of teachers and other workers are not sacrificed;
- take a leadership role in bringing into being new educational administrators who will identify themselves with SADTU;
- accelerate your membership mobilisation and conscientisation – negotiating for not less than 60% of teachers in South Africa by the year 2000; and
- develop the capacities of both men and women capable of representing teachers at all levels of decision-making in education (SADTU 1995).

The challenges identified by Bediako and EI have been at the heart of SADTU's growth and development since its launch. This chapter reviews the progress made by SADTU in meeting them, specifically the internal and external challenges it faced as it set about building the organisation, recruiting members, setting up branches, and framing its vision, mission and operational procedures. A key question that the chapter explores is whether SADTU's organisational goals, especially its professional and unionist dimensions – identified both at its National Congress in 1993 and subsequently in its 2030 Vision document released in 2010 – have been achieved. Does SADTU have the capacity to reach its professional unionism goals under its current organisational structure? In attempting to answer these questions, the chapter highlights the nature and content of organisational learning that has shaped the organisation and its membership, and assesses how well SADTU has responded to contemporary societal changes and challenges.

Organisational challenges: periodisation

The organisational development and efficiency challenges faced by SADTU in seeking to strike a balance between unionism and professionalism have differed based on the changing social, economic and political context, which can be broadly divided into four periods. A summary of the four periods is provided below and elaborated on later in the chapter.

The challenges in the first period, 1990-1993, were mainly developmental in nature, as the organisation established its structures, sought recognition from the apartheid state and fought for collective bargaining rights for teachers (discussed in Chapter 1). In this period, SADTU had to focus on establishing its organisational structures, in particular at branch level. This included the difficult task of integrating the smaller, militant teacher unions that emerged in the 1980s, such as the National Education Union of South Africa (NEUSA), and the older, conservative associations that joined SADTU. In parallel, SADTU worked to achieve recognition as a national non-racial teacher union from the (hostile) apartheid state.

The second period, 1994-1999, coincided with the transition to democracy. SADTU had to redefine its relationship to the democratic state and its role in the restructuring and reform of the education system, paying equal attention to both unionist and professional goals. It was confronted with the challenge of moving from the politics of resistance to the politics of engagement in policy-making, as elaborated in Chapter 3. SADTU aligned itself politically to the African National Congress (ANC). This was reinforced by its affiliation to the Congress of South African Trade Unions (COSATU), which, together with the ANC and the South African Communist Party (SACP), formed the Tripartite Alliance under the leadership of the ANC. However, its political alliance notwithstanding, SADTU recognised that it would have to continue to fight for the rights of teachers, as the democratic state would have to manage the contradictory interests of a range of stakeholders, not all of whom were sympathetic to worker interests. Participation in the political alliance came at a cost, notably the loss of senior leadership to government and a consequential weakening of capacity within SADTU. This would have serious ramifications for its ability to influence education policy-making and reform, an important dimension of a teacher union's professional work (see Chapter 3 for details).

In the third period, 2000–2010, SADTU enjoyed a healthy growth in membership – despite a decline of some 9 000 members between 1999 and 2002. That decline was due largely to SADTU members leaving to join rival unions, such as the National Professional Teachers' Organisation of South Africa (NAPTOSA), which were offering better benefits and services and were not perceived as being openly politically-aligned. Steady membership growth enabled SADTU to achieve financial security and reduce its reliance on international teacher organisations for monetary support. However, the growth in membership had one downside – namely, that rank and file members experienced participation challenges, especially with regard to policy development processes. This coincided with SADTU's traditional communication platforms grinding to a halt, as discussed later in the chapter.

In the fourth period, post-2010, SADTU experienced ups and downs in membership, dropping from a peak of just over 255 000 members in 2013 to just under 249 000 between 2013 and 2016. Subsequently, from 2017 it experienced a rise in membership, peaking at just over 266 000 by December 2019 and dipping again to just over 261 800 at the end of 2021. As before, the decline was due to membership dissatisfaction with the level and quality of both professional and labour/economic services provided, which was compounded by both internal and external communication challenges. Addressing these challenges helped SADTU rebuild its membership numbers. However, the union's major challenge in this period was at the leadership level. Aside from the continued loss of senior leadership to government, SADTU experienced serious fragmentation as members became embroiled in political intrigues and infighting within COSATU and the Tripartite Alliance. This situation exacerbated perceptions that SADTU was neglecting its professional programme obligations at the expense of political alignment.

The challenges that have confronted SADTU since its establishment can best be understood through an overview of the four key goals that SADTU adopted at its Second National Congress in 1993 to guide its development:
- Political – 'Ending apartheid in education [and the] reconstruction and development of a democratic education system'.
- Unionist – 'To enhance teachers' salaries and conditions of service through the establishment of proper collective bargaining councils'.
- Professionalism – 'To build capacity and expertise in education policy'.
- Organisational development – 'To become the largest teachers' union in South Africa through the building of effective union structures at national, regional, branch and school site levels' (SADTU 1993: 21).

Subsequently, in 2010, SADTU adopted its '2030 Vision', based on five strategic pillars, to guide the development of its programmes. Although differently nuanced, there is continuity between the 1993 goals and the 2030 strategic pillars, especially those relating to professionalism and unionism. The five pillars are:
- 'Servicing union members', which focuses on conditions of service and the provision of membership benefits – that is, the goal of unionism.
- 'Creating a learning nation', which focuses on an enabling learning environment to facilitate nation-building – that is, the goal of professionalism, although this is implied rather than stated categorically.
- 'Promoting a development-oriented nation state', which focuses on building awareness of and support for national development objectives – that is, the political goal of transformation.
- 'Creating international partnerships', which focuses on promoting solidarity with teacher unions in other countries,

in particular those within the Southern African Development Community (SADC) region – both a political and professional goal.
- 'Building a delivery based organizational capacity', which focuses on building management capacity and ensuring financial sustainability – that is, the goal of organisational development (SADTU 2010: 13–15).

Significantly, some of these challenges, such as membership services and internal communications, persist to this day, although their form and content may have changed.

Conceptual framework

In line with this book's underlying framework as outlined in the Introduction, this chapter adopts a historical conceptual lens, assessing SADTU's approach to balancing the professionalism-unionism nexus in the context of the organisation's development and the challenges it faced in different periods. Politics and the contestation for power are central constructs, given that teachers regularly clash with the state to assert their professional independence (McPherson and Raab 1988). For their part, teacher unions demonstrate considerable agency in their relations with the state – for example, in the cultivation of political alliances with a view to influencing policy (Murillo 1999). Central to understanding the emergence and development of teacher unions, particularly in the case of SADTU, is recognising the unique hybrid identity of teachers as both workers and professionals. Given their ambiguous class location between the working class and the middle class, teachers display multiple identities based on socio-economic, political and historical factors (Hindle and Simpson 1993; Olin-Wright 1979). Thus, teachers may describe themselves as 'professional workers' or 'worker professionals'.

To thrive and operate effectively in the broader political context, a teacher union needs a strong organisational base. In this regard, the chapter draws on Bascia and Stevenson's (2017) notion of teacher union renewal in the twenty-first century, which highlights four features of renewal that seek to fuse teachers' professional and union identities:

- increasing union membership
- increasing member involvement and participation in union structures and activities
- developing the skills and capacities of members, as both professionals and activists, through professional learning and member education
- developing 'unionateness' [or professional unionism] – the alignment of teachers' professional identity and union membership such that they may be considered as indivisible (Bascia and Stevenson 2017: 9).

Note on methodology

The chapter draws extensively on the author's doctoral thesis, Vusumuzi Kumalo and Dineo Skosana's *History of SADTU*, and the doctoral thesis of Shermain Mannah, former SADTU head of education (Govender 2008; Kumalo and Skosana 2014; Mannah 2008). These studies were qualitative in nature, involving in-depth interviews with teachers from various unions, union officials and policy-makers. The chapter also provides documentary evidence from SADTU's archives and includes data triangulation based on the author's discussions with SADTU officials during a writing retreat at the Wits Rural Facility in July 2019.[2]

Early years: building the organisation

As recounted in Chapter 1, SADTU's organisational roots lie in the emergence and participation of the militant teacher unions in the 1980s in the anti-apartheid struggle led by the United Democratic Front (UDF). These unions, which did not have strong organisational structures as their focus was on challenging apartheid, would ultimately constitute the core of SADTU's organisational base.[3]

Against this background, SADTU's primary aim after its launch in October 1990 was to build its organisational base. At that stage, SADTU's embryonic structure existed only on paper. Aside from the (interim) National Executive Committee (NEC) elected at the launching conference, the rest of the structure at the provincial, regional and branch levels remained a work in progress. In terms of SADTU's founding constitution, the highest decision-making body is the National Congress, which meets every five years, although in the early 1990s it met every two years. Between congresses, decision-making powers are vested in the NEC based on mandates from lower-level structures, at the heart of which are the branches. Thus, building the branches was a key priority in the 1990–1993 period. This included empowering members with skills to establish branch structures, promoting membership participation and training site stewards to effectively perform their functions, including grievance handling, conflict resolution, negotiation and communication skills. The emphasis in the early years was thus inclined towards the unionist functions of collective bargaining and improving teachers' conditions of service. However, SADTU faced enormous challenges – in terms of integration, administration and politics – in building the organisation, as discussed below.

The integration challenge

The main organisational challenge in this period was integrating into a common structure the militant unions and those established associations that had joined SADTU. It required ensuring that both the emergent unions and the established associations, whose orientation was towards professionalism, were represented in the newly formed leadership structure. This was done by accommodating the leaders of the various organisations through the creation of a range of vice-president positions at the national level, in addition to the posts of general secretary, president and treasurer. As Mxolisi Dimaza, a former SADTU member, explains:

> ... we have what we call Vice President of Education, Vice President of Sport. It was meant to [satisfy] people from other Unions, for people to fill some positions. Some of them were Presidents in their Unions and some were Vice Presidents ... we were trying to please people like *abo*Thonjeni, people like *abo*Swartz and so on (cited in Kumalo and Skosana 2014: 57).

It also required accommodating and addressing the uncertainties of the full-time staff who were employed by the established associations. Antony Moonsamy, a former administrator of the (Indian) Teachers' Association of South Africa (TASA) who was transferred to SADTU, reflects on this issue:

> Well, in my mind it was a challenge. I'm an Indian. I said, we will have to take the chance. If it works out for me, then it works out. If it doesn't work out for me, then I'll have to look for another job. But for myself and other colleagues, I tell you we survived. And I've been with the organisation for more than 20 years now ... I was also assisting that time in my Indian organisation to move towards SADTU, so there was no regret for me (cited in Kumalo and Skosana 2014: 61).

Besides the incorporation of TASA staff into the new SADTU structure, staff from other established associations, such as the African Teachers' Association of South Africa (ATASA) and the United Teachers' Association of South Africa (UTASA), and the smaller progressive unions were also integrated into administrative positions at national and provincial levels. However, not all existing staff was absorbed, as positions were limited. Some staff, especially senior officials from established associations, sought opportunities elsewhere. The integration of these established teacher associations, with their focus on professionalism, ensured that the professionalism-unionism balance impacted on SADTU's evolution as an organisation from the outset.

Administrative challenges

The administrative challenges in the early years included lack of an office, inadequate communications infrastructure and insufficient funding. This state of affairs reflected SADTU's origins in the militant teacher unions, which mobilised teachers as part of the anti-apartheid struggle rather than servicing their professional needs as teachers, which meant they did not require an established organisational structure. Difficulties in communicating with the membership and in facilitating the establishment of union structures required national officials to make direct visits to the various regions, which created additional burdens in terms of time and costs.

However, the administrative difficulties were in part mitigated by sympathetic officials in various education departments, as noted by Jobie Motumi, a SADTU organiser in the then Western Transvaal and Bophuthatswana:

> There were no resources. We didn't have a fixed office... we would go to a particular school and in the end there was this teachers' centre... The person who was in charge of the teachers' centre was an educator, it was someone we understood, we organized meetings there... (cited in Kumalo and Skosana 2014: 63).

In addition, in regions where the established teacher associations that joined SADTU were active, their infrastructure and resources were placed at the disposal of the union, and their experience and expertise proved invaluable to the young organisation. For example, in KwaZulu-Natal, TASA made a significant contribution by assisting with stop-order facilities and dual membership registration, which was a transitional measure. Similarly, in the Eastern Cape, the Transkei Teachers' Association (TTA)[4] provided logistical and financial support (Kumalo and Skosana 2014). UTASA, the coloured teachers' federation, also contributed by negotiating a group assurance scheme for SADTU employees.

However, not all the established associations that joined SADTU were equally helpful. For example, although the Ciskei Teachers' Union (CTU)[5] initially provided support and office space in King William's Town, the relationship between the young SADTU members and the old guard of the CTU was not harmonious given the inherent historic tensions and distrust between them. This was compounded by the fact that the CTU was unwilling to open its books and give up all its resources. As Mxolisi Dimaza states:

And they were not telling you all the resources that they had . . . They did not declare cars. The only things they declared mostly is the things that we see in the offices. But as far as the cars which they had, they didn't declare [those]. As far as their finances were concerned, they did not declare [those] (cited in Kumalo and Skosana 2014: 66).

Generally, however, the conservative teacher associations in SADTU contributed to its organisational development. And more importantly, TASA and UTASA, which under apartheid organised Indian and coloured teachers, contributed to strengthening SADTU's non-racial vision. This was reflected in the election of the late Poobie Naicker of TASA as the first deputy president of SADTU, while Shepherd Mdladlana served as the first president.

SADTU also benefited from the support and solidarity of teachers worldwide through two international teacher organisations: the World Confederation of Organisations of the Teaching Profession (WCOTP) and the International Federation of Free Teachers' Unions (IFFTU), which later became EI (Kumalo and Skosana 2014).[6] The funding provided by these international fraternal organisations significantly defrayed SADTU's operational costs between 1990 and 1992, covering staffing, general administration, membership recruitment and services, publications, campaigns and labour relations education, and was critical in enabling the union's organisational development. It is clear that SADTU was focused mainly on unionist, labour-related issues to ensure organisational stability, which would lay the basis for tackling more complex policy and teacher professionalism issues in the ensuing years. A study of teacher union renewal involving seven countries (Chile, Kenya, New Zealand, Poland, Scotland, Turkey and the United States) concluded similarly that teacher union development starts with a focus on basic instrumental issues, such as membership building, and extends thereafter to addressing teachers' professional and union issues, such as developing activist and professional learning skills (Bascia and Stevenson 2017).

Political challenges

SADTU also encountered political challenges in establishing structures in the 1990–1993 period. Among these was the intensification of competition between SADTU and those conservative teacher associations that had formed the separate national teachers' organisation NAPTOSA in 1991. SADTU also faced a hostile and intransigent state opposed to non-racialism and teacher unionism, and the broader political contestation and conflict that prevailed in the early 1990s. While the background to and details of these issues are addressed in Chapter 1 – notably, the political developments relating to the rise of the UDF and its clashes with the apartheid state and self-governing states (Bantustans) – the focus here is on the impact of these issues on organisation building within SADTU.

The hostility to SADTU was especially evident in the so-called self-governing Bantustans – in particular, KwaZulu and the Ciskei, both of which were at war with the ANC (to which SADTU was allied) and would not countenance any challenge to their authority. Samora Nene, a former teacher and one of the founders of SADTU in the Northern Natal region, describes the situation:

> It was difficult in the 1990s for a union to get off the ground because there were ZPs [Zulu Police] and police brutality which made it difficult for us to convene meetings . . . When the union started, we could not form branches of the union in our schools because these schools belonged to the KwaZulu Government. We had to mobilize underground (cited in Kumalo and Skosana 2014: 62).

In both KwaZulu and the Ciskei, SADTU organisers were denied entry into schools, and thus access to teachers, by the school principals, who, together with the older teachers, were members of the political parties that controlled the Bantustans. As Muziwamdoda Dliwayo, a SADTU organiser, recalls:

> We began organizing, we would visit schools, we would go and demand to meet teachers. It was not easy, you would go to a

school and the principal [was] not welcoming. The teachers were scared and we would demand that 'we want to talk to the teachers' and the principal would say 'this is my school, you can't just come in' and we would say 'hey, this is not your farm' (cited in Kumalo and Skosana 2014: 63).

However, the hostility of the apartheid state and the Bantustans also contributed to the growth of SADTU. For example, in KwaZulu many teachers turned to SADTU branches for protection when the KwaZulu minister of education, Lionel Mtshali, made insensitive and scornful remarks – '*labothisha bayakhonkotha kuhle kwemdlwane*' (teachers are barking like small puppies) – in response to SADTU's call for wage parity.

Similarly, in the Western Cape, SADTU grew in response to the apartheid state's restructuring and rationalisation plans, including teacher retrenchments (discussed in Chapter 1). Not surprisingly, the plans raised the ire of teachers and helped to mobilise them into forming SADTU structures in the Western Cape and elsewhere. As John Gutsy, a principal at Robin Hood Special School in Atlantis, recalls:

After that meeting [to discuss the state's proposals], we realised that these people will not take us anywhere, we must become part of a more progressive structure. And me and the other three guys, we were in the executive of the primary sports union. We were only four and we started to organise the SADTU branch. And we started talking amongst ourselves about SADTU and then we [contacted] the provincial [people] and we set up a branch here in Atlantis . . . [in] 1993, almost sixty percent of the teachers joined the union (Kumalo and Skosana 2014: 62).

All told, the integration, administrative and political challenges that confronted SADTU in the 1990–1993 period were formidable. The fact that SADTU was able to overcome these challenges and lay the foundations of the largest teacher union in South Africa by the end of its first decade is testimony to the commitment and resilience of the young teachers entering the profession and the militant unions they formed to fight for the rights of teachers as workers and professionals in the context of the struggle for democracy. This, together with the support of the established teacher associations who identified with the struggle for democracy, as well as the support provided by the two main international teacher unions before their merger into Education International, paved the way for SADTU's organisational growth and success.

Organisational growth and developmental challenges

From its early beginnings as a small, non-racial teacher union, SADTU has grown in leaps and bounds to become the largest teacher union in South Africa. Its growth has been nothing less than meteoric, increasing from some 20 000 members in 1990 to a peak of more than 261 000 in 2021, which is double the total membership of its main rivals, NAPTOSA and the Suid Afrikaanse Onderwysers Unie (SAOU).[7] A significant milestone was achieved by 2013, when SADTU recorded more than 255 000 members, thus gaining a two-thirds majority in the Education Labour Relations Council (ELRC). This achievement was on the back of breaking new ground in terms of recruitment, through targeted programmes focusing on Early Childhood Development (ECD), Adult Basic Education and Training (ABET), Further Education and Training (FET) and non-teaching staff (SADTU 2014b). However, the growth trajectory was not always upwards and there were periods of declining membership, but these was marginal and short-lived.

The servicing of such a large membership requires a high level of organisational capacity and expertise, a reality which affects SADTU's ability to influence policy outcomes (as elaborated in Chapter 3). SADTU has nine provincial offices comprising 53 regions, 485 branches and more than 26 000 school sites (SADTU 2014b). It has a total staff complement of 155 in its national office in Johannesburg and the nine provincial offices. While the majority are women – 112 (or 72 per cent) – it is striking that all the organisers are male. More striking is the low number of professional and research staff – heads of department, specialist professionals, researchers, counsellors and organisers – who comprise 16 per cent (or 25) of the total staff complement, which underlines the professional and policy capacity challenge within SADTU. The professional staff, except for organisers, are based at the national office.[8]

SADTU also has a number of elected officials at national, provincial and branch level who play an important intellectual and leadership role in the union's operations. These elected officials are in many ways the engine of the union, formulating policy and making decisions at various levels: NEC, National General Council (NGC), and provincial and branch levels.

Becoming the largest teacher union in South Africa meant overcoming many difficulties. In addition to the policy capacity and development challenge, these include the impact of political alliances on the organisation, membership services, internal communications, ensuring financial sustainability, and gender equity.

SADTU's political alliances: a perennial challenge

SADTU's origins as part of the broad anti-apartheid struggle which fought for the rights of teachers as workers is reflected in its political programme and goal to end apartheid in education, as well as its commitment to unionism. This was captured in the theme of the Second National Congress in 1993, 'Unionise for Educational Reconstruction and Development', and given expression through SADTU's affiliation to COSATU and its participation through COSATU in the ANC-led Tripartite Alliance.

SADTU's decision to affiliate to COSATU was contentious and, as discussed in Chapters 1 and 2, once again brought the issue that divided the NTUF to the surface: the identity of teachers as professionals and workers, as reflected in internal debates. As former SADTU president Duncan Hindle puts it:

> I think if you look at the whole debate about the affiliation to COSATU, there were different views, different tendencies within the organisation. Some felt very strongly that COSATU was the

right place and obviously that was at a time when the ANC wasn't there so COSATU was the proxy for the ANC . . . COSATU at that time was both a political and a workers' organisation – there wasn't any sense of professionalism or professional unions at that time in COSATU. So it was, in a sense, a very big debate that eventually got carried by a Congress decision, but certainly not an easy one and not a unanimous one in the end (cited in Govender 2008: 265).

These differences in SADTU were also mirrored in the discussions within COSATU in response to SADTU's affiliation application (as discussed in Chapter 2).

However, the decision to affiliate to COSATU, and thereby to participate in the Tripartite Political Alliance under the leadership of the ANC, came at a cost, both in terms of the loss of senior leadership to government structures and as a result of internal leadership battles linked to the politics of the Alliance. While the political alliance with the governing party came with benefits, including career opportunities, it was a double-edged sword as it constrained SADTU's independence as a union, particularly when it came to policy matters. These themes are explored more closely in the sections that follow.

Loss of leadership expertise

At its establishment in 1990, SADTU faced serious capacity constraints in terms of experienced leadership to ensure the development of well-oiled operational machinery across the length and breadth of the country. These constraints were exacerbated in the immediate aftermath of the elections in 1994, when senior leaders of SADTU were released to serve as ANC members in the national and provincial legislatures. Others became senior bureaucrats in the newly established national and provincial departments of education, as well as in statutory structures such as the South African Council of Educators (SACE). As a result, the union was deprived of some of its most experienced leaders. These included, among others, SADTU's first president, Shepherd Mdladlana, and general secretary Randall van den Heever, both elected as ANC members of parliament; Rej Brijraj, vice-president for media affairs, who was appointed as the first CEO of SACE; and Dhaya Govender, national organiser, who became the first general secretary of the ELRC.[9] Subsequently, in 2009, SADTU's general secretary, Thulas Nxesi, was elected as an ANC member of parliament and became minister of labour in 2019. Similarly, several other leadership figures took up positions in provincial government structures in this period, including the vice-president for gender, Nombule Mkulesi, and vice-president for sports, arts and culture, Salome Sithole.[10] In some respects, it could be argued that the union has been a stepping stone for political office.

The main reason for releasing SADTU members was to influence the transformation of the education system in terms of policy and bureaucracy operations. However, as noted in Chapter 3, the movement of senior SADTU officials to government and the education bureaucracy did not necessarily provide a platform for shaping policy to serve union interests, given the nature of the compromises that government was forced to make during the political transition. SADTU members were also members of the ANC as individuals, and no doubt some of them were influenced by their own political career ambitions. Moreover, the release of senior members of SADTU leadership to government was not without its problems, as noted by Hindle:

> The issue of leadership is a difficult one for the Union... However, a strategic analysis should be conducted by this Congress to guide the future release of senior leadership by assessing the gains and costs in an objective fashion. We may find that we have erred in the past by allowing the State to choose who they want and appoint them where they wish, rather than strategically deploying our human resources in identified key areas of government (SADTU 1995).

The loss of leadership would eventually compel the union to embark on a major capacity-building programme to build a strong second and third tier of leadership.[11] This, together with the fact that more recently SADTU has adopted new criteria that require a commitment to stay in the organisation to be eligible for leadership positions, as discussed in Chapter 6, seems to have had a positive impact. Since 2014, only three SADTU provincial leaders and none at the national level have moved into political positions.[12]

Factional battles, democratic centralism and disciplinary action
Since the late 2000s, SADTU has also lost senior leadership as a result of internal battles, which have their roots in the broader political struggles linked to different factions within the Tripartite Alliance. Thus, at least two SADTU presidents, Willie Madisha and Thobile Ntola, have been removed from office because of their links to the losing side in the factional battles within the Alliance (discussed in Chapter 6). Disciplinary action was also taken against some provincial and regional leaders and branches for failing to uphold the union's constitution.[13]

According to the SADTU report on the Eighth National Congress, the internal factional battles in SADTU were also linked to an unwillingness of members to accept the precepts of democratic centralism, which is the central principle underpinning decision-making in SADTU. In essence, the principle means that 'after all views are heard a decision is taken by higher and central bodies' after which there is a 'reasonable expectation that every structure of the organisation must be able and must have the will to implement Union programmes as directed by a higher structure' (SADTU 2014b: 87). This principle has been challenged in the context of factional leadership battles across all provinces, but most starkly in the Eastern Cape:

> ... the Union has been bleeding to such an astronomical extent in the province due to a number of causal factors, including poor levels of service, a glaring failure to implement Union programmes thus eroding the confidence members have in the organisation and its positions, a deliberate and persistent attack on the National Executive Committee based on mistruths and an unwillingness to respect internal organisational processes, be

it of a disciplinary nature or communication to the membership ... The province refused to accept democratic centralism, they have total disregard of the constitution, policies and decisions of the organisation (SADTU 2014b: 93–4).

At the heart of the turmoil in the Eastern Cape was the deep-seated anger among the provincial leadership and members over the expulsion of Ntola, who hails from the province. The provincial leadership is also alleged to be at the forefront of launching a new, alternative union to SADTU, with support from some branches and regions in the other provinces (SADTU 2014b). Thus, political dynamics may impact on the internal coherence and stability of teacher unions, a phenomenon not unique to South Africa. For example, the largest teacher union in Chile, the Colegio de Profesores, is 'known both for its tradition of putting forward counterproposals to government reforms and for its willingness to wage strikes when necessary. Since the return to democratic rule, relations between the teacher union and central governments have been tense but productive' (Bascia and Stevenson 2017: 13).

Organisational independence and the Tripartite Alliance
Loss of leadership may be a small price to pay if it results in the increased influence of SADTU in policy-making. SADTU certainly benefited from its participation in the Tripartite Alliance, as the ANC government was unwilling or unable to take action against SADTU, in particular when it disrupted schooling, for fear of losing votes at the ballot box. However, the union has enjoyed an ambiguous and somewhat tense relationship with the democratic government on policy issues, as discussed in Chapter 3. Its influence has been limited mainly to those aspects of policy that directly impact on teachers, such as performance measurement and evaluation. Where the rights of teachers are not directly affected by policy, such as on aspects of the South African Schools Act, the union's position has been ignored by the ANC-led government. And despite assertions that in such cases SADTU would assume its 'fighting character', this has not always materialised, as noted by Hindle in his address at SADTU's Third National Congress:

> Where policies deserve to be defended, SADTU will stand rock solid by the ANC-led government. But where policies are indefensible, positions are weak, or practices are unacceptable, then SADTU will assume its fighting character, whatever the source of these policies, position or practices ... We will be informed by our principles, and by our knowledge and experience of education. Our independence will never be compromised (SADTU 1995).

Thus, SADTU's membership in the ANC-led Alliance is double-edged. On the one hand, it has afforded the union access to the corridors of political power; on the other hand, it has constrained its independence in policy processes (see Chapter 3 for details). Indeed, globally and over many decades, contestation over control and ownership of education policy is central to teacher union-state relations (Bascia and Stevenson 2017; Govender 2015; McPherson and Raab 1988). Furthermore, as discussed in Chapter 3, SADTU's unionist/labour efforts to pursue members' material interests took precedence over its professional obligations, resulting in further strained relations with government and the ANC ruling party. A key reason for government's disquiet was the adverse effect union strike and protest actions were having on building a culture of learning and teaching in schools in pursuit of quality education.

Policy capacity and influence: a key professionalism-unionism challenge

SADTU's struggle for professional unionism has a long history that is intertwined with its development and growth as a union. Indeed, as this chapter makes clear, organisational capacity and efficiency are key ingredients in building professional unionism. The tension between unionism and professionalism, which dogged the teacher unity talks in the late 1980s, was seemingly resolved by SADTU at its founding conference, where consensus was reached that unionism and professionalism were two sides of the same coin.

In practice, however, SADTU prioritised labour matters for much of the 1990s, while its role in the development of education policy and the professional development of teachers was more limited, as discussed in Chapters 1 and 3. In fact, in its 2030 Vision document, teacher professionalism, although implied, is not a strategic pillar, and neither is the development of education policy. More recently, SADTU has attempted to address the unionism-professionalism imbalance through the establishment of the SADTU Curtis Nkondo Professional Development Institute (SCNPDI) and collaboration with the Department of Basic Education and other teacher unions to advance teachers' professional development, as discussed in Chapters 3 and 5.

SADTU had recognised the need to move away from protest politics to focus on policy development, including the professional development of teachers, at its Second National Congress in 1993:

> A tendency to use rhetoric to gloss over huge issues is an unfortunate legacy of our days of protest, but the participants [at the conference] . . . had no doubts about their intention to govern the future system of education, and the need to prepare for this (SADTU 1993: 45).

In fact, the union boldly asserted that it would be a key player in policy development, as 'South Africa will be looking to SADTU, more than any other organization, to reconstruct education, to somehow transform this failed system' (SADTU 1993: 46). This was something of an overstatement and was certainly optimistic. Although SADTU had developed positions on several policy issues of the day, it was not considered a powerful player in the policy arena (Chisholm and Ngobe 2003). This was largely due to its lack of capacity and policy expertise, which was highlighted at its Third National Congress in 1995, where it resolved to recruit experienced personnel to build SADTU's research capacity, given the 'need for a more sophisticated approach to policy positions and submissions' (SADTU 1995: 54). A report by Glen Abrahams, who was then SADTU's vice-president for education, addresses the matter:

> A number of instances have arisen recently which indicated the need for a more sophisticated approach to issues. The present salary negotiations have required an in-depth understanding and analysis of economic issues – pension funds, restructuring of remuneration principles taking into account broadbanding and multi-skilling approaches, taxation, etc. We have also been asked for our policy positions on the National Qualifications Framework, on consultative structures, on affirmative action, corporal punishment, as well as on ABET and Educare . . . and as in so many cases we do not have the capacity . . . All of this would suggest that the establishment of a research office within the union is imperative . . . (Abrahams 1995).

The concern with the lack of policy capacity was also raised by the then minister of education, Sibusiso Bengu, in his address to the Congress:

> . . . transformation requires involvement of a different kind to the one we are used to. It requires input, deep thinking, research, reflective analysis and hands-on experience . . . SADTU therefore needs to consider more seriously the question of teacher participation in policy debates and related areas (SADTU 1995: 54).

Bengu's statement underscores the pressure that SADTU was experiencing from its allies in government and the Tripartite Alliance to take on a stronger leadership role in the policy domain, and to shift its focus from political-cum-union activism to education development. As emphasised in Chapter 3 and elsewhere, SADTU's relations with government and its allies were often strained, and this had already become evident in the mid-1990s.

It would be some time, however, before concrete action was taken to build SADTU's research capacity. Although an Education Desk with an education officer had been established in 1994, it was only in 1996 that an education administrator was appointed,[14] followed by the appointment of education specialists and a researcher in February 1998.

Although its capacity was limited, SADTU, through the Education Desk, managed to coordinate its response to the plethora of policies emanating from the Department of Education, including participation in the National Education and Training Forum (NETF) Curriculum Committee, which was tasked with cleansing the apartheid curriculum and subject syllabus of racist and sexist content. The Education Desk was supported by provinces and regions, as indicated by Lesego Monyera, former educational officer in the Northern Cape:

> I was responsible for convening the education desk at the provincial level, so I would call all the then . . . four regions . . . I would call and coordinate meetings around this draft white paper, this draft legislation . . . We will discuss the proposal by the department of education; we will craft our own provincial response towards that [for submission] to a national meeting, where each province was represented by each provincial coordinator (cited in Kumalo and Skosana 2014: 75).

In the absence of the necessary capacity and expertise, SADTU drew on the Centre for Education Policy Development (CEPD) and the Wits Education Policy Unit (EPU) for policy analysis support:

> Of course we made use of various progressive institutions like the CEPD, the Wits EPU and so on, but what we guarded against in those years was to verify academic advice and expertise, to check it with the actual mandate that you received from the ground or from the ordinary teacher in the classroom (interview with Glen Abrahams, cited in Govender 2008: 290).

While Abrahams correctly pointed out SADTU's collaboration with external research units, it is arguable whether there was any connection between the advice received and the views of the ordinary teacher in the classroom, as the challenges faced by SADTUs' Education Desk indicate. From 2000 onwards, although SADTU's in-house research capacity increased, it was not sufficient to undertake all aspects of research required to meet the needs of its large membership base and union roles. Thus, SADTU continued to build partnerships with an expanded range of research organisations to facilitate the development of its own research programme to inform its policy positions. Aside from the CEPD and the Wits EPU, these included the National Labour and Economic Development Institute (NALEDI), COSATU's research arm; the Human Sciences Research Council (HSRC); the Child Labour Network; and the Gender Commission (SADTU 2002). This over-reliance on external policy expertise is perhaps one reason why SADTU has been unable to achieve its professional goals to the extent that its rival unions, such as NAPTOSA and SAOU, have been able to do. For example, the policy inputs of both NAPTOSA and SAOU are based on solid research that addresses the technical content of policies, drawing on internal capacity of highly experienced former educationists and bureaucrats, as well as lawyers with expertise in education law and policy, among their senior officials (Govender 2008; see also Chapter 3). Moreover, an over-reliance on external expertise potentially compromises organisational efficiency.

Membership services

Membership services straddle both the professional and unionist programmes of teacher unions, covering three main areas: representation of members in disputes with the employer; collective bargaining to enhance teachers' conditions of service; and professional development (SADTU 2002). In addition, the provision of financial benefits, such as insurance and loan schemes, ranks highly with members.

The first sign that all was not well with regard to membership services was the drop in membership from 218 878 members in 1999 to 210 235 in 2002. Aside from structural factors, such as the impact of teacher rationalisation and administrative weaknesses, difficulties in collecting subscriptions in some provinces and challenges in SADTU's organising strategy, the main reason for this decline was attributed to the quality of services provided to members:

> We also have to look at organizational and administrative weaknesses. We have to ask serious questions about the quality

of service to members. Have we done all we can to represent our members in the bargaining and dispute processes? Without pointing fingers, we have to analyse the subjective and objective factors for this stagnation on the membership front (SADTU 2002: 4).

The reasons for leaving advanced by SADTU members are instructive:
- dissatisfaction with benefits, especially loan schemes;
- dissatisfaction with union service and/or personnel;
- dissatisfaction with the union's record on salaries and CoS [conditions of service];
- opposition to union policy: the ANC Alliance-mentioned view that the union is too close to government to protect members adequately. Also, militant action is costly to members in the form of 'no work, no pay' (SADTU 2002: 4–5).

While the union asserts that the quality of membership services remains an important factor in why members join or leave a union (SADTU 2014b), the decline in SADTU's membership high point post-2013 is attributed to the dynamics of particular provinces. Specifically, the union cites organisational discipline at the leadership level in provinces such as the Eastern Cape, Gauteng and North West as a key contributor to membership dissatisfaction. This relates to the political infighting and subsequent disciplinary actions taken against union leaders, as discussed earlier (SADTU 2014b). SADTU recognised that it needed to develop a strategy to address members' concerns in provinces such as the Eastern Cape and North West. Overall, 'effective and timeous membership service still remains a challenge . . . given the enquiries that are directed to the national office on a regular basis' (SADTU 2014b: 101). An issue that continues to plague the union, and which remains a reason why members might leave to join rival unions, centres on the 'no work, no pay' principle. This is due largely to the absence of a strike fund to compensate striking members; there is also the fear of victimisation by principals. In addition, some members leave because of dissatisfaction with the union's association with the ruling party.[15] It is therefore clear that political factors also influence membership growth and trends, and in SADTU's case, they ultimately impact on its quest for professional unionism.

As a response, SADTU's programme plans for 2003–2006 are equally instructive. Although there was recognition of the need to build research capacity, initiate professional development programmes for teachers and strengthen internal communications, the main focus of the resolutions adopted were political in nature. This was reflected in the organising frame of the resolutions – 'Deepening the working-class content of the National Democratic Revolution and the Tripartite Alliance' – which included the following:

- to establish political schools and political/socio-economic commissions;
- to participate in municipalities;
- to defend the labour movement and its leaders from attacks; and
- to build the SACP by allocating resources for joint programmes.

There appears to be a preference to address political challenges rather than the quality of membership services, as suggested by plans to educate members on the importance of the Alliance and strengthening the SACP. This suggests that there were tensions between the leadership and the membership, a reality underpinning one of the biggest challenges faced by SADTU – namely, grassroots involvement in policy work. In the early to mid-1990s, participation by rank and file members was hampered by the fact that provincial and, in particular, branch-level organisational structures were not fully operational. As a result, there was a reliance on provincial and national officials to represent and carry the mandates of members. However, this was not always possible because of logistical and organisational challenges, as explained by Hindle:

> [There were] enormous challenges and that was also part of the capacity constraints, financial in part, but just logistical and organisational. The union was still in a fairly precarious state

then – we had very few officials, certainly at provincial or local levels who were full-time, so we were running an organisation – a big organisation – largely on voluntary commitment. The union did try to facilitate, as far as possible, consultations and discussions at the lower levels of the organisation and there were those who made use of the opportunities within the union to have their say on these matters; but I have no doubt that many, many members didn't even get to see or hear about these debates [relating to school governance and funding] (cited in Govender 2008: 273).

In general, SADTU branch meetings afforded members a limited opportunity to make inputs and suggestions regarding broader education policy matters, as branch meeting agendas often dealt with what were seen as more pressing issues, such as salaries and promotions.

In fact, the ineffective functioning of organisational structures continued post-2000, as indicated by the challenges faced by SADTU's Education Desk, which was the national facilitating structure for provinces on all education policy matters. First, the participation of provincial structures in the work of the Desk had become erratic, depending on the issue concerned and the adequacy of financial resources for provincial operations. Of particular concern was the poor response from provincial structures when policy documents or discussion papers were circulated. The process proved to be time-consuming, affording provinces little time to respond. In step one, a draft policy document is sent to provinces for inputs; in step two, provincial inputs are sent back to the national office for consolidation; and in step three, either the general secretary or deputy makes a final input before forwarding the document to the education department.[16] Second, SADTU officials representing the union in various stakeholder forums had not been interacting with the Desk on a consistent basis: decisions taken at such forums were often not relayed to the Desk, which in certain instances led to the Desk and SADTU representatives contradicting the decisions taken. In attempting to resolve these problems, several recommendations were made, including the need to develop an effective communication strategy and consolidate reporting mechanisms to ensure accountability for mandates given and the sharing of information with relevant structures (SADTU 2002, 2014b).

The challenges of non-participation by members was further exacerbated by the particular model of representative democracy that SADTU adopted – namely, democratic centralism. Under this model, decision-making powers are concentrated in national structures, in particular the Education Desk and the National Executive Committee, which is the union's highest decision-making structure between national congress and general council meetings. This resulted in members being out of touch with key policy developments and, arguably, the national leadership being out of touch with members' views and concerns. As Bascia and Stevenson 2017) assert, teachers' engagement in union policy-making/democratic structures is an important activity that can enhance professional unionism; they also suggest that this engagement presents an opportunity for the development of teacher agency and leadership, which teacher unions should consider.

This is not to suggest that the union's leadership is totally oblivious to members' concerns. For example, as emphasised by SADTU's national education officer, Brenda Ndelu, and North West province education convenor, Mkhuseli Mafunda, the union has been collaborating with other unions to improve the quality of its membership services relating to wellness programmes and its teacher professional development services through the SCNPDI.[17] The union has also taken firm steps to address the fallout following the leadership fracas post-2000, discussed earlier. This, together with targeting educators in non-school sectors, such as technical and vocational education and training (TVET) colleges, has resulted in membership reaching an all-time high of just over 261 000 members by December 2021. Overall, there is an expectation on the part of many members that much more can be done, and that organisational decision-making structures are not agile enough to respond to the needs of a diverse membership. This suggests that SADTU needs to be more responsive to the needs of membership diversity as part of its professional programme so that it is not seen to be favouring members' unionist/economic interests at the expense of their developmental and professional interests.

Communications

As intimated above, effective communication with members constitutes an important part of organisational efficiency that ultimately impacts on a union's ability to strike a balance between professionalism and unionism. In the mid-1990s, SADTU's primary method for keeping members informed of policy development, which was coordinated by its media department, was through two publications, the SADTU newsletter, *Educators' Voice*, and its journal, the *New Teacher*. These were discontinued in 2010. It seems the newsletter was discontinued due to poor distribution because of a lack of reliable address lists, as well as the high publishing costs. More recently, in July 2019, the union launched the *Teachers' Journal* to provide a learning platform for its members. The main purpose of the journal, which was first mooted in 2017, is to help 'education workers as professionals to write articles and share experiences that will assist with finding solutions for some of our challenges in the education system' (SADTU 2017: 23).

However, currently and going forward, SADTU has prioritised the development of technology platforms that allow members to communicate through the union's website and via email. The focus on technology to facilitate communication is reflected in the development of SADTU's Information Communication Technology (ICT) Master Plan, which makes provision for training in the use of technology, including supporting members to gain access to laptops and other electronic devices (SADTU 2014b).

It is clear from these initiatives that SADTU is intent on improving communication with members, including facilitating professional learning and information sharing through the use of both digital and traditional media. The optimal use of technology and social media should help facilitate grassroots participation, as well as advance progress towards achieving SADTU's professional goals.

Financial independence

An essential requirement for organisational growth and development in order to meet a union's professional and unionist goals is a sound financial base. At its establishment in 1990, SADTU had a limited resource base. Because it lacked recognition from apartheid authorities, it was unable to access membership subscriptions, the lifeblood of any trade union. Between 1990 and 1992, SADTU relied on funding from its international allies – WCOTP and EI – for its organisational and operational activities. However, by 1993, SADTU had won recognition from the apartheid state, albeit within the different racial departments of education rather than as a national non-racial teacher union (as discussed in Chapter 1). This enabled SADTU to access membership subscriptions, resulting in EI shifting from covering SADTU's operational costs to supporting the union's programmes in August 1993.

By 1999, SADTU was financially independent and sustainable, with membership subscriptions constituting its primary source of income – close to 75 per cent. This was supplemented by ELRC levies (10 per cent) and insurance commissions (11 per cent). However, in 2001, there was a significant decline in membership subscriptions – down to 60 per cent – which coincided with the decline in membership numbers between 1999 and 2002 discussed earlier. Moreover, SADTU's annual savings had diminished significantly. This led to concerns over future financial sustainability and the long-term future of the union. Ironically, SADTU decided that in the interests of its financial viability, it had little choice but to embrace capitalism by setting up its own investment company, SADTU Investment Holdings (SADTU 2002).

Today, the union continues to reflect a sound financial position, including investments and the acquisition of new premises for its headquarters, known as the SADTU Village, in Kempton Park, Gauteng. Subscriptions remain the union's major source of income at 50 per cent, agency fees (31 per cent),[18] insurance commissions (4 per cent), donations (2 per cent) and other income (13 per cent) (SADTU 2014a).[19] The question to be asked, therefore, is whether SADTU is making efficient and effective use of its finances in service of members' hybrid needs, including professional and labour/economic needs.

Gender issues

Gender equity and concerns have remained high on SADTU's agenda. Teaching is one of the few professions in which women were and still are represented in large numbers. In 1991, women made up 71 per cent of the teaching profession in the Department of Education and Training primary schools and 42 per cent in secondary schools. However, women were rarely promoted to head of department and principal posts, and were also discriminated against in terms of salaries and conditions of service. The remuneration scales were unequal, and women did not enjoy the same benefits as their male counterparts in relation to housing subsidies, medical aid and pensions.

In its attempt to fight for gender equity, SADTU held a conference in Durban in 1991 to raise awareness around women's oppression and developed a programme of action for women teachers. This led to the launch of a Gender Desk in 1993 (SADTU 1995). SADTU, together with NAPTOSA and other unions, made notable gains in addressing gender inequality and discrimination between 1993 and 1998. These included salary parity between women and men; increased maternity leave (four months) and the extension of maternity leave for single and divorced women; and equality in housing subsidies, which were extended to all women (SADTU 1998). SADTU has also linked the promotion of attitudes and practices for minimising HIV transmission with its campaign for greater gender equality and the empowerment of women. These included demands for women to be free to choose their preferred contraceptive methods and persuading male teachers to participate in HIV/AIDS education programmes (Govender 2004).

However, the gains in equality in salaries and conditions of service were not mirrored in internal organisational structures; nor did these structures reflect women's professional and leadership aspirations:

> The key point we would like to raise is that the struggle for gender equality needs a consistent and honest approach from all of us. We still have our membership comprising of men and women on a 40/60%, while the contrary is mirrored in decision making structures (SADTU 2002: 121).

In the assessment of SADTU's Gender Desk, certain fundamentals had to be addressed if the situation of female teachers was to be alleviated and social changes in gender relations achieved. These included addressing the enormous imbalance of women in leadership and decision-making positions; the male-dominated culture of caucusing and lobbying; male teachers' patriarchal and sexist attitudes; and monitoring the implementation of gender equity, childcare and sexual harassment policies (Govender 2004). Thus, besides addressing women teachers' labour and economic needs, there was a need to address women's broader social concerns to facilitate their growth as teacher professionals.

Since 2002, there has been considerable progress in gender representation in the organisation. By 2014, all SADTU structures had complied with a 2010 congress resolution that there must be a 50/50 gender representation (SADTU 2014b). Moreover, a similar requirement was set for representation at workshops, trainings and meetings. However, the challenge remains in top positions. The majority of chairpersons and secretaries at branch, regional, provincial and national levels are male; women are more likely to be elected to various portfolios in deputy positions. Similarly, all the provincial organiser positions are held by men, and there are only two women in the ten-member national negotiating team (SADTU 2014b).

According to some union officials, this inequality is due to the domestic pressures on women members in their roles as mothers and wives/partners.[20] Bascia and Stevenson (2017: 7) concur: 'For teachers with caring responsibilities, managing work and family and being involved in the union can appear impossible.' Similarly, Shermain Mannah (2008: 155-6), asserts that 'the tension between gender consciousness and a heightened consciousness triggers a conflict between their [women's] private and public realities'.

There is little doubt, however, that SADTU's Gender Desk is very active. This is reflected in the participation of SADTU's female members at various international and regional conferences, such as the EI's Second World Congress in Dublin (April 2014) and a UNESCO-led workshop on gender-based violence in schools in Botswana (August 2014) (SADTU 2014). To facilitate greater progress in resolving gender challenges, SADTU adopted the following resolution at its 2017 NGC meeting:

> A gender policy to provide guidelines for institutionalising and operationalising gender as a key development strategy for achieving gender equality, equity and women's empowerment within SADTU [to be implemented]. The National Executive Committee should be tasked with ensuring that the gender policy is implemented by all Union structures (SADTU 2017: 21).

Thus, in spite of tremendous strides being made in material benefits for women teachers, a key challenge for SADTU is to confront the fundamental patriarchal and exclusionary relationship between male and female teachers, and to ensure that inclusive gender policies addressing the subordinate status of women teachers are in place (see Chapter 6 for further discussion). Monitoring the implementation of gender-related policies, both within the union and in the broader society, remains another ongoing challenge. Nevertheless, there has been considerable progress in meeting this challenge, as expressed by Mannah (2008: 170):

> Although I do not envisage any feminist revolution in SADTU in the immediate future, I maintain that the last 17 years have been important years of cumulative experience, learning and irreversible change for women in the union. As one woman states, 'We have begun to recognise that women are an intrinsic part of the organisation'; we have claimed our voices in the union.

Conclusion

There is little doubt that, since its formal launch in 1990, SADTU has made huge organisational strides towards achieving its professional unionism goals as spelt out in its programmes. Nevertheless, much more needs to be done to optimise organisational efficiency and effectiveness.

Overall, SADTU has struggled to strike a balance between unionism and professionalism as its commitment to unionism continues to take precedence over its professional commitments, although there has been a significant reduction in SADTU-initiated teacher strikes in recent years. Simultaneously, SADTU's professional development focus to benefit teachers has grown substantially, as has its concern with education quality issues. A related and long-standing lesson for SADTU is the imperative of creating a learning culture within the union, especially building the organisational capacity and skills of its members. This includes deepening the union's research and policy capacity to better serve its professional goals, and thus reversing its persistent tendency to rely on external policy expertise.

One of the biggest challenges is competition for membership, a constant challenge faced by unions globally. A key mediating factor here is the quality of services rendered to members. While SADTU has strived to make greater use of technology to enhance communication with members – especially around access to professional development opportunities and learning – it has struggled to compete with rival unions, such as NAPTOSA, in providing quality services to its members. This was a major reason for the decline in membership in the early 2000s and again in 2013. The situation appears to be changing in the last few years, as the union seeks to address some of these gaps. It is important for the union to undertake continuous and rigorous reviews of its membership benefits package so that it is able to respond to diverse membership needs, as well as to changes in the socio-economic and political milieu. In terms of the latter, SADTU membership is not a homogeneous mass – while many members might choose to remain because of the material benefits of belonging to the largest union in the country, others are choosing to leave the union due to its continued ideological positioning and political alliances. As discussed in Chapter 3 and elsewhere, SADTU's political alignment with the ANC-led Tripartite Alliance has serious implications, and lies at the heart of negative public perceptions of SADTU's bona fides in realising its development as a professional union. Moreover, as Bascia and Stevenson (2017) suggest, teacher unions play a key role in defending members' working conditions while simultaneously promoting teachers' professional status and development. They argue that this can be achieved by strengthening unions' grassroots activism and building democratic engagement through formal and informal structures to involve members with diverse interests and experiences.

In South Africa's current political and economic conjuncture, characterised by endemic levels of state capture and corruption as well as economic meltdown, SADTU will be challenged to meet the diverse socio-economic, political, labour and professional needs of its members. Given the union's general financial stability, due largely to members' fees and the dividends derived from its investment vehicle (SIHOLD), SADTU has reason to be optimistic about the future. However, more judicious use of its financial capacity will be required in the years ahead – notably, through the institutionalisation of monitoring, evaluation and accountability systems in order to make thorough assessments of programme implementation and relevance, as well as organisational agility and effectiveness.

Organisational learning is one thing, but without visionary and transformational leadership, the translation of lessons into action will remain a major challenge (see Chapter 7). In this regard, SADTU has faced serious challenges in the post-2000 period. The union was forced to take disciplinary action against senior leadership, including two of its presidents, over political factional battles and corruption charges, resulting in fragmentation within provincial and regional structures. Thus, a major leadership and management challenge in the years ahead, therefore, centres on the dexterity and vision of SADTU's leadership in crafting a political programme for influencing policy while retaining relative autonomy from government and its political allies. This requires SADTU to pay more attention to its professional rather than its political goals in its quest to become a truly professional union.

Fundamentally, SADTU's biggest challenge is the development of an organisational blueprint that blends traditional unionism with what might be termed twenty-first-century unionism – that is, giving attention to both unionist and professional issues, and responding appropriately to new social and economic challenges. While the union has embarked on this path, it needs to accelerate the upgrading of its digital and technological infrastructure to improve its operations and better serve its members, and to be in a position to confront new education sector challenges being unleashed by the Fourth Industrial Revolution.

Notes
1. Education International is a global union federation that brings together organisations of teachers and other education employees from across the world. It represents some 383 member organisations and more than 32 million teachers and education support personnel in 178 countries. See also note 6.
2. The officials were Brenda Ndelu, SADTU education officer, and Mkhuseli Mafunda, SADTU North West province education convenor.
3. Of the racially based teacher organisations, the (African) African Teachers' Association of South Africa (ATASA), the (Indian) Teachers' Association of South Africa (TASA) and the (coloured) United Teachers' Association of South Africa (UTASA) joined the new union. The white teacher organisations, under the umbrella of the Teachers' Federal Council (TFC), did not join. However, soon after SADTU's launch, two ATASA affiliates – the Transvaal United African Teachers' Association (TUATA) and the Natal African Teachers' Union (NATU) – and a UTASA affiliate – the Cape Teachers' Professional Association (CTPA) – withdrew and joined NAPTOSA, which would become the second-largest teacher union in South Africa (Govender 1996).
4. An ATASA affiliate.
5. An ATASA affiliate.
6. WCOTP, established in 1952, was the world body of teacher organisations that considered themselves professional associations rather than trade unions, whereas IFFTU had a trade union focus. Following years of debate, WCOTP and IFFTU merged into Education International in 1993 to form a single body with both a professionalism and unionism focus. Its members are therefore historically more professionally focused (e.g. NAPTOSA) or more unionist oriented (e.g. SADTU).
7. SAOU represents (white) Afrikaans-speaking teachers.
8. SADTU's national office consists of the following departments: National Administrator and Secretariat, Finance, Legal Department, Corporate Services, Communications, Membership Services, Research, Education and Gender Desks.
9. Other high-ranking SADTU leaders who left the union include Duncan Hindle, former president, who joined the Department of Education in 1995 and ultimately become director general there until 2009, and Ronnie Swartz, SADTU Western Cape leader, who became head of the Western Cape

Department of Education from 2002 to 2009 and has also served in various management capacities in Gauteng province.
10. Discussion with Brenda Ndelu, SADTU education officer, and Mkhuseli Mafunda, SADTU North West province education convenor, during the writing retreat at Wits Rural Facility, 18 July 2019.
11. *SADTU News*, June 1996.
12. In 2014, George Masegela, SADTU's Northern Cape provincial chairperson, became mayor of Ga-Segonyana. Following the May 2019 national elections, there were only two known deployments: SADTU Limpopo province chairperson Ronnie Mosoeka, who became a member of parliament, and Free State province deputy secretary Zanele Sifuba, who became Speaker of the Free State provincial legislature.
13. Disciplinary action was taken against Papa Ndaba, former regional secretary of Maluti in the Free State; Lawrence Tsajwa, the former provincial secretary of North West; the branch executive committees of four branches in the Maluti region; and the regional office bearers of the Motlanti Mmekwa region of North West (SADTU 2014b).
14. *SADTU News*, September 1996.
15. Discussion with Brenda Ndelu, SADTU education officer, and Mkhuseli Mafunda, SADTU North West province education convenor, at the writing retreat at Wits Rural Facility, 18 July 2019.
16. Discussion with Brenda Ndelu, SADTU education officer, and Mkhuseli Mafunda, SADTU North West province education convenor, at the writing retreat at Wits Rural Facility, 18 July 2019.
17. In a discussion with the author during the writing retreat at the Wits Rural Facility, 18 July 2019.
18. An agency fee refers to union commission in lieu of participation in the Public Service Bargaining Council from monies deducted from the salaries of all teachers, and paid on a proportional basis to all registered unions. As the union representing the largest proportion of members, SADTU receives the largest share of agency fees.
19. Email to author from SADTU, 14 August 2019.
20. Discussion with Brenda Ndelu, SADTU education officer, and Mkhuseli Mafunda, SADTU North West province education convenor, at the writing retreat at Wits Rural Facility, 18 July 2019.

References

Abrahams, G. 1995. 'Education Report'. Addendum to the Secretariat Report of the SADTU Fourth National Congress, 6-9 September 1998. SADTU National Archives, Matthew Goniwe House, Johannesburg.

Bascia, N. and H. Stevenson. 2017. *Organising Teaching: Developing the Power of the Profession*. Brussels: Education International.

Chisholm, L. and P. Ngobe. 2003. 'Gearing up for an Integrated Education and Training System'. In *South African Education Policy Review, 1993–2000*, edited by L. Chisholm, S. Motala and S. Vally. Sandton: Heinemann.

Govender, L. 1996. *When the 'Chalks are Down': A Historical, Political and Social Interpretation of Teacher Militancy in South Africa*. Pretoria: HSRC.

———. 2004. 'Teacher Unions, Policy Struggles and Educational Change, 1994–2004'. In *Changing Class: Education and Social Change in Post-apartheid South Africa*, edited by L. Chisholm. Cape Town: HSRC Press.

———. 2008. 'Teachers' Participation in Policy Making: The Case of the South African Schools Act'. PhD thesis, University of the Witwatersrand, Johannesburg.

———. 2015. 'Teacher Unions' Participation in Policy Making: A South African Case Study.' *Compare* 45(2): 184–205.

Hindle, D. and L. Simpson. 1993. 'Teachers Don't Talk in Class! A Class Analysis of Teachers and Their Organization in South Africa'. In *Kenton-at-Broederstroom, 1992: Conference Proceedings*, edited by S. Pendlebury, L. Hudson, Y. Shalem and D. Bensusan. Johannesburg: Education Department, University of the Witwatersrand.

Kumalo, V. and D. Skosana. 2014. *A History of SADTU, Part 1: An Education Giant is Born*. Johannesburg: SADTU.

Mannah, S. 2008. 'The Experiences of Women Leaders in the South African Democratic Teachers' Union (SADTU)'. PhD thesis, University of KwaZulu-Natal, Durban.

McPherson, A. and C.D. Raab. 1988. *Governing Education: A Sociology of Policy since 1945*. Edinburgh: Edinburgh University Press.

Murillo, M. 1999. 'Recovering Political Dynamics: Teachers' Unions and the Decentralization of Education in Argentina and Mexico'. *Journal of Interamerican Studies and World Affairs* 41(1): 31–57.

Olin-Wright, E. 1979. *Class Structure and Income Determination*. New York: Academic Press.

South African Democratic Teachers' Union (SADTU). 1993. 'Secretariat Report'. Second National Congress, July. SADTU National Archives, Matthew Goniwe House, Johannesburg.

———. 1995. 'Secretariat Report'. Third National Congress, August. SADTU National Archives, Matthew Goniwe House, Johannesburg.

———. 1998. Annexure E to 'Programme and Minutes of SADTU's Third National Congress, July 1995'. Fourth National Congress, September. SADTU National Archives, Matthew Goniwe House, Johannesburg.

———. 2002. 'Secretariat Report'. Fifth National Congress, September. SADTU National Archives, Matthew Goniwe House, Johannesburg.

———. 2010. '2030 Vision'. Internal document. SADTU National Archives, Matthew Goniwe House, Johannesburg.

———. 2014a. 'Finance Report Book 5'. Eighth National Congress, October. SADTU National Archives, Matthew Goniwe House, Johannesburg.

———. 2014b. 'Secretariat Report Book 2'. Eighth National Congress, October. SADTU National Archives, Matthew Goniwe House, Johannesburg.

———. 2017. 'National General Council (NGC) Book 4'. SADTU National Archives, Matthew Goniwe House, Johannesburg.

5

Dilemmas of Unionism and Professionalism in the Promotion of Teacher Accountability

MICHAEL CROSS AND SIBONOKUHLE NDLOVU

Since the late 1990s, SADTU has been under increasing public scrutiny and criticism fuelled by the perceived tension between its pursuit of members' rights and its role in meeting the public obligations of teachers in the schooling system and the education sector at large. In the public and media domain, the poor quality of outputs and outcomes in schooling is blamed on the intransigence of SADTU in narrowly furthering the interests of its members at the expense of learners. Despite its best efforts, SADTU has been unable to alter the negative public perception of its role in schooling, which is the result of the manner in which it has pursued its goals, and its political role and participation in the Tripartite Alliance led by the African National Congress (ANC), which has governed South Africa since 1994.

At the centre of this tension is SADTU's role in managing a delicate balance between unionism and professionalism and its impact on teachers' professional identity and accountability on the one hand, and between cooperation and contestation in its relations with government in pursuit of post-apartheid education reconstruction and development on the other. Internally, the challenge of teacher professionalisation has occupied centre stage, with many members complaining about the lack of recognition of their rights – professional, occupational and academic. Historically, a major constraint to teacher professionalisation has been the fact that SADTU members suffered from a working-class syndrome – that is, resignation to just working as a teacher with little or no commitment to developing a strong professional identity, an attitude that still persists among some teachers. This is illustrated by the views of a teacher as expressed in 2017:

> The teacher union I belong to is SADTU, and I think one of the prime reasons I am the member of the particular union is that ... I think when I became a worker, as a worker you have certain rights and to ensure that these rights are upheld, you need [an] umbrella body to ensure these rights are being upheld. So one of the prime reasons I joined the union or a particular union, is to ensure that my rights as an educator is always upheld (cited in Sibiya 2017: 69).

This chapter assesses the role that SADTU has played in the development of teacher professionalism, teacher professional identity and teacher accountability. It argues that this role has been constrained by SADTU's approach to unionism and professionalism, and that a new strategy is needed if SADTU is to play a pivotal role in facilitating teacher professionalism, identity and accountability. The new approach should be based more firmly on the concept of professional unionism, which (i) prioritises the interests of the learner, as demanded by government and the public at large; and (ii) recognises that the precondition for the latter is a cooperative rather than conflictual relationship between the different stakeholders in the education system. An enabling factor in this regard is the legacy of dialogue, consultation and negotiation that has characterised SADTU's internal unionist politics. This legacy has facilitated social dialogue and provided teachers with an independent voice. It can certainly play a critical role in educating teachers and in building their collective capacity to support the teaching profession for quality education and for investment in education as a public good (ETUCE 2016). There is growing recognition within SADTU both at membership and leadership level, as indicated below, of the need for teacher professionalism and that this requires addressing grievances through negotiations rather than the militant strategy of strikes associated with unionism:

I do not view things blindly like some of my union colleagues. The Department of Education as an employer, should develop all teachers professionally for the sake of uniformity and not the unions . . . and that will be a correct thing to do (SADTU member cited in Sikhosana 2004: 56).

We need to always balance the two because a strike has got to be last resort, which breaks the deadlock. People have to go back to the negotiation table to find a solution because the strike is not a solution but a weapon used to make sure that you find a solution, when a solution has to be found. So [since the struggle] we have changed a lot. So the legacy is that we started seeing a lot of change because of negotiations.[1]

Teacher unionism, professionalism, autonomy, identity and accountability: conceptual perspectives

The tension between unionism and professionalism in relation to teachers and teacher organisations is not unique to SADTU and contemporary South Africa. It permeates the debates about the role of teacher organisations globally and historically. Both in the United Kingdom and the United States, for example, the debate around professional unionism was quite prominent in the 1980s (see the Introduction to this book). The different ideological outlooks of teacher unions influence their approach and priorities in relation to unionism and professionalism. On this matter scholars appear to be divided. Some emphasise unionism and argue that the role of teacher unions is to prioritise and focus on the improvement of working conditions, including job security (Sanger 1990). Others contend that the main focus and priority should be to advance and develop teachers' professionalism, including influencing educational reform in terms of educational standards and teaching content (Sibiya 2017; Villegas-Reimers 2003). There are also scholars who argue that teacher unions should move beyond the unionism versus professionalism divide and focus on advancing social justice and democracy (Van der Walt 1998).

The historical evidence suggests that the distinction between unionism and professionalism is not binary. The prioritisation of unionism or professionalism varies across time and space and is dependent both on the changing social and political context and, importantly, the ideological orientation of different teacher organisations. Teacher unions first emerged in the nineteenth century, when teaching was institutionalised in public schooling systems. The main focus of teacher unions in this period was 'expanding and protecting the prerogatives of teachers by promoting the professional dimensions of teachers' work' in response to the emphasis on 'scientific' expertise by bureaucratic administrators in charge of public schooling (McCollow 2017: 3). In this sense, although they called themselves unions, they were more akin to collective associations, as they rarely engaged in traditional union activities such as collective bargaining and industrial action and did not identify with the broader trade union movement and associated political parties. This is not to suggest that the early teacher unions did not highlight or concern themselves with bread-and-butter issues. However, such involvement was limited and often related to bureaucratic control issues. For example, the National Union of Teachers (NUT) in Britain was formed in 1870 in response to the planned introduction of a 'system of payment by results, which was both a remuneration and a control issue' (McCollow 2017: 3).

However, in the twentieth century, as labour struggles led to changes in industrial legislation, teacher unions took advantage of this and shifted their focus to improving pay and conditions of service through collective bargaining, including strike action (McCollow 2017). Evidence from the United States indicates that collective bargaining has improved teachers' salaries and conditions of service (Gindin and Finger 2013). Indeed, the growth of teacher unions in the United States was directly linked to industrial teacher unionism, and members view salaries and conditions of service as the most important focus of union activity (McCollow 2017).

The underlying reason for the tension between unionism and professionalism is due in large part to the ambiguous occupational status of teachers as employees. As Raewyn Connell argues, although 'teachers are workers, teaching is work, and the school is a workplace', this is complicated by the fact that teaching primarily occurs in the public sector and is regarded as 'white-collar' or 'knowledge work' (cited in McCollow 2017: 3). This implies that teachers are not workers in the traditional sense of the term but are professionals with a well-defined set of knowledge, skills and expertise that is acquired through training in the craft (Vaillant 2005). Furthermore, professionals develop a professional identity, which, as scholars agree, involves having a self-image and sense of belonging to a particular profession based on a common set of attitudes, values, beliefs and behaviours (Higgs 1993; Ibarra 1999; Paterson et al. 2002). Thus, professional identities vary based on the specific characteristics and traits associated with particular professions.

The view of teaching as a profession and teachers as professionals is, however, open to contestation. Unlike other professions such as law and medicine, teaching is not characterised by a high degree of autonomy (Hargreaves 2000). The role of teachers in professional practice is limited and restricted. It is shaped by the organisational goals of the education system, which provides the framework for directing and monitoring the classroom practice of teachers (Demirkasimoglu 2010). Teachers are required to implement a predetermined and designed curriculum that conforms to specified national standards, and their performance is measured and regulated through public examinations. Teachers are expected to conform to the requirements as stipulated, rather than exercising their own decisions and creativity. The only aspect of classroom practice in which they can exercise autonomy is in the teaching methods they use. This lack of autonomy and blind compliance to government prescripts leads to the deprofessionalisation of teachers (Evans 2008; Samuel 2008). It also raises questions, not only about the role of teachers as drivers of educational change, but also about their accountability for performance outcomes.

However, limited autonomy does not necessarily imply that teachers as professionals lack agency to transcend the imposed limits. As Judyth Sachs (2001) argues, this agency is dependent on the professional identity that teachers develop in response to both internal and external factors. She identifies two distinct identities: one in which teachers are compliant and over-reliant on the state's prescribed frameworks, and the other in which teachers identify as activists. In the former, teachers have little power over their work, and they identify more as workers rather than professionals, while in the latter, teachers view themselves as professionals who engage with the state to improve the quality of education. The activist identity is fuelled by the desire to build conditions for democratic schools that promote the free and open flow of information; faith in the individual and collective capacity of teachers to advance solutions that can resolve problems; critical reflection and analysis of policy formulation and implementation; transformation of the role of schools as social institutions to promote democracy in public life; and so on.

The development of a strong professional ethos and identity is integrally linked to, and cannot be separated from, teacher accountability. Accountability means 'to render an account of, to explain and to answer for' (Wagner 1989: 2). It refers to accounting for the performance of the roles, duties and responsibilities assigned to particular occupations or jobs to those responsible for the assignation, usually the line manager in an industrial or commercial setting. However, accountability in education is complex. It involves different stakeholders at different levels of the education system – teachers; school principals; departmental officials at district, provincial and national levels (in South Africa); and government – all of whom are accountable for the performance of the education system. Accountability will not be complete if it is only required from teachers alone. It is a shared obligation in which all stakeholders have to contribute by fulfilling their roles and responsibilities.

Teachers are accountable to learners, school principals, parents, the communities they serve, and government as the employer. However, the main stakeholder to whom teachers are accountable is the learner. Teachers' performance or non-performance of their roles, duties and responsibilities impacts directly on learners, as reflected in the achievement or non-achievement of learning outcomes. Indeed, the acknowledgement of responsibility for learner performance is at the centre of teachers' accountability (Maphosa et al. 2012).

A teacher's accountability to the learner is intrinsic to and embedded in the teacher's professional identity. It includes the acquisition of and proficiency in subject content knowledge, which is foundational to teaching, and pedagogical knowledge, which includes teaching and assessment methods that take into account the prior knowledge of learners and the diversity of learner backgrounds. Accountability also relates to the teacher's capability to exercise professional judgement in selecting the content knowledge to teach and the teaching and assessment methods to use (Phasha and Moichela 2011; Rusznyak 2015; Winch 2014). Yael Shalem (2014: 7) states this point clearly:

> Teachers have to exercise professional judgement when selecting emphasis for the content to be taught, designing a sequence of contents in a specific topic, choosing correct examples to demonstrate a concept, interpreting learners' errors, dealing with cultural differences in learners and so forth.

SADTU and teachers' unionism and professionalism

In South Africa, the crisis in public education has resulted in negative public perceptions about prevailing school practices and the teaching profession in general. These perceptions have varied in different time periods. In the early to mid-1990s, they centred on the problem of dysfunctional schools and un- and underqualified teachers, which was a reflection of the apartheid legacy. This led to the initiation of several professional development programmes to build capacity among both teachers and school principals, as well as the reorganisation of district offices in the different provinces (Christie 1998). In the late 1990s to mid-2000s, attention was drawn to a generalised crisis in schooling outcomes, which resulted in the replacement of the matriculation certificate by a new Senior Certificate, automatic promotion and progression through the different school grades, and the review of the outcomes-based education (OBE) curriculum philosophy. More recently, a major concern has been the spread of corruption at all levels of the school system as manifested in irregularities in national school examinations, the appointment of teachers and school principals, the functioning of school governing bodies, and so on.

The crisis in public schooling reflects the broader social, economic and political context that has engulfed South African society since the transition to majority rule in 1994. Particularly relevant are the fiscal constraints and inability of the democratic state to restructure the economy to address the systemic inequalities, unemployment and poverty inherited from apartheid (Luiz 2007), challenges that continue to this day. These factors – in particular, the fiscal constraints – adversely impacted on public schooling as the demand for parity in salaries and conditions of service between black and white teachers ultimately left little in the fiscus to address school infrastructure backlogs and the quality of teaching and learning. However, in the public mind, the schooling crisis is blamed on SADTU. It is widely felt that, given its role in the struggle against apartheid education, the union has not lived up to societal expectations. It was believed that SADTU would be a key driver in transforming and improving the quality of education by advancing teachers' professionalism, professional identity and, consequently, accountability. The societal expectations and pressures created a dilemma for SADTU. On the one hand, it was committed to the reconstruction and development of the education system and associated professional development issues. On the other hand, SADTU had to safeguard the hard-won collective bargaining rights of teachers, including improved salaries and conditions of service. SADTU attempted to resolve this dilemma, which pitted unionism versus professionalism, by arguing that the two were not mutually exclusive (as discussed in Chapter 1).

In practice, however, SADTU prioritised its unionist goals and has fallen short with regard to its professional goals, especially the teacher accountability dimension. This is not surprising given its origins in the teacher unions that fought against apartheid education – in particular, the apartheid state's proletarianisation and deprofessionalisation of black teachers. In this context, unionism has been a necessary and effective strategy for SADTU to address the legacy of segregation and discrimination against black teachers in terms of salaries and conditions of service in comparison to their white counterparts (Maile 1999; Moll

1989). It is precisely this unionist focus that not only ensured that teachers' rights to collective bargaining and strike action were guaranteed in the Labour Relations Act of 1995, but also ensured parity in salaries and conditions of service between black and white teachers.

The emphasis on unionism rather than professionalism has shaped the teachers' identity of SADTU members and has contributed to the negative image of the union in the public domain. This is not because of SADTU's unionist focus per se, but because of the form and manner through which SADTU pursues its unionist goals, the behaviour of some of its members, and SADTU's inability and/or unwillingness to hold its members accountable for their actions, as outlined below.

First, in support of its demands for improved working conditions and salaries, SADTU has more often than not resorted to strike action over lengthy periods. Aside from depriving learners of learning, these strikes have been characterised by violence and intimidation of those who do not support them (Sibiya 2017; Sikhosana 2004). At a provincial level, SADTU members have often embarked on strike action not related to legitimate demands but because of dissatisfaction with, for example, appointment processes for promotion posts when SADTU members are unsuccessful.

The union's proclivity to embark on strike action in the late 1990s and early to mid-2000s contrasts starkly with its approach to gaining recognition from the apartheid state in the early 1990s. In its fight for recognition as a national non-racial teachers' union, SADTU avoided strike action because of the public outcry against teacher strikes, which disrupted learning. Instead, the union limited its protest action to mass meetings, demonstrations and petitions (as discussed in Chapter 1). This suggests that the increasing resort to strike action after 1994 may be the consequence of the loss of organisational memory resulting from the absorption of SADTU's most senior and experienced leaders into parliamentary and bureaucratic positions (detailed in Chapter 4). More recently, however, within the context of the labour relations framework of the Education Labour Relations Council (ELRC), the frequency of strikes has declined.

Second, at the school level, there have been instances of SADTU members causing disruption and making schools ungovernable by defying the authority of and intimidating principals and head teachers, as they are seen as puppets who impose policies on teachers without consulting them (Sikhosana 2004). This makes it difficult for principals to control or enforce accountability on errant teachers, thus diminishing the effective functioning of schools and leading to a decline in school discipline (Sayer 1989). The inability of principals to enforce accountability is compounded by the fact that officials at district level rarely take action against the transgressors, even when complaints are laid against such teachers (Heystek and Lethoko 2001; Sibiya 2017).

Third, at the provincial level, there have been instances of nepotism in relation to recruitment for promotion posts involving SADTU members. In 2009, for example, SADTU members in Gauteng went on strike because those who were expected to be promoted to vacant principal posts were not considered by the provincial education department. In one instance, there was support for a candidate who was a clerk with extensive experience in clerical administration but no teaching experience or qualifications (Sibiya 2017; Zengele 2009). Similarly, in the North West province in 2009, information relating to advertised promotional posts was provided to SADTU applicants prior to the interviews for the posts, thus giving them an unfair advantage over non-SADTU applicants (Letseka and King-Mackenzie 2012).

Fourth, there have been instances of SADTU members using union structures to pursue their personal interests, such as securing political positions in government, or even for personal enrichment (Samuel 2014). Allegations of corruption and fraud, notably the selling of educator posts, led to the appointment of a Ministerial Task Team (MTT) to investigate the matter. In its report, the MTT found that although the cases of wrongdoing were limited and involved teachers from all teacher organisations, its investigation was hampered by what appears to be a culture of secrecy among teachers and departmental officials, which is linked in part to fears about personal safety and adversely impacts on the ethics of accountability (DBE 2016). The report also raised concerns about what appears to be the undue influence of SADTU through cadre deployment across a number of provincial education departments.

> Data submitted to the Task Team suggests that cadre deployment by Unions has weakened the education system. It has been alleged, for example, that SADTU determines who and for how long HODs [heads of department] in many provinces stay in office, and that it deploys cadres into levels of provincial education departments regardless of their qualifications. However, SADTU is not alone in exercising cadre deployment. Such domination and influence has been made possible, it was submitted, by the feeble and dilatory conditions of Districts and Circuits, permitting Unions to move into areas in which they have no business. In the view of the Task Team, this amounts to the exercise of undue influence (DBE 2016: 25–6).

The report suggests that the undue influence is further entrenched by the fact that senior public servants are also members of SADTU, and thus unable to distinguish between their obligations to learners and the public and their loyalty to the union (DBE 2016). The result is the deflection of focus away from policy and professionalism:

> Conflict between Department and Union is rarely over policy, it is over power and control. This has significant implications. In this process, the educational heart of Unions has been lost, as is the case, to a lesser extent, with the Department itself. It is in this context that things are going wrong and creating crises. The Task Team accepts fully the differences between the interests of the Department as the employer and the roles that Unions should play on behalf of their members. But in South Africa there are bigger issues for us all to address. Instead, for example, of using 'transformation' as a pretext for gaining control of schools and offices, there should be joint and co-operative efforts to address the manifold challenges and developments that are desperately needed in our education system (DBE 2016: 122).

In its submission to the MTT through its lawyers, SADTU contested the allegations regarding cadre deployment and undue influence:

> The MTT makes this finding without any evidence ... [The MTT] does not indicate how the education system has been weakened, and in respect of which provinces ... The MTT does not even indicate how SADTU determined which HOD's position; for how long an HOD in a province would stay as a result of SADTU's actions; and which HOD's by name are affected or involved. The MTT does not even give an example of any official who is a SADTU cadre deployed in a province without qualifications ... the MTT simply accepted the negative statements by NATU [National Teachers' Union], NAPTOSA [National Professional Teachers' Organisation of South Africa] and the single HOD in the North West province as facts. It is logical that NATU and NAPTOSA, as SADTU's competitors would have nothing positive to say about SADTU (DBE 2016: 245-6).

The allegations have, however, dented SADTU's professional image and fuelled negative public perceptions of the union. The stand-off between the Department of Basic Education (DBE) and SADTU remained unresolved in this matter, producing considerable acrimony. There is clearly a need for SADTU and the DBE to engage each other, as they do on other matters in the ELRC and other forums, to attempt to resolve issues that adversely affect teacher union-government relations, as well as the professional status of educators, long before such matters reach the stage where task teams or commissions of enquiry are the only alternative.

The post-1994 context also diminished SADTU's lack of focus on professional issues in three ways. First, despite the progress made towards transformation, most schools generally remain trapped in the apartheid legacy. Second, in the immediate aftermath of its formation, SADTU was involved in the thick of struggle and did not have the space to build its capacity as an organisation (detailed in Chapter 4). This lack of capacity was exacerbated by the fact that, like other grassroots organisations, SADTU suffered from a leadership crisis due primarily to the flight of its senior leadership to posts in government and the private sector (as discussed in Chapter 3).

Third, the slow pace in facilitating the professionalisation of teachers is due in part to SADTU's assumption that implementing the professional development of teachers could be left to the new democratic government. At the same time, SADTU continued to oppose any policies introduced by government – in particular, evaluation and performance appraisal policies – which could contribute to the professional development of teachers on the grounds that these were reminiscent of apartheid-era bureaucratic controls that had been successfully resisted by the progressive teacher unions. The union failed to recognise that teachers' autonomy is dependent on developing their professional attributes in terms of knowledge and pedagogy, attributes that were underdeveloped under apartheid and remain so to this day. Moreover, SADTU lost sight of the fact that the professional development of teachers is central to the transformation of the education system. As Hamsa Venkat and Nic Spaull's (2015) analysis of the Southern and Eastern Africa Consortium for Monitoring Educational Quality (SACMEQ) III (2007) test results indicated, Grade 6 learners were taught by teachers who were at the same grade level as the learners, and some were below the learners' level in terms of their grasp of mathematical concepts. The lack of subject content knowledge, as Nick Taylor argues, compromises teachers' accountability as 'teachers cannot teach what they do not know' (2010: 24). Remedying this situation requires a focus on enhancing teacher training and upgrading un- and under-qualified teachers who are still in the system (Hammet 2008; Tlhakola 2013). Although SADTU cannot be held accountable for the lack of teachers' training and upgrading, which is the responsibility of government, the union does have a duty to ensure that the government meets its obligations in this regard.

SADTU and teachers' accountability

The impact of SADTU's unionist goals on the functioning of the education system helps explain the negative image of SADTU in the public mind. However, more important is the union's inability and/or unwillingness to hold its members accountable for their actions. Thus, in SADTU's submission to the MTT, the union accepts that its members may be involved in the selling of educator posts. However, its view is that since such wrongdoing is not SADTU's policy, the union cannot be held responsible for the actions of its members. SADTU has a similar response to issues of accountability with regard to time-on-task, teachers attending union meetings during school hours, drunkenness, sexual harassment, and teacher absenteeism, which is widespread and leads to learners either being left to their own devices to roam the school grounds or, as the *Economist* reports, being 'padlocked' inside the classroom.[2]

The underlying reason for the absence of teachers' accountability and the union's reluctance to accept responsibility for this is, as the MTT found, the de facto control by SADTU of six of the nine provincial departments of education. Hence, the MTT's conclusion that 'it is not improbable to say that schooling throughout South Africa is run by SADTU' (DBE 2016: 25–6). The MTT report argues that this is the result of the Tripartite Alliance's policy of cadre deployment, which has resulted in a situation whereby political affiliation and organisational membership trump professional and administrative skills and qualifications in the appointment of senior officials, as well as the fact that senior departmental officials continue to hold SADTU membership. In its response to the MTT report, the union rejected such findings, pointing to the lack of supporting data and evidence to justify such claims.

According to some analysts, South African teacher unions have blocked various policy initiatives to enhance teachers' professionalism and accountability, including:
- Standardised student testing, particularly the Annual National Assessments, which are necessary to track the performance of the system and inform parents of their children's learning progress;
- Teacher testing (even for matric markers) to identify teacher capability constraints and inform pre-service and in-service training;

- Pay-for-performance schemes such as the original occupation-specific dispensation proposal necessary to reward effort and attract a stronger pool of teacher candidates into the system; and
- Performance contracts for school principals to establish clear requirements against which their performance can be assessed and underperformance effectively dealt with (Van der Berg et al. cited in Govender 2017: 249).

For its part, the government has attempted to introduce a teacher appraisal system – the Integrated Quality Management System (IQMS) – to facilitate the professional development of teachers, monitor performance and enforce accountability (De Clercq 2008, 2011). However, the IQMS has been consistently opposed by SADTU on the grounds that teachers' development should precede performance appraisal and evaluation, and that the latter should not be linked to pay progression. Teachers also perceive the IQMS as an attempt to blame them for the shortcomings of the education system.

SADTU may be correct in pointing out the inadequacies of the IQMS – in particular, that its focus is not on teachers' professional development but rather on fault-finding and ritualistic performance practices that do not contribute to teachers' identity, professionalism and accountability. This claim is supported by an empirical study of the implementation of the IQMS, which found that integrating professional development with appraisal leads to the neglect of development in favour of appraisal, which is associated with incentives (Mosoge and Pilane 2014). Furthermore, the study found that the departmental teams responsible for the IQMS lack knowledge and expertise to mentor, coach, manage and monitor teachers' performance. However, pointing out the flaws in the IQMS is one thing; what SADTU needs to do in its pursuit of enhancing teachers' professional development is to develop alternative options to the IQMS for consideration.

SADTU's de facto control of the majority of provincial education departments partly explains the inability of the government at the national level to hold SADTU accountable, despite the attempts made by the minister of basic education. Another factor is that SADTU, through its affiliation to the Congress of South African Trade Unions (COSATU), is part of the Tripartite Alliance led by the ANC. As the governing party, the ANC is dependent on SADTU – which is not only the largest teachers' union in South Africa, but also the second-largest affiliate of COSATU – for the electoral support of its members. The ANC is thus reluctant to rock the boat by implementing policies that directly impact on teachers and which are opposed by SADTU. As various scholars have suggested, SADTU's participation in the Tripartite Alliance has created an over-politicised environment in education, leading to an emphasis on political struggle rather than professional engagement to enable the reconstruction and development of the education system (Carnoy, Chisholm and Chilisa 2012; Van der Berg et al. 2016). To focus on professional engagement, SADTU may need to end its political affiliation to the Tripartite Alliance (Sibiya 2017).

Teacher accountability: role of the South African Council for Educators

The South African Council for Educators (SACE) is the professional body responsible for registering teachers and regulating their professional conduct and ethical behaviour (De Clercq 2011). Registration with a professional body, which involves pledging allegiance to the rules of conduct and behaviour of a particular profession, is intrinsic to the development of a professional identity (Trede, Madelin and Bridges 2012). Thus, SACE has a critical role to play in contributing to teachers' professionalism, identity and accountability.

However, evidence suggests that SACE has played a less than robust role in dealing with teachers' transgressions of its professional and ethical code. This is due primarily to SADTU's dominance of the council. As the largest teachers' union, SADTU is able to ensure that its members are appointed to critical positions in SACE. For example, the first CEO and chairperson of SACE were senior officials in SADTU. The union recognises and is aware of the lack of professionalism among its members (Heystek and Lethoko 2001). However, SADTU protects and is not willing to take disciplinary action against its members, arguing that their lack of professionalism is the result of grievances linked to their conditions of service. In SADTU's view, addressing the latter is a precondition for enhancing teachers' professionalism.

Teachers' accountability: role of government

The focus on SADTU's role in teachers' accountability should not detract from the accountability role of government. The precondition for teachers' accountability is the provision of a conducive and supportive working environment, which enables teachers to practise their craft effectively (Maphosa et al. 2012). In this regard, government has been found wanting, as the inherited apartheid-induced inequalities between black and white schooling remain in place. The lack of government accountability in relation to black schooling is reflected in, among other things, teachers not getting paid on time, inadequate distribution of textbooks, dilapidated infrastructure, large class sizes, lack of computer and science laboratories, and inadequate teacher training and support (Eloff and Kgwete 2007).

Such government shortfalls have adverse impacts on teachers' and learners' performance for which SADTU cannot be held responsible. In fact, it could be argued that SADTU has a responsibility to highlight these shortcomings, including taking industrial action as appropriate. As one SADTU member stated:

> We know how to put pressure on the Department of Education, in order to hasten the delivery of textbooks and stationery for effective teaching and learning. It is mainly the child and the principal that benefits from our victory (cited in Sikhosana 2004: 42).

This suggests that strikes are undertaken not only for improving conditions of service but also for demanding educational provision. However, while there may be isolated cases of strike action in support of educational provision, most strikes have been related to conditions of service. SADTU's lack of action in support of improved educational provision is reflected in its absence from various civil society initiatives to hold government accountable for providing educational services, particularly school equipment and infrastructure. These initiatives, which have gained momentum in recent years, have been led by non-governmental organisations such as Equal Education and Section27. SADTU's non-participation in these initiatives is due to the union's membership of and participation in the Tripartite Alliance. In short, SADTU is not willing to be associated with initiatives that are critical of an ANC-led government (see also Chapters 3 and 7).

SADTU and professional development

There is an increasing recognition by SADTU that restoring the status of teaching as a profession and enabling teachers to take responsibility for improving the quality of educational provision requires giving equal weight to both unionism and professionalism. The union has also recognised that although its policies and strategic frameworks speak to the need to facilitate the professional development of its members, it has been found wanting in policy implementation. To rectify the gap between policy and implementation in relation to professional development, the SADTU Curtis Nkondo Professional Development Institute (SCNPDI) was established in 2013. The focus of the SCNPDI is to address the competency and skills challenges facing teachers and school principals. This includes both subject content and pedagogical knowledge and skills, as well as leadership and management skills, in the context of the diverse backgrounds of learners in terms of race, ethnicity, language, class and religion. These skills are sorely lacking, specifically among older teachers in black schools, who in most cases, as a result of apartheid education, entered the profession as unqualified teachers, or at best with the equivalent of a Grade 10 school-leaving certificate and a teaching qualification.[3]

The SCNPDI had trained a total of 400 heads of schools in curriculum-related issues, and 19 000 Foundation Phase teachers had also been trained in subject content and pedagogical skills between 2011 and 2013. Overall, more than 50 000 teachers were reached as part of the Teacher Union Collaboration (TUC) initiative in this period (SADTU 2013). Between 2014 and 2022, more than 26 000 teachers were trained by the SCNPDI, covering diverse subjects including professional learning communities, governance, policy and leadership, mathematics training for primary school teachers, reading improvement training, and robotics and coding training.[4] An exciting innovation in this regard has been the partnership that SADTU entered into with the Apartheid Museum in Johannesburg to develop and support the knowledge and pedagogical skills of history teachers (Tlhakola 2013). The SCNPDI has also developed relevant teaching-support materials such as science kits for physics and the life sciences, and DVDs on different subjects.

The focus on the development of knowledge and pedagogical skills is pertinent given the link between professionalism and accountability. It also contributes to the development of a positive self-image and identity, which is grossly lacking in South Africa's education system. In general, SADTU's professional development programmes have had a positive impact, particularly in enhancing teachers' skills to improve classroom practice.[5] Nevertheless, it seems that their workshop-based nature may not be best suited to improve teachers' knowledge and skills (Steyn 2013). This is supported by a participant in one workshop-based professional development programme offered by a university who stated: 'You can train us until we are blue in the face, we are still going to struggle' (Walton et al. 2014: 322).

SADTU appears to have recognised the limitations of workshop-based approaches to professional development. This is indicated by SADTU's piloting, in partnership with the National Education Collaboration Trust (NECT), of a professional learning community (PLC) approach to facilitating professional development. PLCs involve a bottom-up approach in which teachers themselves work together as a community to develop their subject content and pedagogical skills, taking into account the needs of learners in specific contexts (Darling-Hammond and Richardson 2009). It entails sharing knowledge, expertise and making adaptations and changes from existing traditional practices of pedagogy that teachers hold on to. Studies of PLCs in other countries indicate that they provide a platform for a purposeful conversation and engagement among teachers to explore new pedagogical possibilities that are enriching and have a meaningful impact on daily classroom practice and student performance (Desimone 2009; Feldman 2017). The simultaneous focus of PLCs on the needs of both teachers and learners strengthens teachers' accountability as it places learners at the centre of the learning process, thus enabling teachers to value the prior knowledge of learners and to recognise that they are the co-constructors of knowledge with learners. In addition, the value of PLCs as a bottom-up approach is that it is not imposed on teachers from above and addresses the weaknesses in the IQMS that SADTU has identified. It contributes to a positive self-image through ongoing self-improvement, which, as Michael Samuel asserts, is a key characteristic of a 'professional teacher' (2014: 617).

SADTU has recognised that it has previously privileged unionism over professionalism, which has negatively impacted on its public image. Its commitment to address this imbalance is reflected in the steps the union has taken to strengthen its role in the professional development of its members. However, aside from implementation challenges, SADTU's emerging focus on professionalism remains hidden – hence the continued public perception that SADTU is an obstacle to building a quality education system.

However, despite the dilemma and notwithstanding the need to improve its communications strategy (discussed in Chapter 4), it may be opportune for SADTU to rethink its current approach to unionism and professionalism, which is underpinned by the notion that unionism and professionalism are two sides of the same coin. The main shortcoming of this approach is that it continues to privilege the rights of teachers, albeit with regard to professional development, without balancing the latter with the rights of learners and the concerns of parents and society in general. It is this imbalance between the rights of teachers as workers and professionals with the rights of learners that SADTU needs to reset through a new approach.

Conclusion: professional unionism as a new approach

The new approach, which will enable SADTU to strike an appropriate balance between unionism and professionalism without privileging either, as well as between the rights of teachers and learners, is captured by the concept of professional unionism. At the centre of professional unionism is the principle that learners and the education of learners are the essential components of the education system. This principle is underpinned by two key requirements. First, teachers must look beyond their personal interests and prioritise the needs of learners. Second, beyond their differences and diversity of interests, all stakeholders in education must work together collaboratively to enable the provision of quality education. It requires abandoning the 'them versus us' perspective and committing to work together in mutual understanding for the good of learners (Kerchner and Caufman 1995; Samuel 2008). Professional unionism also entails channelling the positive militant energy accumulated in the tradition of unionism, not only for the defence of teachers' rights, but also for the promotion of learners' rights and the common good of society in education.

Professional unionism will enable SADTU to overcome the current conflictual environment within schools that pits teachers against both principals and departmental officials. It will contribute to the strengthening of teachers' professionalism and identity through shared and collaborative professional development programmes. Moreover, it will strengthen and enhance the accountability of all stakeholders through an agreed framework clearly identifying the roles and responsibilities of different stakeholders in addressing the challenges that confront the education system, including teachers' conditions of service. Professional unionism reconciles the struggles for quality education and learners' rights with the broader emancipatory struggles linked to the transformation of the education system and broader society, which was the impetus behind the formation of SADTU in 1990. In short, professional unionism will allow SADTU to reconcile its commitment to teachers' professionalism and accountability without compromising its unionist foundations, and to contribute to the transformation of education. Professional unionism has worked successfully in Britain, Canada and the United States, and it may also work in South Africa. Success depends on all responsible stakeholders placing education goals above narrow employment and workplace interests, and embracing a full commitment to accountability and professional identity.

Notes
1. Interview with SADTU leader, 5 July 2019.
2. 'School's Out', *The Economist*, 25 April 2019, special report.
3. Under apartheid, after completing Standard 8 (Grade 10), students could enrol for either a two-year or three-year teaching diploma (Reeves and Robinson 2010).
4. Email communication from Renny Somnath, SADTU education officer, 19 October 2022.
5. Email communication from Renny Somnath, SADTU education officer, 22 October 2022.

References
Carnoy, M., L. Chisholm and B. Chilisa. 2012. *The Low Achievement Trap: Comparing Schooling in Botswana and South Africa*. Cape Town: HSRC Press.
Christie, P. 1998. 'Schools as (Dis)Organisations: The "Breakdown of the Culture of Learning and Teaching" in South African Schools'. *Cambridge Journal of Education* 28(3): 283–300.
Darling-Hammond, L. and N. Richardson. 2009. 'Research Review/Teacher Learning: What Matters'. *Educational Leadership* 66(5): 46–5.
De Clercq, F. 2008. 'Teacher Quality, Appraisal and Development: The Flaws of the IQMS'. *Perspectives in Education* 26(1): 7–18.
———. 2011. 'Teacher Appraisal Reforms in Post-1994 South Africa: Conflicts, Contestation and Meditations'. PhD thesis, University of the Witwatersrand, Johannesburg.
Demirkasimoglu, N. 2010. 'Defining "Teacher Professionalism" from Different Perspectives'. *Procedia Social and Behavioural Sciences* 9: 2047–51.
Department of Basic Education (DBE). 2016. 'Report of the Ministerial Task Team Appointed by Minister Angie Motshekga to Investigate Allegations into the Selling of Posts of Educators by Members of Teachers' Unions and Departmental Officials in Provincial Education Departments'. Pretoria: DBE.
Desimone, L.M. 2009. 'Improving Impact Studies of Teachers' Professional Development: Towards Better Conceptualisation and Measures'. *Educational Researcher* 38(3): 181–99.
Eloff, I. and L.K. Kgwete. 2007. 'South African Teachers' Voices on Support in Inclusive Education'. *Childhood Education* 83(6): 351–5.
European Trade Union Committee for Education (ETUCE). 2016. 'Empowering Education Trade Unions: The Key to Promoting Quality Education'. https://www.csee-etuce.org/images/attachments/Final-Background--document_EN.pdf (accessed 16 March 2022).
Evans, L. 2008. 'Professionalism, Professionality and the Development of Educational Professionals'. *British Journal of Education Studies* 56(1): 20–38.
Feldman, J. 2017. 'The Role of Professional Learning Communities in Facilitating Pedagogical Adaptation and Change'. *Journal of Education* 67: 65–82.

Gindin, J. and L. Finger. 2013. 'Promoting Education Quality: The Role of Teachers' Unions in Latin America'. Background paper commissioned for the Education for All Global Monitoring Report 2013/4, 'Teaching and Learning: Achieving Quality for All', UNESCO, Paris.

Govender, L. 2017. 'Teacher Unions and Transformation: More Political than Educational'. In *Reimagining Basic Education in South Africa: Lessons from the Eastern Cape*, edited by W. Ngoma, L. Govender and A. Mc Lennan. Johannesburg: MISTRA and Real African Publishers.

Hammet, D. 2008. 'Disrespecting Teachers: The Decline in Social Standing of Teachers in Cape Town, South Africa'. *International Journal of Educational Development* 28(3): 340-7.

Hargreaves, A. 2000. 'Four Ages of Professionalism and Professional Learning'. *Teachers and Teaching: History and Practice* 6(2): 151-82.

Heystek, J. and M. Lethoko. 2001. 'The Contribution of Teacher Unions in the Restoration of Teacher Professionalism and Culture of Learning and Teaching'. *South African Journal of Education* 21(4): 224-7.

Higgs, J. 1993. 'Physiotherapy, Professionalism and Self-directed Learning'. *Journal of the Singapore Physiotherapy Association* 14(1): 8-11.

Ibarra, H. 1999. 'Provisional Self: Experimenting with Image and Identity in Professional Adaptation'. *Administrative Science Quarterly* 44(1): 764-91.

Kerchner, C.T. and K.D. Caufman. 1995. 'Lurching Towards Professionalism: The Saga of Teacher Unionism'. *The Elementary School Journal* 96(1): 107-22.

Letseka, M. and E. King-Mackenzie. 2012. 'Public-Union Sector and the Crisis of Education in South Africa'. *Creative Education* 3(7): 1197-1204.

Luiz, J. 2007. 'The Battle for Social and Economic Policy'. *Discourse* 35(2). Wits Business School, University of the Witwatersrand, Johannesburg.

Maile, S. 1999. 'Policy Implementation and Governance: The Rise of Trade Unionism in Education'. Paper presented at SAELPA Annual Conference, 20-22 September.

Maphosa, C., E. Mutekwe, S. Machingambi, N. Wadesango and A. Ndofirepi. 2012. 'Teacher Accountability in South African Public Schools: A Call for Professionalism from Teachers'. *Anthropologist* 14(6): 545-53.

McCollow, J. 2017. 'Teacher Unions'. In *Oxford Research Encyclopaedia of Education*, edited by G. Noblit. DOI: 10.1093/acrefore/9780190264093.013.201.

Moll, I. 1989. 'Towards One South African Teachers' Union'. *South African Labour Bulletin* 14(1): 60-74.

Mosoge, M.J. and M.W. Pilane. 2014. 'Performance Management: The Neglected Imperative of Accountability Systems in Education'. *South African Journal of Education* 34(1): 1-18.

Paterson, M., J. Higgs, S. Wilcox and M. Villeneuve. 2002. 'Clinical Reasoning and Self-directed Learning: Key Dimensions in Professional Education and Professional Socialisation'. *Focus on Health Professional Education* 4(2): 5-21.

Phasha, N. and K.Z. Moichela. 2011. 'Inclusive Education in South Africa'. In *Handbook of African Educational Theories and Practices: A Generative Teacher Education Curriculum*, edited by A.B. Nsamenang and T.M.S. Tchombe. Bamenda, Cameroon: Human Development Resource Centre.

Reeves, C. and M. Robinson. 2010. 'Am I "Qualified" to Teach? The Implications of a Changing School System for Criteria for Teacher Qualifications'. *Journal of Education* 50: 1–33.

Rusznyak, L. 2015. 'Knowledge Selection in Initial Teacher Education Programmes and Its Implication for Curricular Coherence'. *Journal of Education* 60: 7–29.

Sachs, J. 2001. 'Teacher Professional Identity: Competing Discourses, Competing Outcomes'. *Journal of Education Policy* 16(2): 149–61.

Samuel, M. 2008. 'Accountability to Whom? For What? Teacher Identity and the Force Field Model of Teacher Development'. *Perspectives in Education* 26(2): 3–16.

———. 2014. 'South African Teacher Voices: Recurring Resistance and Reconstruction for Teacher Education and Development'. *Internalisation Research and Pedagogy* 40(5): 610–21.

Sanger, M. 1990. 'The Union Has Arrived'. *Work in Progress* 70(71): 35–40.

Sayer, J. 1989. *The Principalship*. New York: Macmillan.

Shalem, Y. 2014. 'What Binds Professional Judgement? The Case of Teaching'. In *Knowledge, Expertise and the Professions*, edited by M. Young and J. Muller. London: Routledge.

Sibiya, T.P. 2017. 'Key Stakeholders' Experiences and Perspectives on the Role of the South African Democratic Teachers Union (SADTU) in Education'. Master's dissertation, University of KwaZulu-Natal, Pietermaritzburg.

Sikhosana, O.T. 2004. 'Principals' Perceptions of the Role of Teacher Unions in the Effectiveness Management of Schools in Ndwedwe and Maphumulo Circuits, KwaZulu-Natal'. Master's dissertation, University of KwaZulu-Natal, Pietermaritzburg.

South African Democratic Teachers' Union (SADTU). 2013. 'Co-ordinating the Professional Development of Teachers'. *Infinity* 1: 12–15.

Steyn, G.M. 2013. 'Building Professional Learning Communities to Enhance Continuing Professional Development in South African Schools'. *Anthropologist* 15(3): 277–89.

Taylor, N. 2010. 'What's Wrong with South African Schools?' Paper Presented at the JET Education Service Conference 'What's Working in School Development?', 28–29 February, Boksburg.

Tlhakola, M.A. 2013. 'Perceptions of Educators about the Involvement of the South African Democratic Teachers' Union in Professional Development'. Master's dissertation, University of Pretoria.

Trede, F., R. Madelin and D. Bridges. 2012. 'Professional Identity Development: A Review of the Higher Education Literature'. *Studies in Higher Education* 37(3): 365–84.

Vaillant, D. 2005. 'Education Reforms and the Role of Teachers'. *PRELAC Journal: Teacher Involvement in Educational Change* 1:38–51.
Van der Berg, S., N. Spaull, G. Wills, M. Gustafsson and J. Kotze. 2016. 'Identifying Binding Constraints in Education: Research on Socio-economic Policy'. Pretoria: Department of Planning, Monitoring and Evaluation.
Van der Walt, L. 1998. 'Trade Unions in Zimbabwe: For Democracy, Against Neo-liberalism'. *Capital Class* 22(3): 85–117.
Venkat, H. and N. Spaull. 2015. 'What do We Know about Primary Teachers' Mathematical Content Knowledge in South Africa? An Analysis of SACMEQ 2007'. *International Journal of Educational Development* 41: 121–30.
Villegas-Reimers, E. 2003. *Teacher Professional Development: An International Review of the Literature*. Paris: UNESCO International Institute for Educational Planning.
Wagner, R.G. 1989. *Accountability in Education: A Philosophical Inquiry*. London: Routledge.
Walton, E., N.M. Nel, H. Muller and O. Lebeloane. 2014. '"You Can Train Us until We are Blue in Our Faces, We are Still Going to Struggle": Teacher Professional Learning in a Full-Service School'. *Education as Change* 18(2): 319–33.
Winch, C. 2014. 'Know-how and Knowledge in the Professional Curriculum'. In *Knowledge, Expertise and the Professions*, edited by M. Young and J. Muller. London: Routledge.
Zengele, V.T. 2009. 'The Involvement of Teacher Unions in the Implementation of the Employment of Educators Act 76 of 1998'. PhD thesis, University of South Africa, Pretoria.

6

Leaders, Leadership and Change in SADTU

MICHAEL CROSS AND DAVID MATSEPE

This chapter maps out the leadership discourse of SADTU and its leaders, and the lessons and inferences that can be extracted from SADTU's experience to inform its future as a professional teachers' union. It is concerned with the nature and purposes of organisational leadership and its impact on the union's organisation, its members and the education system at large. The chapter focuses on five important dimensions: (i) a systematic approach to the history of SADTU; (ii) the background and social and educational context which influenced SADTU's leaders and informed and shaped the nature of their leadership practices; (iii) the changing roles of SADTU leaders within the union and beyond; (iv) the relationship of SADTU leaders to the SADTU membership in particular and teachers in general, and the positive impact of this relationship on enhancing and promoting better outcomes, not only for SADTU members, but also for the wider school communities of teachers and learners; and (v) the leadership legacy and the lessons that can be drawn to serve as a source of inspiration for the future of SADTU as a teachers' union.

A key characteristic that has defined the role of SADTU leaders throughout its history is their active presence in all domains of organisational activities. The term 'active presence' refers to purposeful, regular and continuous efforts by leaders to achieve their organisational goals. This active presence within organisations – in particular, social movement organisations – is felt through the constant mobilisation, motivation, encouragement and engagement of members in the various activities of the organisation. It enables leaders to impact, both directly and indirectly, on members and to influence organisational performance through the promotion of organisational learning. An active presence allows leaders to provide strategic direction and to negotiate and renegotiate the organisation's vision and goals in light of changing circumstances, all of which positively impact on members' commitment, behaviour and achievements (Robinson, Hohepa and Lloyd 2009).

The chapter assesses the role and impact of the active presence of SADTU leaders by examining three generations of its leadership. The first generation emerged from the militant teacher unions of the 1980s that were an integral component of the anti-apartheid struggle and laid the basis for the formation of SADTU as a national non-racial teachers' union in 1990. This coincided with the intensification of the anti-apartheid struggle in the mid-1980s led by the United Democratic Front (UDF), the Congress of South African Trade Unions (COSATU) and, in education, by the National Education Crisis Committee (NECC). As SADTU's former education and research officers Shermain Mannah and Jon Lewis observed, the NECC realised that education was critical to achieving liberation and building a democratic future, and it encouraged teachers and students to challenge the system of Bantu Education from within (Mannah and Lewis 2008). This led to the emergence of the progressive teacher unions, which would later coalesce into SADTU in 1990 (discussed in Chapter 1). These unions and their leaders adopted a strong unionist approach in dealing with educational change and policy, but also identified with community struggles for a better life.

The second generation of leadership (1990–2000) addressed the role of SADTU in the transition to democracy by redefining its role and shifting its focus from resistance to apartheid to nation-building, reconstruction and development. Following the union's launch in October 1990, which coincided with the unbanning of the ANC and other political organisations, SADTU leaders played an important part in South Africa's transition to democracy. As highlighted later in this chapter, senior leadership figures would serve in the ANC-led democratic government and bureaucracy in order to contribute to the transformation of the education system from its narrow, racist origins to one that would serve all South Africans. In the main, SADTU in this period was viewed positively in the public domain as it was seen to be advancing the educational interests of the black child and contributing to the transformation of the education system.

The third generation (2000-present) addressed the leadership crisis that confronted SADTU in the mid-2000s by embracing professional unionism to enhance its role in the transformation of the education system. In this period, as discussed in Chapter 4, SADTU's leaders have come under increasing pressure to respond to the growing public criticism that the union was complicit in contributing to the deteriorating quality of education in many of South Africa's schools. This is a key criticism that SADTU's leaders continue to face, based on the view (outlined in the Introduction) that the union privileges unionism over professionalism.

The chapter is based on both primary sources (interviews with SADTU leaders and documents from SADTU archives), and secondary sources (studies of SADTU and other social movements). The main argument put forward here is that as SADTU evolved as an organisation, it appears to have found it difficult to draw fully on the political energy, organisational discipline, value framework, and adaptability that characterised earlier generations of SADTU leaders. These attributes not only united teachers into a very powerful union but also led them successfully through the difficult moments of the struggle against apartheid education, including winning recognition as a national non-racial teachers' union and building the foundations and articulating the vision for the democratisation and transformation of the education system (elaborated in Chapter 1). One of SADTU's current leaders, Deputy General Secretary Nkosana Dolopi, reflected on these moments:

> ... there are 'chapters' [issues] that we must never close like the right to strike in a capitalist society – South Africa is a capitalist society – and there are 'chapters' that should have been closed, for example the abuse of strikes and/or disruptive behaviour that impacts negatively on learners in especially deprived communities in pursuit of selfish goals.[1]

It is this disconnect from the leadership lessons of the past that this chapter addresses to help find answers to the critical question posed by the current president of SADTU, Magope Maphila: 'With so much positivity, why is SADTU known by things that are not so positive?'[2]

Theoretical and conceptual parameters

The theoretical framework for this chapter rests on the principle that leadership in social movements is based on conscious social interaction between leaders and the communities/organisations in which they operate. It draws on important constructs from socio-constructivism – namely, the role of social interaction between leaders and members of social movements (Burkitt 2008); the prevailing dynamics and forms of socialisation (Giddens 2006); and the emerging political consciousness, dialogue and discourse as well as the contextual specificity of the terrain where leaders operate (Dlamini, Smit and Loock 2014). This framework is underpinned by Burkitt's (2008: 3) contention that leaders 'are born in social relations with others and the self is formed through social relations with others and through the relations to the own self', whose agency determines the form and style of leadership. Thus, socialisation through specific social relations with others and the own self shapes an individual's and group's consciousness that informs the style and modes of leadership. In line with critical leadership studies (CLS), the chapter recognises that 'leadership is a relational, socially constructed phenomenon rather than the result of a stable set of leadership attributes that inhere in "the leaders"' (Sutherland, Land and Böhm 2014: 1). Thus, leadership styles are forged in groups or social contexts in which significant processes of interaction, dialogue and socialisation occur (Giddens 2006). They entail a system of beliefs, attitudes and values that underpin social and political practices within particular social and cultural milieus through which behaviour can be influenced.

From this perspective, leadership in social movements is about the social capital that individuals invest in or bring into the organisation, and which is reflected back through refinement in individual members and beyond. Put differently, leaders create social movements, and these recreate their leaders through dialogue and discourse translated into organisational learning in a dialectical relationship. Central to leadership in social movements is individual and collective agency and adaptability in response to internal dynamics as movements grow in size and complexity and in response to complex and changing circumstances and challenges that they confront. Thus, it is necessary to consider the historicity of leadership as a dynamic, adaptable and changing phenomenon by considering its key historical or evolutionary moments. This chapter freezes these critical moments in SADTU by examining three generations of its leaders.

As a social movement union, SADTU strives for change for the public good of its members, teachers in general and learners. In this regard, the chapter draws on transformational leadership theory as an analytical frame (Huey 1994; Nirenberg 1993). Transformational leadership is most often associated with creating vision and goals, setting direction, restructuring and realigning the organisation, developing and empowering members, and connecting with the external community. These specific practices reflect, but also add to, three functions of leadership typical of social movements: (i) mobilising, motivating and inspiring; (ii) organising and clarifying roles and objectives; and (iii) bargaining/negotiating, action planning and implementing. Leaders' direction-setting practices significantly influence members' individual sense of efficacy, solidarity, loyalty and organisational commitment. For example, helping members develop and inspiring a shared sense of purpose through meaning-making enhances their work, whereas holding (and expressing) unreasonable expectations has negative effects on members (Yukl 1989). Meaning-making refers to the 'multitude of processes involved in creating, re-creating, uncovering, preserving, maintaining, nurturing and evolving meaning' around organisational goals, opportunities and challenges (Wilkens 1983: 85). Leaders can also assist the work of members by providing discretionary space, promoting regular access to a range of professional learning and development opportunities, distributing leadership across the organisation, and practising what they preach.

Given that liberation struggles and organisations are prone to creating an obsession with the role of prominent leaders, it is necessary to caution against a narrow celebration of individualistic, heroic notions of leadership advocated by the leader-follower discourse (Seale and Cross 2019), which downplays the social and relational dimensions of leadership. In a changing organisational context, transformational leadership (Huey 1994), shared leadership (Avolio, Walumbwa and Weber 2009), team/collective and/or participatory leadership (Black and Gregersen 1997) play an important role depending on the social and political circumstances. Despite the role prominent leaders played in the context of the anti-apartheid struggle, SADTU has placed emphasis on collective leadership and collective responsibility. This is not to suggest uniformity or to underplay the importance of personal experiences, qualities, preferences, styles, motivations and approaches between the different layers of SADTU leaders. Drawing on the above conceptual framework, some of the main leadership issues and dynamics that confronted SADTU leaders and the organisation over the years are discussed below.

First-generation leadership: leading teachers into a united teachers' union

The process leading to the establishment of SADTU as a national non-racial teachers' union was triggered by the 1976 Soweto uprising of school students against Bantu Education. The revolt placed the struggles of teachers beyond the confines of schools, collective bargaining and workplace demands, to embrace the wider struggles for democratisation in all spheres of society as advocated by the liberation movement. Leadership in this period included the predominantly young and highly politicised black teachers who came of age post-1976, such as Curtis Nkondo and Thulas Nxesi (Webster and Adler 2001). Other important teacher union leaders of this generation included Shepherd Mdladlana from the Democratic Teachers' Union (DETU) and Ronald Swartz from the Western Cape Teachers' Union (WECTU).[3] These unions, among others, formed the plethora of militant teacher organisations that sprang up across the country in the 1980s as the struggle against apartheid intensified (Webster and Adler 2001). Their leaders were influenced by three key factors. First, they believed that their status as teachers was undermined by the apartheid state, resulting in teacher deprofessionalisation and proletarianisation. In short, they were reduced to the status of workers. Second, they were opposed to the racially and ethnically based apartheid education system, including the race-based conservative teacher associations. Third, they saw themselves as part of a wider alliance of progressive social movements, which bound together militant school and university students, unionised workers and community activists under the umbrella of the Mass Democratic Movement (MDM), which led the struggle against apartheid. And, importantly, the MDM was also involved in developing alternatives to minority rule. In education, SADTU, through its participation in the NECC, embraced the idea of people's education for people's power, at the centre of which were attempts to introduce alternative democratic governance systems in the schooling system representing parents, teachers and students, as well as alternative teaching and learning practices.

The linking of the struggles of teachers as workers against capitalism with the broader struggles of the community against apartheid became an important principle of SADTU (Letseka, Bantwini and King-McKenzie 2012). It enabled SADTU to incorporate the shop-floor discourse of unionised workers and the democratic discourse of the liberation movement into teachers' unionism without members losing their identities as teachers and their specific structural location in society (Dlamini, Smit and Loock 2014). As Dolopi put it:

> As a worker at a school your life doesn't end there . . . When you immediately leave the gate of the school, you are confronted with the same challenges that every citizen in the community faces. The questions of health, the questions of electricity, the questions of water, the questions of transport, roads and all those kinds of things. So, you can't have a situation whereby you close yourself and say I am only a teacher. Yes, you are a teacher at school . . . but the same things that face those . . . people in the community, you are also experiencing them.

How did these struggles shape the leadership discourse within SADTU? SADTU leaders, like other activists who emerged as leaders, developed a system of beliefs, principles, values and attitudes from their everyday social and cultural struggles and practices, which formed part of their leadership language and discourse. This included a commitment to promoting inclusivity, unity within the organisation and participatory democracy in decision-making (Kumalo and Skosana 2014). Depending on their effectiveness in everyday struggles, these values came to be internalised and widely shared within the organisation as a whole. For SADTU leaders, leadership discourse did not come from any form of training, but through everyday meaning-making derived from trial and error in mobilising and organising teachers through mass meetings, mass actions, marches, boycotts, rallies, stay-aways, strikes and other forms of protests. This approach was underscored by a two-day programme at SADTU's official launch in October 1990 – a formal conference followed by a mass rally involving grassroots members and the broader public (Kumalo and Skosana 2014). The rally activities and actions provided the context through which leadership ideas were constructed and reconstructed, formed and re-formed or interrupted, and added and expanded into leadership discourses as SADTU leaders and members achieved shared meaning in values, principles, approaches and styles to adopt. These discourses embraced the values of freedom and equality and the vision of a transformed education system in the service of democracy and social and economic development.

In giving effect to these values, a central challenge that confronted the first generation of leaders, and which persists to this day, is that of uniting a diverse membership and advancing gender equity. Mobilising and recruiting teachers employed by racially and ethnically based education departments and teacher associations required an inclusive leadership with sensitivity to political and sociocultural diversity, including the use of militancy as a mobilising and unifying tool. For this reason, provision was made for a large number of vice-presidents to accommodate leaders from different regions and associations. As SADTU General Secretary Mugwena Maluleke stated:

So that's why there were a lot of vice-presidents. People would ask: 'Why the vice-president for this, vice-president for that?' And there were many deputy presidents. So it was just to say for each and every culture . . . let us have a vice- president who would represent that particular culture . . . So thanks to that type of leadership . . . [we] could say it was an inclusive leadership . . . They understood that they needed to lead as a collective; they would differ when needed but with the intention of building a single unit and that is the legacy they left for us: a legacy based on collective and inclusive leadership; and a legacy that made sure the structures needed were purposeful and were fit for that particular purpose at the time. So, as we evolved, the organisation started reducing on the structure because the organisation became jelly and . . . we were beginning to create our own culture.[4]

While SADTU successfully created an inclusive leadership at its founding, it was less successful in ensuring gender diversity. The first national leadership of SADTU was male-dominated. To rectify this, in 1998 SADTU introduced a quota system for leadership positions to ensure a 50-50 model of gender representation for executive positions. Although this was an important achievement in terms of gender representation, the quota system imposed an artificial cap that prevented women from occupying leadership positions beyond the 50 per cent limit. Thus, the quota system was revised in 2010 with a more progressive resolution that did not put a ceiling on the election of female leaders.[5] One of the lessons learned from other unions is that sometimes well-intentioned policies do not automatically translate into implementation. For these policies on gender to be meaningfully realised, the union needs to begin with organisational introspection in order to change its culture, values, norms and attitudes so that members embrace equal gender-power relations. Thus, SADTU decided on a practical strategy of setting up a Gender Desk, where issues of school-related gender-based violence are given priority. SADTU's policy on gender states that 'gender violence is one of the worst manifestations of gender discrimination and violates a wide range of children's rights'. In fact, education can empower and transform the lives of all young people, especially girls, yet widespread gender-based violence in and around schools seriously undermines the achievement of quality, inclusive and equitable education for all children (SADTU 2017).

In SADTU's endeavour to advance gender equality, the rationale for supporting its establishment was grounded in the union's conceptual shift from a 'women's structure' to a 'gender structure'. This shift in emphasis and focus was driven by the need to improve gender equity and power relations within the union and the education sector more broadly. Fast-forward to 2022, when SADTU's head of research, David Matsepe, contends that gender relations between males and females within the union have made strides, and that gender equity is on a positive and constructive trajectory.[6] In the period 2019–2022, the SADTU Gender Desk has been one of the most active in the union, having mobilised teachers to be involved in a range of activities, including health screening during the Covid-19 pandemic, engaging men to help address gender-based violence and femicide issues, and research and leadership training in partnership with COSATU (SADTU 2022: 77–87). In terms of gender equity at the leadership level, however, the situation remains male-dominated. The SADTU National Working Committee (NWC) is made up of the eight most senior leaders of the union. The current president, deputy president, general secretary and deputy general secretary are all male, while the more junior positions of vice-president for gender, sports, education and national treasurer are all female, which gives an impression of tokenism. The National Executive Committee (NEC), the highest decision-making structure between national congresses and to which the NWC reports, is also male-dominated. There are 26 NEC members, including the eight NWC members, nine provincial chairpersons and nine provincial secretaries. Of the eighteen provincial representatives on the NEC, only three are female.[7] It is clear that females remain under-represented within the union's most senior leadership structures, a reality that does not bode well for a profession where the majority are women.

Second-generation leadership: managing the transition

SADTU was imbued with what Eddie Webster and Glen Adler refer to as 'social movement unionism', which arose out of three political traditions of the labour movement in its relationship with the liberation movement in South Africa: (i) the national democratic tradition; (ii) the shop-floor tradition; and (iii) the Black Consciousness/Africanist tradition (Webster and Adler 2001). SADTU, in line with COSATU – to which it was affiliated – combined the national democratic tradition, which spoke to the oppression of all black people irrespective of their class position, with the shop-floor tradition, which spoke to the exploitation of workers. And both traditions emphasised the importance of democratic participation. In practice, this meant that the SADTU leadership privileged the implementation of democratic structures, including inclusivity, consultation and participation (Dlamini, Smit and Loock 2014); promoted working-class leadership and accountability; and reconciled shop-floor or unionist concerns with education quality issues within the framework of an emergent professional unionism. This is evidenced in the organisational structures of SADTU, including provincial and branch-level structures, to optimise grassroots members' participation, as well as its specialist education and research committees to focus on curriculum and policy development (see Chapter 4 for a detailed discussion).

The adoption of the national democratic tradition – with its focus on the democratisation of South African society as captured in the Freedom Charter and its impact on the wider mobilisation of all sectors of society, including teachers and workers – would later enable COSATU (and SADTU) to have considerable influence on the country's politics by bringing together factory, township, school and community struggles (Freund 2007; Southall and Webster 2010; Wolpe 1988). This broader role in the struggle for democracy was reflected in SADTU leaders' strong contestation of narrow professionalism, as suggested by Maluleke:

> There was contestation about what it is to be professional – whether a militant or radical person can be professional ... Then we can see people beginning to understand. Then people

> began to say: 'Look, you cannot teach and fight at the same time.' We are professional as leaders and this union is a union of professionals, but because we want to liberate our people, we have got to fight. In a capitalist society, like South Africa, you are not going to get medical aid until you fight for it. You are not going to get resources enough to enable you to do your best unless [you] fight for it.

It is on this political and ideological basis that the SADTU leadership managed the transition to democracy and national reconstruction and development. The transition represented by far the most inspiring and prolific moment in SADTU's history in terms of its engagement in the process of national reconstruction, and more specifically in the development of labour relations legislation and education policy. Under the banner 'Unionise for educational reconstruction and development' and inspired by the discourse of 'people's education for people's power', SADTU leaders concentrated their efforts on three challenges: (i) attainment of national and international recognition of SADTU (Kumalo and Skosana 2014; SADTU 1991); (ii) participation in the transitional negotiations to stop the unilateral restructuring of the education system by the apartheid state and to help develop policies for the democratisation of the education system (Amoako 2014); and (iii) active engagement in the post-1994 elections and national reconstruction and development (Govender 2004).

With regard to education, SADTU's vision is well encapsulated in the metaphor of the union's first president, Membathisi Shepherd Mdladlana: 'people with ears', which speaks to the ability to listen and be accountable to the public:

> We need a new education department with new personnel that understand public accountability. A new department that will be governed democratically by people who believe in consultation. People with ears. People who are prepared to listen to its teachers through negotiations and not through strikes and marches.[8]

According to Maluleke, this generation of leaders in the early 1990s was confronted with a fundamental question in the context of national reconstruction: 'Do you believe in the negotiations or do you believe in the streets?' They did not believe that the challenges faced by teachers, which were inherited from apartheid, could be resolved in every instance by resorting to mass action either in the streets through protest marches or through strikes. This meant that the methods used in the fight against apartheid education were not always appropriate in the context of national reconstruction and development, as Maluleke affirms:

> The strike is not a solution but a weapon used to make sure that you find a solution, when a solution has to be found ... Whilst we had said that we were going to be disruptive, and we were going to be ungovernable, we needed to prepare for governance, and preparing for governance must be based on skills, knowledge, and leadership that is visionary ... So I can say, from there throughout they were leading in the boardroom ... in meetings with governments, in meeting with stakeholders.

This meant not that strike action could not be utilised in the context of a democratic state, but that it should be resorted to only after all attempts at negotiations have failed – in Maluleke's words, 'you cannot remove the pressure from the pedal'. Indeed, between 1995 and 1997, strikes played an important role in addressing a range of challenges faced by teachers, including salary parity between black and white teachers, conditions of services such as school safety, improvement of school infrastructure, as well as pension and housing subsidies, to mention but a few.

It is important to note that this generation of SADTU leadership contributed both to the organisation's development as a union fighting for the rights of teachers as workers and to its role in the development of post-apartheid education policy. As discussed in Chapter 1, a key priority in the period immediately after the union's launch was to secure recognition of SADTU as a national non-racial teachers' union. SADTU not only succeeded in gaining recognition, but also played a central role in winning collective bargaining rights for teachers with the establishment of the Education Labour Relations Council (ELRC) and the promulgation of the Education Labour Relations Act in 1993. In addition, on the international stage, through the efforts of SADTU President Shepherd Mdladlana and General Secretary Randall van den Heever, SADTU was admitted as a member of Education International (EI). Established in Stockholm in January 1993, EI stands for the advancement of teachers' interests and welfare; the defence of trade unions, professional rights and the right to education; and for the promotion of peace, democracy, social justice, equality and the fight against all forms of racism. The organisation thus provided an enabling context for the furtherance of international unity and solidarity of teacher unions.[9] It was an appropriate home to provide support to and hone the organisational skills of SADTU leaders, given its approach that linked global education struggles to the broader struggles for a just world.

Although SADTU did not develop any substantive education policies of its own in this period, it contributed to the development of post-apartheid education policies through its representation and active participation in the policy development process initiated by the MDM (discussed in detail in Chapter 3). This process yielded the National Education Policy Investigation (NEPI) established by the NECC, and the ANC's Policy Framework for Education and Training (the so-called Yellow Book), the Implementation Plan for Education and Training (IPET) and the Reconstruction and Development Programme (RDP). SADTU was also active in the curriculum revision (or cleansing) project, which was initiated by the National Education and Training Forum (NETF). Moreover, post-1994 the union contributed to the development of the new democratic government's education policies through engagement with the ANC Education Study Group in parliament (many of whose members were previously senior leaders in SADTU), including making submissions on policy frameworks as part of the formal public parliamentary consultative processes. SADTU's role in these processes is summed up by Dolopi:

> We were actively involved in policy formulation . . . whether it be SASA [South African Schools Act], whether it's the [Employment

of] Educators' Act, whether it be the Employment Equity Act, whether its Basic Conditions of Service Act, whether its Labour Relations Act, all these pieces of legislation . . . SADTU was involved in all . . . [P]olicies, I mean you can count them, White Paper, ECD [Early Childhood Development], all these White Papers, we were involved in. Even higher education policies, we were involved in the formulation of the policies.

While SADTU's participation in these processes was not always significant, it was generally facilitated by several factors, as outlined below.

Seasoned and visionary leaders in key positions

A primary factor was undoubtedly the emergence of a generation of leaders with demonstrated mobilisation, conscientisation and leadership skills forged in the struggle against apartheid, and a firm commitment to unite teachers and find alternatives to apartheid education. It was from this pool of seasoned leaders that the first senior leadership of SADTU was elected at its launch in October 1990. Among these first leaders were Membathisi Shepherd Mdladlana – president; B.B. Mabandla – deputy president; Randall van den Heever – general secretary; and Thulas Nxesi – assistant general secretary. Five vice-presidents were elected: Ismael Vadi – media; Pinkie Mpowane – gender; Squire Khumalo – sport; Vivian Carelse – culture; and Duncan Hindle – education. As this list makes clear, gender representation remained a challenge for SADTU. Nonetheless, this national leadership was supported by young, politically aware and committed teacher-activists at regional and branch levels. Notably, these leaders were elected at national level only after carrying out political and education work at lower levels of the organisation.

SADTU's early participation in policy-making also enabled its leaders to build strong linkages and networks with leaders of the MDM. This not only ensured the election of some of SADTU's leaders to the first democratic parliament in 1994, but also enabled SADTU's representation in almost all the bodies and structures established to advise the democratic government in the development of education policy. As Dolopi described it:

> It was really a very democratic process where we were represented in the teams . . . we were represented through the Alliance and at times advising discussions of portfolio committees . . . we [were] invited to study groups of the ANC, were part of those, and [we would] participate in the study groups, sponsor ideas, and so on and so forth. So that was the level of involvement, to an extent then that these Acts almost represented our aspirations.

The senior leaders elected to parliament included Mdladlana, Van den Heever and Vadi – all of whom served on the first Education Portfolio Committee in the National Assembly, which navigated the policy and legislative agenda of the democratic government. Others, such as Duncan Hindle, Thami Mseleku and many of the regional and branch leaders, moved into the newly formed national and provincial education departments. However, although these leaders came from SADTU, they saw their role as creating a new education system in the interests of all rather than narrowly in the interests of its members. Through its leaders, SADTU contributed to giving effect to the MDM's vision for education. Thus, the union's voice was heard in the bargaining and policy negotiating structures even if SADTU as a body was not there. We refer to this as extended representation; that is, SADTU's vision was embraced and articulated by other members of the MDM, yielding SADTU's voice despite the union's physical absence. These developments underscore the transformational leadership character that emerged within SADTU, marking perhaps a high point in the impact of SADTU's leaders on society at large and in the interest of the common good.

Assessing the impact of SADTU's first- and second-generation leadership: relative autonomy or critical distance

SADTU emerged as a relatively autonomous teachers' union with enough political space and distance to operate simultaneously as a partner in the political Tripartite Alliance led by the ANC, the governing party, and as a pressure group for the public good of teachers, learners and society at large. As Mdladlana stated in his 'Keeping Our Distance' address at the SADTU launch in 1990:

> We must keep the distance between ourselves and political parties, otherwise we will be like our colleagues in Mozambique and elsewhere in Africa where teachers' rights are violated. Africa is frightened of militant teachers. Let us also learn from the experience of Transkei where teachers are sjambokked, teargassed and shot by so-called people's leaders. We must not fool ourselves by thinking that the new government will be our Father Christmas with a bag full of toys for teachers.[10]

Overall, this generation of leadership can be defined by their commitment in approach, style and practice to change the status quo for the benefit of the wider society under the guidance of democratic principles and values. These values included:
- transformational leadership and leadership for social justice – the ability to influence change for common good;
- collective and participatory leadership – the ability to listen to, lead and work with other layers of leaders or to delegate important tasks when necessary, without compromising on organisational accountability;
- collective responsibility – commitment to address organisational challenges and problems at any level of organisational structures whenever necessary; and
- organisational responsiveness and the public good – leadership practice as central to organisational learning, the enrichment of members, and the promotion of good outcomes for teachers, learners and society at large.

Thus, the vision, political energy and rich lessons acquired in this context enabled SADTU leaders to redirect union activities to address the challenges of national reconstruction and development without losing its organisational identity as a social movement committed to quality education, public good and social justice.

Third-generation leadership: managing a leadership crisis

In the mid-2000s, SADTU faced a leadership crisis, out of which emerged the third generation of leaders. This crisis was sparked by tensions and conflicts within the Tripartite Alliance, which were in part the result of the Growth, Employment and Redistribution (GEAR) macroeconomic strategy being introduced by the ANC government without consulting its Alliance partners. The lack of consultation and fundamental differences over GEAR precipitated the rise of factionalism, rivalry and political competition between the different ideological streams within the Tripartite Alliance. The differences were not only between the Alliance partners but also within the partner organisations. The outcome of the tensions at the national level was the removal of South Africa's then president, Thabo Mbeki – the architect of GEAR – and his replacement by Jacob Zuma, who was supported by the opponents of GEAR.

The falling-out at the national level was replicated in the Alliance, including within SADTU, with Mbeki supporters ousted and replaced with Zuma supporters. In SADTU, this led to the erosion of the strong identity and political solidarity between leaders and members, which diminished accountability, consultation, collective decision-making, and so on. Values widely shared and pursued by the first and second generation of leaders began to erode. This, together with the social and economic impact of GEAR on the day-to-day lives of teachers, resulted in a climate of mistrust and resentment that placed SADTU leaders at loggerheads with government and public opinion.

The GEAR strategy called for restricted spending on education and social services. Teachers felt the impact in the form of retrenchments and deteriorating working conditions due to burgeoning administrative workloads, overcrowded classrooms, additional teaching periods, lack of teaching materials and a decline in salaries in real terms.[11] This resulted in low teacher morale. On the positive side, SADTU's engagement with government on GEAR led to the realisation that the union should reclaim and retain its role as a pressure group on issues concerning the well-being of teachers in general, school improvement and education quality, as well as wider community issues. On the negative side, this effort towards renewal was constrained by irreconcilable tensions at senior leadership level. In brief, SADTU leaders were putting emphasis on talking about each other instead of talking to each other as they used to. They talked above the organisation instead of talking within and through the organisation, as a result of the emergence of factionalism, tribalism, regionalism and what has been labelled business unionism by some leaders.[12]

Symptoms of the leadership crisis manifested in instability at the level of the office of the president over a five-year period and affected two presidents: William Mothipa 'Willie' Madisha (1999–2008) and Thobile Ntola (2010–2014). Madisha, the longest-serving SADTU president and a former president of COSATU, was part of a young layer of third-generation leaders nurtured by the MDM. Both Madisha and Ntola were expelled from SADTU for instigating divisions within the organisation in the context of the political machinations of the Tripartite Alliance. They found themselves on the losing side in the ongoing factional political battles in the Alliance in the mid to late 2000s. Madisha was accused of acting outside the collective position of SADTU and COSATU by backing Thabo Mbeki's bid for a third term as president of the ANC instead of supporting Jacob Zuma at the ANC's elective conference in Polokwane in December 2007.[13] Subsequently, Ntola sided with Zwelinzima Vavi, the then general secretary of COSATU, who was expelled for calling for Jacob Zuma's removal as president of the country.

There were other charges levelled at the two. Madisha was accused of departing from stated union policy when he publicly declared that SADTU would be shifting its focus from unionism to professionalism and the attainment of professional ethics by getting rid of all members who exhibited unprofessional and unethical behaviour. More seriously, Ntola was accused of 'business unionism', a term used to refer to leaders developing inappropriate relationships with service providers for personal gain at the expense of the organisation. Ntola was allegedly receiving a monthly allowance of R10 000 from one of the union's service providers.[14]

The leadership crisis displayed itself in four main forms. First, there were strong symptoms of factionalism, regionalism and tribalism based on political and regional allegiances. The regional divisions became apparent with the expulsion of Ntola, who comes from the Eastern Cape. As Maluleke put it:

> So, the regions were divided into Xhosa against the Sotho [including Pedi] ... the Western Cape and Eastern Cape and Northern Cape siding together because the President was a Xhosa, and the Deputy President was a Pedi; so on the other side Gauteng, which is no man's land, but predominantly Zulu and Pedi, and Limpopo, which was [previously] Northern Province and part of North West ... because of proximity, siding with the ... group of the Deputy President and ... the general secretary both of whom come from Limpopo province. Some of us were being the mediators all the time because the general secretary [myself] then was an international leader ... So, the administration was swayed to side with one faction [that of the Deputy President].

Second, there was the emergence of business unionism, which, according to SADTU executive members, refers to the use of union resources for personal enrichment. Traditionally, the concept has been linked to union members who are opposed to working-class or revolutionary unionism and who advocate the principle that unions should be run like businesses (Taft 1963). Third, power relations played a significant role, with self-importance increasingly reflected in leadership behaviour. This resulted in contraventions of the union's constitution, such as leaders making decisions on behalf of the organisation without respecting organisational structures, protocols and policies. This led to suspicions and rumours that the leadership was 'selling us out' (*Bayasithengisa laba*), especially in the labour relations bargaining context. Fourth, the struggle for positions fuelled perceptions that leadership posts could be used as a stepping stone or incubation hub that provided easy access to senior positions in government and other statutory structures. This was supported by the fact that senior SADTU office bearers had moved into such positions post-1994.

The consequences of the crisis were felt not only internally, but also within the broader education community by the erosion of SADTU's relationship with external stakeholders and role players, including learners, parents, the education authorities and civil society. Thus, strike action in 2010, for example, was met with fierce public criticism and accusations that SADTU and its leaders had lost their integrity as professionals. There were charges against SADTU of hooliganism and militancy linked to classroom disruptions and blame for violence in schools (Amtaika 2013; Sibiya 2017). This led the then Gauteng ANC provincial secretary, David Makhura, to call SADTU leadership 'rogue and ill-disciplined'.[15] As discussed in Chapters 3 and 5, SADTU's public image has suffered immensely as a result of its privileging unionism over professionalism; it is also clear that SADTU's leadership crisis from the mid-2000s, linked to the political turbulence within the ANC, is another contributing factor to its declining popularity.

The crisis was a wake-up call for SADTU leaders, rallying them to reclaim some of the core values that were fast eroding – in particular, the commitment to collective leadership and responsibility. It also focused leadership attention on creating synergy between the ethics, ethos and values of the union with those that underpin school and educational practice in the country. This meant reinforcing awareness of the SADTU code of conduct within the organisation and the teaching profession more generally through collaboration with the South African Council for Educators (SACE). The focus thus shifted to the need to promote professionalism in education in line with the vision of SADTU's founding leaders. This was given effect through the establishment of the SADTU Curtis Nkondo Professional Development Institute (SCNPDI) to provide professional development training to SADTU members and other teachers. Equally important, the depletion of the leadership resulting from the movement to government drew attention to the need to rethink the criteria for election to leadership positions, which is discussed below.

Reimagining SADTU leadership for the future: drawing on the leadership lessons of the past

SADTU's past experience highlights the need for strengthening the union's current and future leadership. This would require the development of leaders who, inspired by SADTU's earlier leadership legacy, are above all unwavering in motivating and inspiring members to see beyond their own material interests and to focus on the broader interests of learners, parents and the community in developing a quality education system. This implies reclaiming the transformational and moral leadership characteristics displayed by SADTU's first- and second- generation leaders. Moreover, SADTU leaders must recognise that teachers, like other government employees, are first and foremost public servants, without compromising their working conditions and professional autonomy as educators. There is evidence that this form of leadership is gradually being embraced within SADTU. This is reflected in the lessons learnt as crystallised and expressed by SADTU leaders, outlined next.

Interrogating SADTU's ideological stance and political alliances

In its official documents, SADTU has consistently defined itself as a socialist organisation based on its affiliation to COSATU and its support for the South African Communist Party (SACP). However, Duncan Hindle, an ex-SADTU president, states that SADTU's ideology is influenced by the politics of its membership, and that the union sees no inherent contradiction between a strong organisation able to defend and promote the rights and interests of teachers and the professional work of teachers (Hindle 1991). Whether this represents a socialist orientation is debatable, as teachers who join SADTU because of its successes in the labour relations field may not necessarily support its political outlook. This is confirmed by the union leaders who have been adamant in declaring that SADTU has no ideology, as expressed, for example, by Maluleke:

> We are always warned that our founding principle is that we are not ideological. We don't use ideology ... for recruitment or

retention [but] on policy matters ... The union has an ideology because we are leftist oriented, although in our constitution we can't state that the union has adopted a Marxist-Leninist orientation ... that the union is pursuing a socialist ideology ... It is clear the principles were laid out at the Harare Declaration[16] ... Based on this declaration, the union recruits all workers irrespective of their ideological orientation, although the union is socialist oriented [and as a leader] I must be ideologically rooted or grounded to advance the union's socialist-oriented policies. There is no ideology about how to unite the organisation. So, at the top level, yes, I can be ideological as a leader ... but you don't come and say let us adopt the ideology of Marxism-Leninism in the organisation because we are not a political party.

However, this explanation is at variance with SADTU's commitment to socialism as enunciated in various national congress resolutions and the union's political alliances. The issue of ideology remains an area that warrants critical interrogation and clarity on its implications for policy and practice in the context of SADTU's commitment to transformational leadership. Moreover, with regard to alliances, there has been a significant shift in the way these currently operate. Prior to 1994, the MDM, which was an alliance of anti-apartheid organisations, operated on the principle of the relative autonomy of the participating organisations. This provided organisations with the space to pursue their specific goals without any constraints imposed by the MDM. However, post-1994, when the Tripartite Alliance replaced the MDM, the space for organisational autonomy has structurally narrowed (as discussed in Chapter 3). In this context, it has not been possible for SADTU to distance itself from the political and ideological battles that have been a feature of the Alliance in recent years, or to take independent positions on education policy matters other than when these impact on labour relations issues. This suggests that SADTU may not have the autonomy to push government to address critical challenges in education if the union is in conflict with the policies of the ANC-led government.

Similarly, as argued in Chapter 2, the ANC-led government is reluctant to take action against SADTU members, as it is dependent on the latter's electoral support. This symbiotic relationship and its implications for the education system have further dented SADTU's image in the public mind. It seems clear that to be effective in the pursuit of the public good for teachers, learners and society at large, SADTU should reclaim its right to relative autonomy within the Alliance's organisational structures and processes. That is, the union needs the independence to assert its vision and goals even if they are not fully endorsed by the Alliance. This is an issue with which SADTU's current and future leaders must engage in order to boost the union's claims to transformational and ethical leadership (Huey 1994; Nirenberg 1993).

Consolidating the transformational attributes of its leaders

The key attributes and criteria to become a SADTU leader – from branch level to national office – include (i) willingness, capacity and capability to unite the organisation and its members; (ii) sensitivity to diversity and commitment to inclusive leadership; (iii) skills to drive organisational change within SADTU and the education system in general; and (iv) commitment to stay in the organisation and not to see it as merely a stepping stone to political and government posts, which turns the organisation into a simple incubator of political and government officials.[17] As Maluleke expressed it, 'Those aspiring to become leaders need to show that they have what it takes to remain in the organisation and forfeit the opportunity of becoming a director or deputy director, or director general.' This same point was stated more emphatically by SADTU President Maphila:

> There are leadership requirements. You must mature within . . . the structures of the union . . . For you to become a leader in SADTU, at the place where things are happening, which is the school, you must have been a member for at least a year. Once you have been a member for at least a year, you then qualify to serve at the level of a site . . . So to become . . . a leader at the level of

the region, you must have at least served as a branch member. So the region is a coordinating structure of branches ... How does SADTU behave and so on? Once they are elected, we induct them. There is leadership development and we encourage them to study ... So ... for you to serve at the level of the province, you must at least have served at the level of the region. For you to [serve] nationally, you cannot come here unless you have been a leader at a province. So, there are no surprise leaders.

As underscored by both Maluleke and Maphila, it takes some thirteen years to move from ordinary member to school site leadership to national leadership levels, which is currently one year as ordinary member before qualifying to lead at a school site level for two years, with the cycle at the branch and region pegged at three years each and provincial level four years. There is also the possibility of one being re-elected in the same structure at a lower level, which would result in the number of years exceeding the thirteen years slightly or significantly. As a result, many of the leaders in the union serve more than one term in the four lower union structures, that is, at the site, branch, region and province before progressing to national leadership. The protracted leadership pathway is to ensure that leaders have matured and have a deep understanding of the culture and operations of the union when they assume senior leadership positions at the provincial and national levels.

There can be no doubt that the identified leadership attributes are essential for maintaining organisational stability and impacting positively in the education arena. However, SADTU should pay greater attention to those attributes connected to transformational leadership, which would enable it to enhance its relationship with learners, teachers, schools, education authorities and the relevant professional education bodies. This requires that elected leaders be systematically provided with training and skills development in leadership, labour relations and management, as well as in the ethos, culture and underpinning values of the teaching profession. While SADTU has made considerable good on this promise (as discussed in Chapter 3), it remains to be seen whether the transformational leadership that it espouses will permeate all its structures, from the national to the school site level. Future leadership training programmes should reflect the union's commitment in this regard.

'Closing the chapter' of defiance mentality in advancement of professional unionism

The 'chapters we have not been able to close' is a metaphorical reference to issues such as opportunistic and corrupt practices that have not been dealt with and which negatively impact on SADTU's public image. As Maluleke expressed it:

> The chapter we should have closed is the chapter that people have created for themselves, taking advantage of the fact that there was a time when we were in a defiance campaign . . . So the chapter we must close is the chapter that says there are people who are still taking advantage of not working in our schools in the name of our organisation. Did we ever say do not teach? Was the defiance campaign about not working? Was the defiance campaign about not respecting authority? . . . there is a very small number of people who believe that they can leave the school at 10 o'clock and . . . that the principal cannot say anything, and then they use our organisation. Some of them . . . would go to the extent of using the union for particular reasons . . . It's a chapter of defiance mentality that is basically not following the policies and the vision of our organisation – very opportunistic. It's the one that is creating the image problem . . . And that is against our own constitution; that is against our objectives as an organisation.

It is debatable whether SADTU has been firm and proactive enough in closing this chapter. If it is serious about doing so, it needs to take a stronger stance on the accountability and responsibility of SADTU members in discharging their role as teachers (as discussed in Chapter 5). This may require re-engaging with the notion of education as an essential service, and its implications. For SADTU, the compromise between government and teacher organisations, which recognises the right of teachers to strike but with some non-negotiables, appears to be diluted when reconceptualised into revolutionary tasks. Dolopi explained it this way:

> It is revolutionary for me to be [at] school every day. It is revolutionary for me to be prepared every day. It is revolutionary for me to teach every day. It is revolutionary for me to laugh and appreciate the children and avoid sexual relationships and all those kinds of things. So, in government policy, we call them non-negotiables, but we say you can't recognise yourself as a revolutionary if you didn't teach.

This dilemma between teachers' right to engage in strikes and their obligations to learners lies at the heart of the professionalism-unionism tension, and is a critical organisational policy management issue. The manner and extent to which SADTU's leaders resolve this tension is a fundamental challenge, one explored further in Chapter 7.

A listening leadership: reclaiming Mdladlana's call for 'people with ears'
Mdladlana's notion of people with ears points to the need for individual and organisational openness and self-criticism. SADTU's experience has demonstrated beyond doubt that defensive rhetoric has been self-defeating; it does not work. Although Mdladlana's comments were directed at the political and bureaucratic leaders in government, they have become a key leadership value and principle within SADTU itself. As articulated by Maluleke, beyond embodying personal attributes such as humility and resilience, SADTU leaders should strive to ensure that organisational structures are fit to serve organisational purposes rather than themselves. If they develop a boss (authoritarian) mentality, they will chase members away. Above all, they must be people with ears. As Maluleke put it, they must 'listen to leadership, listen to the members, but more importantly listen to . . . opponents', which will open a space for

self-criticism and improvement. Maluleke went on to say that 'one must develop the ability to take criticism from the leaders, from the members, and from yourself . . . That's what we call "methodical doubt".'

The ability to listen is an important leadership characteristic and is consistent with the ethical and transformational leadership values that SADTU's leaders have emphasised. The art of listening helps leaders to make informed choices and achieve shared meaning and common understanding, both between themselves and with their members, through organisational learning (Giddens 2006). Herein lies another challenge for SADTU's leaders: to listen in order to make informed decisions so that the mistakes of the past are not repeated.

Conclusion

This chapter has explored SADTU's rich and inspiring accumulated leadership legacy and the lessons that can be drawn from it to shape the union's future direction. This legacy was shaped in the struggle by bold and courageous leaders in confronting the brutal apartheid regime, in searching for alternatives to the racist and discriminatory school system, in reconstructing and developing the country, and in dealing with the union's internal organisational challenges. Founding leaders were transformational and driven by the need to serve the public good rather than the narrow and material interests of SADTU members. Their legacy is characterised by a commitment to democratic values and principles, including non-racialism and non-sexism, and an uncompromising determination to enhance the quality of education as a precondition for social justice. Drawn from SADTU's rich history, this legacy is perhaps the most important source of inspiration available to the union today as it strives to shape its future in new, innovative and better ways. When history and memory are ignored, there is only amnesia or ignorance (Assie-Lumumba 2018).

The legacy notwithstanding, there are significant challenges that confront SADTU's leadership as it moves forward. First, SADTU needs to address its negative public image by responding firmly to acts of misconduct by its members in several spheres of organisational and professional life. SADTU cannot distance itself from the actions of its members on the grounds that these actions are not in line with union policy. In this regard, SADTU needs to engage in both individual and organisational introspection to detect and take full responsibility for the problems of its own making, particularly the actions of its members. Socialisation through specific social relations with others is critical, helping to shape individual and group consciousness that informs the style and modes of leadership. Thus, there is a need to go beyond merely being defensive by tackling the critique head-on, illustrating by deed and action that SADTU is a learning organisation that is able to reflect on its weaknesses and adapt to changing conditions and times. Leadership is a relational, socially constructed phenomenon, not just a permanent set of leadership attributes that are immune to change. Second, the external environment – in particular, SADTU's participation in the Tripartite Alliance – is increasingly constraining the union from effectively pursuing its democratic, professional and public good agenda, especially in the education arena. SADTU needs to critically engage with the Alliance in redefining its role in terms of the notion of relative autonomy. This would enable the union to contribute more constructively to the broader policy discourse on the professional responsibilities of its members and teachers in general, on the rights of learners and on enhancing the quality of education. Third, SADTU needs to be more proactive in grappling with the implications of teachers' changing social and economic context. These include current challenges such as the impact of the Covid-19 pandemic and the Fourth Industrial Revolution and other emerging technologies, which will not only put new demands on learners and teachers in terms of new skills and pedagogies, but will also fundamentally change the way in which schools are organised. Transformational leadership entails setting direction, realigning organisational goals, developing and empowering members, and engaging with external stakeholders. Of equal importance is the notion of meaning-making around organisational goals, opportunities and challenges. The full weight of the transformative and emancipatory imaginations of SADTU's leaders will be required to address the challenges in education today and the broader issues that confront society as a whole.

Notes

1. All quotations by Nkosana Dolopi are taken from an interview by Michael Cross, 4 July 2019, Kempton Park.
2. All quotations by Magope Maphila are taken from an interview by Michael Cross, 4 July 2019, Kempton Park.
3. Shepherd Mdladlana was elected the first president of SADTU at its launch in 1990 and eventually become an ANC member of parliament in the first democratic government; he subsequently served as minister of labour. Ronald Swartz was a senior official in the Gauteng Department of Education post-1994.
4. All quotations by Mugwena Maluleke are taken from an interview by Michael Cross, 4 July 2019, Kempton Park.
5. Mugwena Maluleke, interview by Michael Cross, 4 July 2019, Kempton Park.
6. David Matsepe, team meeting discussion with Logan Govender, 10 November 2022.
7. At the time of writing, the gender representation of the 18 provincial representatives on the NEC is Limpopo: chairperson = female, secretary = male; Northern Cape: chairperson = male, secretary = female; KwaZulu-Natal: chairperson = male, secretary = female; and the remaining six provinces of Mpumalanga, North West, Gauteng, Free State, Western Cape and Eastern Cape: all males.
8. *SADTU News*, July 1993.
9. *SADTU News*, July 1993.
10. *SADTU News*, July 1990.
11. Andy Duffy, 'Bloody Battle Starts over Schools', *Mail & Guardian*, 9–15 January 1998.
12. Mugwena Maluleke, interview by Michael Cross, 4 July 2019, Kempton Park.
13. Magope Maphila, interview by Michael Cross, 4 July 2019, Kempton Park.
14. SAPA, 'Ntola Expulsion has "Nothing to Do with Vavi": Sadtu', *Sunday World*, 21 May 2014.
15. Katlego Moeng, 'ANC Flays Rogue Soweto Educators', *SowetanLive*, 16 March 2011, https://www.sowetanlive.co.za/news/2011-03-16-anc-flays-roguesoweto-educators (accessed November 2016).
16. The Harare Accord was the outcome of a conference held in Zimbabwe in April 1988 that worked to establish one unified, non-racial national teachers' organisation. It led to the establishment of the National Teacher Unity Forum (NTUF), as described in Chapter 1.
17. Interviews by Michael Cross with Magope Maphila, Mugwena Maluleke, and Nkosana Dolopi, 4 July 2019, Kempton Park.
18. Paraphrased from interviews with Mugwena Maluleke and Magope Maphila, by Michael Cross, 4 July 2019, Kempton Park.

References

Amoako, S. 2014. 'Teacher Unions in Political Transitions: The South African Democratic Teachers' Union (SADTU) and the Dying Days of Apartheid, 1990-1993'. *Journal of Asian and African Studies* 49(2). https://doi.org/10.1177/0021909613479302.

Amtaika, A. 2013. 'Replaying Memories of the Past: Reflecting on the South African Teachers' 2010 Protest'. *International NGO Journal* 8(5): 108-16.

Assie-Lumumba, N.T. 2018. 'Africa and the Advancement of Higher Education at Home and Globally: Memory and Imperative for Renewal through Purposeful Fusion'. Third Annual Eric Molobi Memorial Lecture, University of Johannesburg.

Avolio, B., F. Walumbwa and T.J. Weber. 2009. 'Leadership: Current Theories, Research, and Future Directions'. Management Department Faculty Publications, 37. https://digitalcommons.unl.edu/managementfacpub/37.

Black, J.S. and H.B. Gregersen. 1997. 'Participative Decision-Making: An Integration of Multiple Dimensions'. *Human Relations* 50(7): 859-78.

Burkitt, I. 2008. *Social Selves: Theories of Self and Society*. 2nd ed. London: Sage Publications.

Dlamini. A., B. Smit and C. Loock. 2014. 'The Influence of Union Leadership on Principals' Identity'. *Pensee Journal* 76(3): 215-27.

Freund, W. 2007. 'Organised Labour in the Republic of South Africa: History and Democratic Transition'. In *Trade Unions and the Growing of Democracy in Africa*, edited by J. Kraus. New York: Palgrave Macmillan.

Giddens, A. 2006. *Sociology*. 5th ed. Cambridge: Polity Press.

Govender, L. 2004. 'Teacher Unions, Policy Struggles and Educational Change, 1994-2004'. In *Changing Class: Education and Social Change in Post-apartheid South Africa*, edited by L. Chisholm. London and New York: Zed Books.

Hindle, D. 1991. 'Blackboard Power: The New Teacher Politics'. *Indicator SA* 9(1): 71-4.

Huey, J. 1994. 'The New Post-heroic Leadership'. *Fortune*, 21 February, 42-50.

Kerchner, C. and J. Koppich. 1993. *A Union of Professionals: Labour Relations and Educational Reform*. New York: Teachers College Press.

Kumalo, V. and D. Skosana. 2014. *A History of the South African Democratic Teachers' Union (SADTU)*. Johannesburg: SADTU.

Letseka, M., B. Bantwini and E. King-McKenzie. 2012. 'Public-Union Sector Politics and the Crisis of Education in South Africa'. *Creative Education* 3(7): 1197-1204.

Mannah, S. and J. Lewis. 2008. 'South African Teacher and Social Movements Old and New'. In *The Global Assault on Teaching, Teachers, and Their Unions: Stories for Resistance*, edited by M.F. Compton and L. Weiner. New York: Palgrave Macmillan.

Nirenberg, J. 1993. *The Living Organization: Transforming Teams into Workplace Communities*. Burr Ridge, Illinois: Irwin Professional Publishing.

Robinson, V., M. Hohepa and C. Lloyd. 2009. 'School Leadership and Student Outcomes: Identifying What Works and Why Best Evidence Synthesis Iteration [BES]'. Wellington, New Zealand: Ministry of Education.

Seale, O. and M. Cross. 2019. 'Towards Systemic and Integrated Leadership Development for Deans in South African Universities'. Mimeo.

Sibiya, T.P. 2017. 'Key Stakeholders' Experiences and Perspectives on the Role of the South African Democratic Teachers' Union (SADTU) in Education'. Master's dissertation, University of KwaZulu-Natal, Pietermaritzburg.

South African Democratic Teachers' Union (SADTU). 1991. 'Steps Taken by SADTU to Gain Recognition'. Issued by SADTU, 10 May.

———. 2017. 'Report on Gender Policy'. October.

———. 2022. 'NGC Secretariat Report'. Presented at the National General Council Meeting, Emperors Palace, Johannesburg, 4–6 October.

Southall, G. and E. Webster. 2010. 'Unions and Parties in South Africa: Cosatu and the ANC in the Wake of Polokwane'. In *Trade Unions and Party Politics: Labour Movements in Africa*, edited by B. Beckman, S. Buhlungu and L. Sachikonye. Cape Town: HSRC Press.

Sutherland, N., C. Land and S. Böhm. 2014. 'Anti-leaders(hip) in Social Movement Organizations: The Case of Autonomous Grassroots Groups'. *Organization* 21(6): 759–81.

Taft, P. 1963. 'On the Origins of Business Unionism'. *ILR Review* 17(1): 20–38. https://journals.sagepub.com/doi/10.1177/001979396301700102.

Webster, E. and G. Adler. 2001. 'Exodus without a Map? The Labour Movement in a Liberalizing South Africa'. In *Labour Regimes and Liberalization: The Structure of State-Society Relations in Africa*, edited by B. Beckman and L.M. Sachikonye. Harare: University of Zimbabwe Publications.

Wilkens, A. 1983. 'Organizational Stories as Symbols which Control the Organization'. In *Organizational Symbolism*, edited by L. Pondy, P. Frost and G. Morgan. Greenwich, Connecticut: JAI Press.

Wolpe, A. 1988. *Within School Walls: The Role of Discipline, Sexuality and the Curriculum*. London: Routledge.

Yukl, G. 1989. 'Managerial Leadership: A Review of Theory and Research'. *Journal of Management* 15(2). https://doi.org/10.1177/014920638901500207.

The following interviews with SADTU officials were conducted by Michael Cross:
Magope Maphila, president, 4 July 2019, Kempton Park.
Mugwena Maluleke, general secretary, 4 July 2019, Kempton Park.
Nkosana Dolopi, deputy general secretary, 4 July 2019, Kempton Park.

7

SADTU's Future Role in the South African Education Landscape

AHMED ESSOP

As explained in previous chapters, SADTU emerged out of the militant teacher unions that were at the forefront of the struggle in the 1980s for the democratisation and transformation of South Africa's education system. The militant teacher unions, which defined teachers as workers, combined economic concerns – equity in salaries and conditions of service – with professional concerns – the upgrading of teacher qualifications and skills and the scrapping of bureaucratic controls on teachers. Moreover, they recognised that teachers' demands as workers and professionals for the democratisation of the education system could not be separated from the broader struggle for democracy, which brought together student, teacher, community and trade union organisations under the umbrella of the Mass Democratic Movement (MDM). Thus, in its origins SADTU can be regarded as an example of a social movement union, the key features of which are described by John McCollow (2017: 6): 'it is locally based; encourages collective actions that go beyond strike or workplace activities; builds alliances in the community and beyond; embraces emancipatory politics; and develops transformative visions'.

As a social movement union, SADTU had a critical role to play in contributing to the transformation of the education system. At its launch congress in October 1990, Nelson Mandela indicated that the establishment of SADTU represented a 'beacon of hope. Hope that we are putting behind an end to the decades of darkness which apartheid education has condemned our people to . . . Hope that we are laying a firm basis for a single and democratic education system' (Mandela 1990). He challenged teachers by defining their rights and duties in a democratic education system:

> It is your duty also to be democratic in the classroom. You have to answer the question – are you developing a kind of intellectual among those in your custody? Are you initiating a new kind of relationship with your pupils? Is this relationship based on mutual respect and trust or is it one which relies on bullying? (Mandela 1990)

However, the expectation and promise that SADTU would lead the transformation of the education system did not materialise beyond the early years in the transition to democracy (as discussed in Chapters 2, 3 and 6). In post-apartheid South Africa, SADTU retreated to a narrower industrial focus befitting a traditional trade union to protect the workplace-based rights of its members. More often than not, industrial actions, such as strikes, were undertaken with little concern for the rights of learners and with the ever-present threat of violence and intimidation (Sibiya 2017). Jay Naidoo, the former general secretary of the Congress of South African Trade Unions (COSATU) and convenor of the National Teacher Unity Forum (NTUF), which led to the establishment of SADTU, recalls that he was 'horrified by the apparent silence' of the senior leadership of SADTU in 2008 in response to allegations that, during a strike against the Gauteng provincial education department's 'attempts to hold teachers accountable for shirking work', a senior SADTU leader in Gauteng threatened learners with 'extreme violence' if they came to school during the strike (Naidoo 2010: 329).[1]

In recent years, SADTU has lost public support and shoulders much of the blame for the perennial crisis in South African education. There is a growing perception that the challenges confronting the schooling system – in particular, the lack of improvement in the quality of educational outcomes – are to some extent the result of SADTU's focus on protecting the workplace-based rights of its members. The fact that the union fails to balance this emphasis with a focus on protecting the rights of learners has contributed to undermining the professional and caring dimensions of the role of teachers. The negative public perception of SADTU is compounded by the union's political role through its participation, as an affiliate of COSATU, in the Tripartite Political Alliance led by the African National Congress (ANC). As one of the largest unions in COSATU, SADTU has been caught up in the factional intrigues and political machinations that have characterised the Alliance, which has distracted it from its role in the transformation of the education system. The criticism that SADTU as a teachers' union is an impediment to addressing the crisis and reforming the education system is not peculiar to South Africa. Negative views of teacher unions are linked to the debate on education reform globally. As McCollow suggests:

> Internationally, education unions face significant challenges in the early decades of the 21st century. Neoliberal economic and industrial policies and legislation have eroded the capacity of unions to collectively organise and bargain, and the global education reform movement (GERM) has created a hostile environment for education unions and their members. Despite these challenges, education unions remain the most important critics of GERM and of global neoliberal social policy generally (McCollow 2017: 1).

In South Africa's prevailing social, economic and political context, SADTU's collective bargaining role is not under threat and its response to neoliberalism has been weak. Significantly, however, its inability to straddle the balance between unionism and professionalism has undermined the role it played in the early 1990s in contributing to fashioning the vision for the transformation of the education system. Thus, more than three decades into democracy, SADTU finds itself at a crossroads. What is its future, especially considering the current fissures in the body politic and, in particular, in the ANC-led Alliance, which is being driven asunder by rival factions vying for the spoils of state power to further their own social and economic interests?

This chapter argues that SADTU's future as a key role player and stakeholder in education is dependent on the union reimagining its role and reclaiming its historical promise in transforming the education system. This requires SADTU to rethink its understanding of and its role in five key issues, which have been distilled from earlier chapters and are discussed below, namely:
- reclaiming its roots as a social movement union: advocating and campaigning for education transformation;
- transcending the unionism versus professionalism divide;
- contributing to the development of education policy;
- redefining its political role in the Tripartite Alliance; and
- renewing its leadership and organisational capacity.

Reclaiming SADTU's roots as a social movement union: advocating and campaigning for education transformation

As indicated earlier, SADTU in its origins can best be described as a social movement union. It fought for the rights of teachers as part of a broader movement – involving parents, students, teachers and other stakeholders – calling for the transformation of the education system. This social movement, which was led by the National Education Coordinating Committee (NECC), dissolved in 1994 with South Africa's first democratic elections on the assumption that the transformation of the education system could be safely left to the ANC-led government. This seemed a safe inference, since many of the key leaders involved in the NECC, SADTU and other progressive organisations had moved into the bureaucracy and the legislature at national and provincial levels. However, although the new government did introduce a wide-ranging policy and legislative agenda to transform the education system, it was less successful in addressing key challenges associated with the inequalities of the past, which continue to bedevil the education system today. Thus, more than 28 years since the dawn of democracy, many children, especially in rural areas, continue to attend schools in dilapidated structures; schools that do not have sanitation systems and depend on pit latrines, which has resulted in injury and death; and schools without adequate textbooks, libraries and laboratories.

The fight for addressing these inequalities, and for holding government to account in discharging its responsibilities, has in recent years been taken up by civil society organisations, spearheaded in education by, among others, Equal Education and Section27. This fight has included campaigns on a wide range of issues, including safety and sanitation in schools, scholar transport, textbook provision and school infrastructure. It has also involved legal challenges to force government to meet its constitutional obligations regarding the right to basic education. For example, in November 2013 the minister of basic education promulgated minimum norms and standards for school infrastructure as a result of a successful legal challenge mounted by Equal Education (Equal Education 2018). However, SADTU has been conspicuously absent from this effort to pressure government to fulfil its promise of creating an equitable education system in line with the constitutionally enshrined rights. This lack of participation contrasts both with SADTU's pre-1994 role and with the role that teacher unions play in other parts of the world. In Latin America, for example, teacher unions have established national and regional pedagogical movements which mobilise public support and campaign for education reform (Gindin and Finger 2013).

It is imperative that SADTU reclaim its past role as a social movement union and advocate and campaign for the transformation of the education system, including holding government to account if it fails to discharge its responsibilities. It should do so through supporting and actively participating in the social movement for educational change that is being driven by civil society organisations. Indeed, SADTU should be leading the social movement for education change. And through its role in education, SADTU has a critical part to play in addressing broader societal challenges that impact on teachers and learners, such as sexual harassment, gender-based violence and xenophobia. SADTU should be at the forefront of developing campaigns to raise awareness of these issues among its members given their role in the socialisation of the young, including ensuring that these issues are dealt with appropriately in the classroom and the curriculum. This will enable the union to reconnect with the broader community and build public confidence by linking the protection of teachers' rights with broader processes for education transformation and social justice. SADTU should also use its participation in international and regional networks, such as Education International (EI) and the Southern African Development Community (SADC), to drive and support regional initiatives for educational change and reform.

Transcending the unionism vs professionalism divide

The attempts in the late 1980s to create a national teachers' organisation, bringing together under one umbrella both the militant teacher unions and the conservative teacher associations, failed mainly because of different views of the role of teachers. The militant teacher unions emphasised the role of teachers as workers and focused on fighting for better salaries and improved conditions of service through collective action, including strikes. The majority of conservative teacher associations, which coalesced into SADTU's main rival, the National Professional Teachers' Organisation of South Africa (NAPTOSA), emphasised the role of teachers as professionals and focused on putting the interests of learners first. This divide between unionism and professionalism is as old as the teaching profession and continues to characterise teacher organisations globally. As McCollow summarises:

> What the collective interests of teachers entail and how they should be pursued have been and remain active questions and matters for debate within these organisations. Different unions at different times have responded differently to these questions, for example, in relation to the degree to which an industrial versus a professional orientation should be adopted, and the degree to which a wider political and social justice agenda should be embraced. They are human organisations – composed of individuals and groups in differing circumstances, with different backgrounds and different priorities – shaped by various internal and external historical, political, social, legislative, and economic factors that vary across localities and time (McCollow 2017: 2).

This suggests that the distinction between unionism and professionalism is not mutually exclusive. They are closely related to each other and cannot be separated – a conducive working environment and satisfactory conditions of service are necessary to enable teachers to discharge their role as professionals. As Kenyan teachers have argued, if students are to have optimal conditions for learning, then teachers must have optimal conditions for teaching (Sang 2002).

The protection and promotion of teachers' rights as workers and professionals was adopted as a guiding principle to facilitate the establishment of a national teachers' organisation in 1988 (largely at the instigation of COSATU, as discussed in Chapter 1). But it was not until its first national congress in 1991 that SADTU recognised, as part of its programme of action, that unionism and professionalism were two sides of the same coin:

> Many teachers have been conditioned into accepting the definition of professionalism which says teachers do not have the right to protest. The rights to organize and protest are basic human rights and we make no apology for calling on teachers to protest against undemocratic service contracts. The state expects teachers to act professionally while they treat us in the most unprofessional manner possible. For them, professionalism means towing [sic] their line and we are not prepared to do that.
> ... There are two inescapable realities about teachers. One is that they are educators and the other is that they are workers. Teachers have no option but to fight for their rights as employees and at the same time exercise the responsibilities of the profession of teaching. It would be the most misguided view of professionalism to conclude that teachers by reason of their commitment to education would accept low salaries, unsatisfactory conditions of service and discriminatory practices ... SADTU fully accepts that teachers have a serious responsibility to provide an education of the highest standard to pupils in the classroom ... [and] that teachers also have democratic rights,

in particular the right to bargain for improved benefits for the profession (cited in Rensburg 1996: 164-5).

This shift toward balancing unionism and professionalism was influenced both by COSATU and by the fact that NAPTOSA, with its emphasis on professionalism and the rights of learners to uninterrupted schooling, was not only gaining public favour but also posed a threat in the competition for membership, which impacted on SADTU at different times in the late 1990s and 2000s (as discussed in Chapter 4).

In practice, however, SADTU was forced to focus on union-related issues given the context and realities on the ground pre-1994. In particular, SADTU faced a hostile state that refused to recognise it as a national non-racial teachers' union, and which embarked on initiatives to unilaterally restructure the education system, including retrenchments and a freeze on teaching posts. The focus on union-related issues continued post-1994. This was necessary because although recognition, collective bargaining and the right to strike were entrenched in legislation, macroeconomic policy and associated budgetary constraints in the mid-1990s required collective action to ensure market-related salaries and improved conditions of service for teachers. It was also necessary to defend teaching posts given the post-provisioning model introduced by government, which resulted in the rationalisation of posts through voluntary severance packages, with adverse consequences for the school system. Following mass teacher protests during 1994 and 1995, agreement was reached on post-provisioning and teacher retrenchments. In August 1999, teacher unions embarked on a national strike, mainly over salary increases (Govender 2004). The strike, which also focused on addressing the inequalities of the apartheid past, resonated with the public and did not result in the erosion of popular support. This is consistent with international evidence indicating that collective bargaining in the second half of the twentieth century delivered real improvements in teachers' remuneration and conditions of service (McCollow 2017).

As argued in Chapter 5, SADTU's lack of focus on professional issues was in part the result of two factors. First, it paid little attention to building its organisational capacity in the initial years after its establishment because of its involvement in the anti-apartheid struggle. The lack of capacity was further compounded by the fact that the union lost many of its senior leaders to government at the dawn of democracy. Second, SADTU did not initially pay attention to developing programmes for the professional development of teachers, as it assumed that this would be done by the new democratic government based on the ANC's education and training policy. However, when the government introduced policies that would facilitate the professional development of teachers, such as evaluation and performance appraisal policies, SADTU, together with other teacher unions, opposed these as attempts to reimpose apartheid-era bureaucratic controls on teachers, given their punitive rather than developmental focus. SADTU failed to recognise that the evaluation and performance appraisal policies were a first step in facilitating the building of teachers' professional capacity in relation to their knowledge and pedagogic skills, which were not developed under apartheid.

The historical context notwithstanding, it is clear that if SADTU is to regain public confidence and support, it needs to reclaim and give effect to its view, as expressed at its first national congress in 1991, that unionism and professionalism are not mutually exclusive. This requires recognising that having wrought significant changes in the working conditions of teachers, SADTU must reset the balance to ensure that both unionism and professionalism are given equal attention, which is captured by the notion of professional unionism (discussed in Chapter 5). It requires rethinking the role of industrial action, specifically strikes, which should be embarked on only as a last resort and, even then, in a manner that does not lead to the large-scale disruption of schooling. Indeed, as suggested in Chapter 6, it may require re-engaging with the notion of schooling as an essential service. It also requires ensuring that legitimate day-to-day union activity does not impact on the school day. Moreover, SADTU needs to rethink its role in contributing to the professionalisation of teaching. Although professional development is the responsibility of the individual teacher, with the state providing an enabling and supportive environment, SADTU has a critical role to play in both promoting awareness and encouraging its members to avail themselves of development opportunities on offer. These opportunities include union-initiated professional development programmes, both formal and informal, in partnership with the state and higher education institutions.

There is evidence, albeit limited, based on the experience of teacher unions in Latin America that active participation in, and facilitation of, professional development by teacher unions contributes to improving the quality of education through developing teacher skills and knowledge accumulation (Gindin and Finger 2013). Contributions by unions to teachers' development take two main forms: (i) organising workshops and training activities to enhance classroom practice and offering credit-bearing extension courses in partnership with universities; and (ii) issuing publications, both in print and online, that disseminate information on pedagogy and policy issues (Gindin and Finger 2013). SADTU is moving in this direction as indicated by the establishment of the SADTU Curtis Nkondo Professional Development Institute (SCNPDI) in 2013 to 'serve as a vehicle through which SADTU can contribute to the professional development' by training its members and other teachers (SADTU 2014: 50). The Institute has initiated a range of programmes including content training, both formal and informal, based on identified knowledge gaps; leadership, management and governance training for principals, deputy principals and heads of department; and research into teachers' well-being. These programmes have been undertaken in partnership with universities, non-governmental organisations and government. The Institute is a step in the right direction, as is the recent launch of the *Teachers' Journal*, which aims to provide a learning platform for members to address professional development challenges (see Chapter 3). Additionally, SADTU should consider creating online resources to facilitate ongoing professional development.

Finally, professionalism also requires paying attention to the ethics – norms, values and principles – of teaching as a profession. That SADTU is doing so is reflected, at least in theory, in its Code of Professional Conduct and in the Code of Professional Ethics developed by the South African Council for Educators (SACE), which regulates the teaching profession. The latter stipulates, among other things, that teachers:

- refrain from any 'form of sexual harassment (physical or otherwise) of learners' and colleagues, including forming sexual relationships with learners;
- do not abuse their position for 'financial, personal or political gain';
- are not 'negligent or indolent in the performance' of their professional duties;
- refrain from 'indulging and/or being in possession of intoxicating, illegal and/or unauthorised substances including alcohol and drugs within the school premises and/or whilst on duty';
- refrain from 'engaging in illegal activities'; and
- behave in a way that 'enhances the dignity and status of the teaching profession and that does not bring the profession into disrepute'.[2]

However, the code is more often than not observed in the breach, as indicated by ongoing media reports of physical and sexual abuse of learners by teachers, and other unprofessional practices. These include the selling of posts as outlined in the report of the Ministerial Task Team (MTT) (DBE 2016) that implicates SADTU members. SADTU agrees that the selling of posts is 'widespread though under reported [which can be] attributed to the fact that the sellers and buyers of posts operate in high secrecy and, in certain instances, accompanied by intimidation or threats of intimidation' (DBE 2016: 241). However, SADTU insists that since the practice is not union policy, the organisation cannot be held responsible for the actions of individual members who 'use the name of the union to further their own interests' (DBE 2016: 252). This is a defensive and unhelpful stance, especially as SADTU is the dominant teachers' union and many senior officials in provincial education departments are SADTU members. It begs the question, what is SADTU doing to root out what it concedes to be a widespread practice? In its defence, SADTU argues that it has distanced itself from the practice, written to the relevant regulatory bodies to investigate the allegations and, through the media, requested its members to provide the

Department of Basic Education with information regarding the selling of posts (DBE 2016). This is a weak response, and one not befitting an organisation that is committed to upholding the dignity and status of the teaching profession. If anything, it points to an organisational culture that is not sensitive to professional ethics. If this is to be reversed, it is imperative that SADTU take an active role in creating awareness and educating its members regarding their ethical obligations. And while SADTU may not be held legally responsible for the action of individual members, it can and should investigate the allegations and institute disciplinary action, including expelling members who are guilty of such transgressions. Finally, as the largest teachers' union represented in SACE, SADTU needs to push for greater action by SACE against teachers who are guilty of transgressing its Code of Professional Ethics.

Contributing to the development of education policy

Teacher unions have an important role to play in the development of education policy. The pedagogical knowledge and experience of their members at the coalface of the education system – the classroom – can contribute to enhancing and strengthening the development of policies to improve the quality of schooling. However, more often than not, teacher unions limit their policy focus to responding to policies that are perceived to impose bureaucratic controls that erode the autonomy of their members. This has primarily been the approach adopted by SADTU post-1994. In the wide-ranging pre-1994 education policy process initiated by the ANC and coordinated by the Centre for Education Policy Development (CEPD), SADTU's involvement was twofold: (i) participation of senior members in the task teams established for different aspects of the education system; and (ii) participation in the consultative processes leading up to the adoption of the ANC's Policy Framework for Education and Training in early 1994.

In the immediate post-1994 period, SADTU's participation in the consultative parliamentary processes for transforming the apartheid policy and legislative edifice of the education and training system was limited. This was due to the lack of organisational capacity and the inexperience of SADTU and other anti-apartheid organisations in engaging with parliamentary processes, as well as to the fact that they deferred to the ANC-led government, which, it was assumed, would implement the policies that would further their interests. Indeed, the non-participation of SADTU and other anti-apartheid organisations raised concerns within the ANC Education Study Group in parliament – many of whose members were previously senior officials in SADTU – that the MDM was not taking advantage of the opportunity provided by the election of an ANC government to intervene in the democratic process. For example, in 1995 the majority of submissions received by the Portfolio Committee on Education on the South African Schools Bill, the first major piece of legislation, were from organisations representing the 'interests of the white minority either in public or independent schools' (Education Portfolio Committee 1995 cited in Essop 2006).

However, the perceived absence of SADTU in education policy debates continues to this day, except in relation to teachers' appraisal and evaluation policies. In the latter case, SADTU has commissioned research, developed alternatives and engaged vigorously with the policy proposals of government. That appraisal and evaluation remain a contested policy area has played no small part in SADTU being blamed for the failures of the education system. The perception is that SADTU's interest in policy is limited primarily to issues that impact on members' conditions of service – that is, policies that speak to its unionist focus. In fact, the underlying reasons for the lack of proactive involvement in policy development are in part the continued lack of capacity – SADTU has a very small research division – and, more importantly, the absence of a clearly articulated vision for the transformation of the school system, which precludes the development of enabling policies and strategies. It seems clear that, going forward, SADTU needs to play a proactive rather than reactive role in the development of education policy. This means SADTU must articulate its vision for the transformation of the education system and develop enabling policies and strategies which contribute to and influence the policy development processes initiated by government. To achieve this, SADTU needs to build and strengthen its capacity to undertake policy research – indeed, the research division of SADTU should be the engine room of the organisation. The union also needs to develop internal mechanisms that enable the active participation of its members in policy development.

Moreover, it is in SADTU's interest to advocate for the institutionalisation of government policy development processes to facilitate the active participation of all role players and stakeholders. It should be emphasised that participation does not equal co-option. In any institutionalised policy process, SADTU and other stakeholders would maintain their independence and would also have to recognise that union interests may not necessarily get translated into policy, given other competing interests. Although the National Education Policy Act, promulgated in 1996, provides for the establishment of a National Education and Training Council (NETC) – which would be the institutional mechanism for stakeholder participation in policy – it has not been implemented to date. This suggests that government may have had second thoughts on stakeholder participation in the policy arena. But the question remains: why has SADTU not demanded the establishment of the NETC? Could it be that SADTU, as part of the ANC-led Alliance, enjoys a cosy relationship with government and benefits from the exclusion of other stakeholders?

Redefining SADTU's political role in the Tripartite Alliance

SADTU is linked to the ANC-led Alliance through its affiliation to COSATU, which, as argued in Chapter 2, has been both positive and negative. SADTU has benefited from the experience and expertise of COSATU in building strong trade unions and in collective bargaining. However, SADTU's preoccupation with predominantly unionist rather than professional concerns has been influenced in part by COSATU's primary focus, given its factory-floor membership, on industrial unionism. Indeed, there were concerns in COSATU when SADTU applied for membership that it may not be appropriate for a teachers' union, which needed to focus on both industrial and professional issues, to be affiliated to COSATU (discussed in Chapter 2). In accepting the affiliation of SADTU, Naidoo reflects that COSATU may have been 'responsible for blurring the line between professional and worker'

(Naidoo 2010: 330). This statement has proved prescient, as SADTU's unionist trajectory has demonstrated.

More importantly, COSATU's participation in the ANC-led Alliance has impacted adversely on SADTU. As one of the largest unions in COSATU, it has been dragged into the factional intrigues and political machinations of the Alliance at great cost to itself, as indicated by the fact that at least two SADTU leaders – Willie Madisha and Thobile Ntola – lost their positions under volatile circumstances as a result of these political battles (see Chapters 4 and 6). The adverse impact of these political battles on the delivery of education was expressed by an official in the Eastern Cape: 'Some comrades from SADTU won't cooperate with a Departmental official if the latter is seen to be part of the opposing faction' (cited in Govender 2017: 245).

Furthermore, except in relation to collective bargaining and accountability issues, SADTU's link to the Alliance has also resulted in a cosy relationship between the union and the governing party. SADTU rarely participates in civil society campaigns to hold government accountable as the union is not willing to be critical of government's failings, especially when the issues are raised by organisations not linked to the Tripartite Alliance. Likewise, government avoids taking policy decisions which put it on a collision path with SADTU, given the union's role in the electoral mobilisation of teachers in support of the ANC. This relationship is underscored in the MTT report, which notes that a number of senior public servants are also members of SADTU and unable to distinguish between their obligations to the public and to learners, in particular, and their loyalty to the union and the ANC as the governing party (DBE 2016). This symbiotic relationship ensures that any differences or conflict between SADTU and provincial departments, as the MTT argues, 'is rarely over policy, it is over power and control' (DBE 2016: 122).

The MTT claims that in six of the nine provinces, political authority in education is effectively in SADTU's control, which has enabled SADTU and other unions to block various policy initiatives (Van der Berg et al. 2016). Although SADTU contends that there is no evidence to support such claims, they place a burden on the union to defend its professional image (as discussed in Chapter 5). The six provinces identified by the MTT are all provinces which incorporated various ex-Bantustan education departments. This is important as the power and control that SADTU exerts is in part, as Sarah Meny-Gilbert (2019) argues, a legacy of education governance in the ex-Bantustans. The authority of the Bantustan education administrations was weak, and power and control were effectively held by traditional authorities through patronage networks, which included principals and teachers, as well as the conservative teacher associations. This patronage network, now including SADTU, continues to exert power and control over provincial education departments (Meny-Gilbert 2019). Moreover, this patronage relationship, as Karl von Holdt points out, tends to be accommodated in the democratisation of developing societies as the state is the key instrument for access to and redistribution of resources:

> The state constitutes the primary agency for redistribution and class formation, not only in the sense that it makes and implements policy for society, but also that it controls the biggest revenues, budgets, assets and payroll in a country, as well as access to . . . other lucrative opportunities. This makes the state itself the key site for black economic empowerment, and the constitutional constraints on the redistribution of assets in the private sector have driven the struggle for asset accumulation and elite formation into the state (Von Holdt 2013: 594).

This context – in which delivery of basic education is a provincial competence and there is a reciprocal benefit to being part of the ANC-led Alliance – helps explain the role of SADTU in exercising power and control in provincial education departments. The control of the education budget at the provincial level provides 'lucrative opportunities' not only through the selling of posts but, more importantly, through the manipulation of tenders, which is a key mechanism for asset accumulation.

The implications of unravelling the symbiotic relationship between SADTU and the ANC are enormous. It would require SADTU to delink from both COSATU – unless the latter withdraws from the Tripartite Alliance – as well as the ANC. This is unlikely given the broader social and political context and the benefits that both COSATU and SADTU derive as part of the Alliance. The alternative, as discussed in Chapters 3 and 6, is for SADTU to insist on its relative autonomy both within COSATU and the Tripartite Alliance, which would enable it to reassert its leadership as a social movement union. This would allow SADTU to provide direction and help to mobilise the broader community – in particular, poor and working-class communities – in support of building a quality education system. However, the fact that, to date, external pressure from parents and civil society demanding greater accountability has had limited impact on SADTU suggests that the pressure for change and charting a new direction must come from within – that is, from the union's membership. Whether this will happen is an open question.

Leadership and organisational renewal

The ability of SADTU to reclaim its roots and to reimagine its future as a social movement union committed to the transformation of the education system is dependent on the nature and character of its leaders. This requires the active presence of leaders in setting the vision, goals and strategic direction of the organisation and in mobilising, motivating and engaging members to achieve the vision and goals set (see Chapter 6). It requires transformational leaders who put the public good – the building of a quality education system – above the narrow and material interests of the organisation and its members. It also requires leaders with the ability to read the pulse of the citizenry at critical conjunctures in a country's history and engage in appropriate introspection and resetting of organisational goals and priorities to enable SADTU to remain socially and politically relevant.

Conclusion

This chapter has argued that the continued relevance of SADTU as a key role player and stakeholder in education is dependent on the union reimagining its role and reclaiming its historical promise in contributing to the transformation of the education system. This requires SADTU to reclaim its roots as a social movement union and take the lead in campaigning for the transformation of the education system through building and strengthening its alliance with civil society organisations. SADTU needs to reset the balance between unionism and professionalism and redefine its role in the Tripartite Alliance by insisting on its relative autonomy as an organisation. Achieving these ends requires SADTU to build and strengthen its leadership and organisational capacity.

Notes

1. The school was KwaBhekilanga Secondary School in Alexandra, a township on the outskirts of Johannesburg.
2. SACE's Code of Professional Ethics is available online at https://www.sace.org.za/assets/documents/uploads/sace_48175-2022-05-09-133889%20%20SACE%20%20ETHICS%20%2004%2005%202022%2012%20pager.pdf (accessed June 2018).

References

Department of Basic Education (DBE). 2016. 'Report of the Ministerial Task Team Appointed by Minister Angie Motshekga to Investigate Allegations into the Selling of Posts of Educators by Members of Teachers' Unions and Departmental Officials in Provincial Education Departments'. Pretoria: DBE.

Equal Education. 2018. 'Statement: Victory for EE and SA's Learners as Court Orders Government Must #FixTheNorms'. 19 July. https://equaleducation.org.za/2018/07/19/statement-victory-for-ee-and-sas-learners-as-court-orders-government-must-fixthenorms/ (accessed July 2018).

Essop, A. 2006. 'Education Policy in the Transition to Democracy in South Africa: Reflections of a Policy Activist Turned Bureaucrat'. Unpublished manuscript.

Gindin, J. and L. Finger. 2013. 'Promoting Education Quality: The Role of Teachers' Unions in Latin America'. Background paper commissioned for the Education for All Global Monitoring Report 2013/4, 'Teaching and Learning: Achieving Quality for All', UNESCO, Paris.

Govender, L. 2004. 'Teacher Unions, Policy Struggles and Educational Change, 1994–2004'. In *Changing Class: Education and Social Change in Post-apartheid South Africa*, edited by L. Chisholm. Cape Town: HSRC Press.

———. 2017. 'Teacher Unions and Transformation: More Political than Educational'. In *Reimagining Basic Education in South Africa: Lessons from the Eastern Cape*, edited by W. Ngoma, L. Govender and A. Mc Lennan. Johannesburg: MISTRA and Real African Publishers. Johannesburg

Mandela, N. 1990. 'Address to SADTU Launch'. 6 October. https://archive.nelsonmandela.org/index.php/za-com-mr-s-1124 (accessed June 2018).

McCollow, J. 2017. 'Teacher Unions'. In *Oxford Research Encyclopedia of Education*, edited by G. Noblit. DOI: 10.1093/acrefore/9780190264093.013.201.

Meny-Gilbert, S. 2019. 'State "Infrastructural Power" and the Bantustans: The Case of School Education in the Transkei and Ciskei'. *African Historical Review* 50: 1–2, 46–77. DOI: 10.1080/17532523.2019.1580422.

Naidoo, J. (2010) *Fighting for Justice: A Lifetime of Political and Social Activism*. Johannesburg: Picador Africa

Rensburg, I.L. 1996. 'Collective Identity and Public Policy: From Resistance to Reconstruction in South Africa, 1986–1995'. PhD thesis, Stanford University, Stanford, California.

Sang, A.K. 2002. 'Interest Groups in Education: Teachers' Perceptions of the Effectiveness of the Kenya National Union of Teachers'. PhD thesis, University of Cape Town.

Sibiya, T.P. 2017. 'Key Stakeholders' Experiences and Perspectives on the Role of the South African Democratic Teachers' Union (SADTU) in Education'. Master's dissertation, University of KwaZulu-Natal, Pietermaritzburg.

South African Democratic Teachers' Union (SADTU). 2014. 'Secretariat Report'. Eighth National Congress, 2–5 October.

Van der Berg, S., N. Spaull, G. Will, M. Gustaffson and J. Kotze. 2016. 'Identifying Binding Constraints in Education: Synthesis Report for the Programme to Support Pro-poor Policy Development (PSPPD)'. Research on Socio-Economic Policy, Department of Economics, University of Stellenbosch.

Von Holdt, K. 2013. 'South Africa: The Transition to Violent Democracy'. *Review of African Political Economy* 40(138): 589–604.

Conclusion

MICHAEL CROSS AND LOGAN GOVENDER

This book provides a critical assessment of SADTU's role in and contribution to the transformation of South Africa's education system. One of its objectives is to draw out the lessons that could inform and assist SADTU in charting a path for the future, taking into account the challenges that confront it as an organisation. These include teachers' working conditions rooted in the apartheid past as well as the new challenges flowing from globally inspired curriculum and assessment reforms and local political and socio-economic dynamics. However, beyond the organisational and policy lessons that have been highlighted, the book has foregrounded important conceptual and methodological insights, and issues relating to the researcher-subject relationship in the writing of organisational histories. Throughout the conceptualisation of the project, a major challenge was the need to reconcile what appeared to be passionate pragmatism of a social movement union – often blinded by historically laden emotional and ideological convictions – with the evidence uncovered from research. In this regard, as the research team engaged with data from interviews and documents, and interfaced with SADTU members in workshops or corridor commentary, different and contradictory signals were detected. There were those who expected the task to be a mere celebration of SADTU's successes. There were others who, for different reasons, saw an opportunity to expose and vilify the organisation. These issues pointed to the need for a critical perspective, higher degrees of intellectual vigilance and adequate epistemological breaks. As Michael Cross and Amasa Ndofirepi (2017: 84) point out:

Despite the claim of scientific objectivity, researchers can never separate themselves completely from their social condition because of their particular social location. As a result, they may not see beyond their own subjectivities and dispositions and may project these onto the object of enquiry rather than seeing more 'truthful' attributes, and may thus fail to fulfil the epistemic imperative of 'truthful knowledge'. Such distortions are more likely in societies that have undergone profound colonisation and racial segregation, as is the case with many African societies where coloniality of the social is inseparable from coloniality of knowledge and research at large.

While the underlying conceptual marker, professional unionism, remains critical to understanding teacher union agency and teacher union relations with the state, it is clear that the manner in which teacher unions appropriate notions of professionalism and unionism is historically bound. Thus, while unionism may provide the framework in the context of power relations, challenging undemocratic regimes and/or helping to advance teachers' economic needs, it has proven inadequate on its own as an ideological tool in the context of a developmental state, particularly a state whose social basis is made up of coalitions and an alliance of political parties with different and somewhat conflicting interests and ideologies. Professionalism, with its emphasis on expert knowledge, pedagogical skills, and continuous teacher education and development, has compelled teachers and their organisations towards collaboration and constructive engagement with the state in order to enhance their professional roles and education quality.

This move towards engagement takes place despite the material and infrastructure challenges faced by many teachers in relation to content knowledge, pedagogical skills and teacher development initiatives. The professional development endeavours are evident in the importance attached to the Teacher Union Collaboration (TUC) programmes involving several unions and government, as discussed in Chapter 3. Such initiatives confirm and support the claim that SADTU has made since its establishment in 1990: its members are professional workers and, in the context of apartheid's legacy, the teacher identity markers of worker and professional are intertwined. SADTU's insistence on the complementarity of these markers and its success in advancing the material interests and conditions of service of its members have been entrenched among and accepted by its members, and even by the conservative teacher associations that in the past eschewed any identification with unionism. Simultaneously, teacher unions today can claim some credit for advancing South Africa's teacher professionalisation project, specifically around teacher development. According to Jeanne Gamble (2010), about a decade ago professional development appeared to be stalling due to persistent challenges related to teachers' knowledge and competency, as well as public perceptions regarding the quality of teachers and the role of teacher unions. Adopting a longer historical lens, Linda Chisholm (2019: 173) suggests that teacher unions post-1994 have played an important role in teacher development work, and 'have striven to keep pace with as well as to influence and shape where possible new policy developments'.

However, contestation over both education and economic policies in South Africa, as elsewhere in the world (see, e.g., Bascia and Osmond 2013), constitutes a central feature of the teacher union-state relationship. This is so despite SADTU's affiliation to the Congress of South African Trade Union (COSATU), a member of the Tripartite Political Alliance led by the governing party, the African National Congress (ANC). In this regard, the key lesson for SADTU is the importance of maintaining and exercising its relative autonomy within the Alliance, as the interests of teachers may not always coincide with the interests of the governing party as reflected in the state and its institutions.

The importance of relative autonomy is that it underpins teacher union agency both in terms of protecting the rights of teachers as workers and professionals, and in advancing the public good relating to education quality. This dual role is captured by the notion of social movement unionism, which requires teacher unions to expand their alliances beyond political parties and union federations to include civil society organisations, especially those representing the poor and marginalised in society. It is precisely this dual role as a social movement union that characterised SADTU at its establishment and facilitated its early successes both in advancing the material interests of its members and in the struggle for the transformation of the education system. It is clear, therefore, that for SADTU to be relevant, and if it is to recapture its leading role in education transformation, it needs to forge closer working relations with civil society organisations such as Equal Education and Section27, and support their campaigns for education quality and social justice. Only when it does this can SADTU and its members claim to be organic intellectuals – not above the rest of society – or teacher-activists, as was the case during the liberation and pro-democracy struggles prior to 1994.

Moreover, as suggested in Chapter 3, SADTU should consider whether its affiliation to COSATU and its association with the ANC-led Tripartite Alliance are major constraining factors preventing the organisation from realising its full potential as a professional teachers' union that prioritises the promotion of education quality in the interest of the public good over the narrow labour and economic needs of teachers. This consideration by SADTU is especially pertinent in the context of the widespread critique of the South African basic education system's failure to adequately prepare learners for the twenty-first century, for which capable, dedicated and highly skilled teachers are essential.

At a methodological level, the power of historical enquiry has proved invaluable as an epistemological lens. There are two important dimensions to this methodology. The first is what a historical approach can reveal about the changing and dynamic nature of the development of social movements. As C. Wright Mills (1959: 156, cited in Govender 2008: 97) succinctly puts it: 'Sometimes there are quite new things in the world, which is to say that "history" does and "history" does not "repeat itself"; it depends on the social structure and upon the period whose history we are concerned with.'

SADTU's growth and development trajectory over the last 30 years represents a historical period, one in which the organisation had to build and then maintain its unionist ideology across historical epochs (pre- and post-apartheid) while gradually committing to a more professional agenda. This combination of old and new historical analysis has helped facilitate a clearer understanding of historical legacies and trends that have shaped teacher unions and teachers' identity and development in South Africa: from broader issues of teacher-state relations, organisational approaches and political alliances, to the more immediate organisational issues of policy capacity, membership competition and loss of critical leadership. 'Simply stated, history helps the policy researcher to maintain a critical perspective of the present' (Govender 2008: 97). It enables the researcher to make adequate connections between the theoretical foundations of our evolving understandings (discursive or epistemological) and the social domain (social action and social relations) (Cross and Ndofirepi 2017) – that is, to home in on the real-life practices of an organisation and its members, and help empower organisations to confront the pressing educational, social and economic challenges of the day.

The second dimension speaks to the value of maintaining a critical perspective in relation to the researcher-subject relationship in the course of the project. Given that SADTU had requested the writing of a book that charts its struggle for professional unionism over the last three decades, it is not surprising that the union would be concerned over potentially negative portrayals. So it came to pass at the writing retreats and workshops when careful distinctions had to be made between academic research, organisational biographies, propaganda and publicity accounts. Thus, the challenge of sustaining analytic objectivity in externally supported research arose on occasion, as it has arisen in similar contexts before.

In particular, given the colonial/apartheid legacy imbuing the South African context, the researcher-subject relationship has been conditioned by the imaginary boundaries of race, class, gender and other exclusionary forms of difference in society, with profound implications for how the researcher thinks about production and validation of knowledge. This important issue was flagged from the outset in engagement of the research team with SADTU in the preparation of the project. It was agreed by both sides that the project should not replicate in any form the dynamics inherited from apartheid-generated hierarchies of knowledge. More specifically, a critical perspective and necessary epistemological breaks were required, forged on the following methodological foundations:

awareness and deep understanding of the social experiences of SADTU and its members in key historical moments and in the context of social movements in South Africa; an understanding that, for the researcher, scholarship is in itself an exercise of power that can have disempowering consequences for the subjects; and the implications of the researchers' positioning in the intellectual field as well as individual dispositions and predispositions that could influence the research outcomes.

Overall, vigilance was needed against any unwarranted flirtation with discursive, epistemological or methodological bias that compromises the value of evidence and the ethical and political responsibility of the researcher. Precautions were taken through dialogue, criticism and analytical introspection to guard against theoretical analysis that does not speak to the individual and collective experiences of SADTU members in their interface with other teachers, the state and civil society organisations. Similarly, of central importance to the researchers was shielding themselves against passion without theory or narrative without analysis by acknowledging that the narratives of success, including celebrations of achievements, and the narratives of failure obtained from SADTU informants remained pointless without deeper understanding of the meanings they articulated. Repeated workshops provided a privileged space for the enactment of these epistemological breaks, which represent crucial steps in analytical rigour.

Finally, and to reflect on questions raised in the Introduction to this book: Where to now for teacher unions? How are teachers and their organisations responding to new challenges, and what possibilities lie ahead? The following prognosis is made. Certainly, in the face of a mounting external accountability regime, teacher unions will continue to invoke both militant and professional strategies in defence of their autonomy, and in demanding a stake in policy-making. In this context, teachers are being exhorted by government and education stakeholders to assume traditional professional roles that emphasise service and loyalty in pursuit of quality education. It is hardly surprising, then, that there is evidence of an emerging teacher accountability counterculture, given the resistance to teachers' performance appraisal and evaluation mechanisms, which has a long history in South Africa going back to the days of Bantu Education. Teacher unions and government must resolve this seemingly impossible contradiction. Otherwise, it will continue to fracture all the good work that is being done to improve the quality of education. In particular, it is critical to review teacher accountability, assessment and development policies that are not responsive to the continuing poor working conditions of teachers, especially in many township and rural communities.

However, in the present local and global conjuncture, teacher unions will need to rise above narrow education and teachers' economic concerns to confront broader issues affecting society. In this regard, teacher unions need to demonstrate leadership and creativity to help calibrate an education system that is responsive to new (and some old) social, economic and development demands. These include, among others, the re-visioning of education prompted by global pandemics, climate-change effects, the Fourth Industrial Revolution, the national reading and literacy crisis, and the deepening scourge of gender-based violence and xenophobia. Teacher unionism in the twenty-first century will not only have to straddle the traditional unionism versus professionalism divide, but will also need to embrace new challenges, which have critical implications for school curricula and classroom pedagogy practices, the social fabric of communities, and the economic growth and prosperity of nation states. Teacher unions' strategies and programmes will thus need re-engineering if they are to remain relevant in the twenty-first century.

In the South African context, SADTU and its fraternal counterparts need look no further than the national reading and literacy crisis, not just for English as lingua franca, but equally in the African home languages, to find a programme worth investing in. The dearth of teachers' knowledge and skills in language teaching, especially in the early foundation phases of schooling, is well documented, as is its importance to learner achievement in later years. Moreover, evidence from projects such as the National Education Collaboration Trust's Primary School Reading Improvement Project (PSRIP) continues to underscore the critical role of qualified and experienced teachers (NECT n.d.). It should be kept front of mind that language competence is the foundation on which creation and innovation thrive, not only in the natural sciences and humanities, but also in the world of technology and robotics.

References

Bascia, N. and P. Osmond. 2013. *Teacher Union-Governmental Relations in the Context of Educational Reform*. Brussels: Education International.

Chisholm, L. 2019. *Teacher Preparation in South Africa: History, Policy and Future Directions*. Bingley, West Yorkshire: Emerald Publishing.

Cross, M. and A. Ndofirepi. 2017. 'Critical Scholarship in South Africa: Considerations of Epistemology, Theory and Method'. In *Knowledge and Change in African Universities*, edited by M. Cross and A. Ndofirepi. Rotterdam: Sense Publishers.

Gamble, J. 2010. *Teacher Professionalism: A Literature Review*. Johannesburg: JET Education Services.

Govender, L.V. 2008. 'Teachers' Participation in Policy Making: The Case of the South African Schools Act'. PhD thesis, University of the Witwatersrand, Johannesburg.

National Education Collaboration Trust (NECT). n.d. 'Primary School Reading Improvement Programme: South Africa Becomes a Nation of Active Readers. A Condition Necessary for Improved Learner Achievement, Active Citizenry and Democracy'. https://nect.org.za/publications/case-studies/psrip_booklet.pdf/view (accessed 1 November 2022).

Index

Abrahams, Glen 137
Action Plan 2014 (Department of Education) 106
African Teachers' Association of South Africa (ATASA) 31, 32, 34, 37, 38, 41, 69, 90, 125, 152 n.3
All Africa Teachers' Organisation (AATO) 37, 118
Amnesty International 3-4
Annual National Assessments 106, 111, 170
Apartheid Museum (Johannesburg) 175
Azanian Confederation of Trade Unions (AZACTU) 71

Bantu Education 27, 34, 184, 188
Bantu Education Act (1953) 31, 90
Bantustans 49-50, 128-9, 230
Bengu, Sibusiso 138
Benin 11
Benoni Teachers' Union (BETU) 33
Bill of Rights for Teachers 46, 47
Bopape, David 30
Brijraj, Rej 133
business unionism *see* SADTU, and corruption

cadre deployment *see* SADTU, and cadre deployment and nepotism
Canada 177

Cape African Teachers' Association (CATA) 31
Cape Teachers' Professional Association (CTPA) 40, 70
Carelse, Vivian 197
Centre for Education Policy Development (CEPD) 139, 140, 226
Child Labour Network 140
Ciskei Teachers' Union (CTU) 126-7
civil society 9, 12, 87-8, 219, 231
climate change 241
collective bargaining 45, 46, 47, 53, 160, 165, 222
collective identity 28, 29, 43
Coloured Teachers' Association 30
Committee on Teacher Education Policy (COTEP) 98, 113 n.6
Congress Alliance 82 n.1
Congress for a Democratic South Africa (CODESA) 92, 99
Congress of South African Trade Unions (COSATU) 27, 37, 38, 39, 40, 70-1, 72-4, 76, 184
corruption *see* SADTU, and corruption
Council for Quality Assurance in General and Further Education and Training in South Africa *see* Umalusi
Council of Unions of South Africa (CUSA) 71

243

Covid-19 pandemic 192, 211
Curriculum 2005 (C2005) 101–3

democratic centralism *see* SADTU, and democratic centralism
Democratic Teachers' Union (DETU) 33, 38, 188–9
Department of Basic Education (DBE) 113 n.12, 168, 173, 194, 225–6
Dliwayo, Muziwamdoda 128–9
Dolopi, Nkosana 185, 196–7, 198, 209

early childhood development 4, 43
East London Progressive Teachers' Union (ELPTU) 33
Education Alliance (ANC) 87, 94–5, 96, 97, 98, 99, 111
Education Collaborative Framework (ECF) 24 n.4
Education for an Aware South Africa (EDASA) 33, 38
Education International 42, 108, 113 n.11, 118, 127, 130, 146, 152 n.1, 152 n.6, 196, 220
Education Labour Relations Act (1993) 47, 53, 93, 196
Education Labour Relations Council (ELRC) 6, 8, 47, 53, 78, 93, 104, 105, 107, 130, 165, 168, 196
Education Study Group (ANC) 95, 97, 111, 196, 227
Education, Training and Development Practices Sector Education and Training Authority (ETDP SETA) 108
Educational Policy Unit (Wits) 139, 140
Educators' Voice 145
e-learning 6
Equal Education 4, 174, 219, 238
examinations 161, 163

Federal Council of Teachers' Associations 30
Federation of South African Trade Unions (FOSATU) 71, 77–8
Fourth Industrial Revolution 211, 241
Freedom Charter 69–70, 71, 193

Gender Commission 140
gender-based violence 23, 191, 192, 219, 241
global education reform movement (GERM) 217
Govender, Dhaya 133
government schools
    apartheid 35–6, 44–5, 215
    and corruption 163
    finance 164
    infrastructure and facilities 3–5, 6, 100, 174, 218, 219
    outcomes 157, 216
    public perceptions of 163
    and race 4
    statistics 5
Gramsci, Antonio 87–8
Growth, Employment and Redistribution (GEAR) programme 94, 200
Gutsy, John 129

Harare Accord on Teacher Unity (1988) 38, 71–2, 212 n.16
hegemony (concept of) 87–8, 111
Hindle, Duncan 113 n.10, 152 n.9, 197, 198, 204
history (in school curriculum) 107, 175
HIV/AIDS 147
Human Sciences Research Council (HSRC) 140

Implementation Plan for Education and Training (IPET, 1994) 92, 196
independent schools 5

Indian Teachers' Association of South Africa *see* Teachers' Association of South Africa
inspectors and subject advisers 48-9, 91
Integrated Quality Management System (IQMS) 105-6, 171, 176
Integrated Strategic Planning Framework for Teacher Education and Development in South Africa (ISPFTED) 108
International Federation of Free Teachers' Unions (IFFTU) *see* Education International

Kenya 89, 221
Khumalo, Squire 197
KwaBhekilanga Secondary School (Alexandra) 232 n.1
KwaMashu (Durban) 39
kwaThema Teachers' Union (KWATU) 33

labour movement 58, 77-8, 79, 193
Labour Relations Act (LRA, 1995) 165
Latin America 11, 219, 224
leadership 186-8
Learner Transport Policy 4
learners
    assessment and performance 162, 169; *see also* SADTU, and learner assessment
    dropout rate 5-6
    interests and rights of 158, 176, 177
Lehoko, Khetsi 70
liberation movements 188
literacy 241-2

Mabandla, B.B. 197
Madisha, William Mothipa (Willie) 134, 201, 229
Mafunda, Mkhuseli 144, 152 n.2
Makhura, David 203
Malawi 11

Maluleke, Mugwena 190-1, 193-4, 195, 202, 204-5, 206, 207, 208, 209
Mamelodi Teachers' Union (MATU) 32
managerialism 16-17
Mandela, Nelson 54, 215-16
Maphila, Magope 186, 206-7
Mapungubwe Institute for Strategic Reflection (MISTRA) 5
Masegela, George 153 n.12
Mass Democratic Movement (MDM) 38-9, 62 n.21, 69, 70, 71, 86, 92, 189, 196, 205, 215, 227
mathematics (in school curriculum) 175
Matsepe, David 192
Mbeki, Thabo 200, 201
Mda, A.P. 30
Mdladlana, Membathisi Shepherd 127, 132, 188, 194, 196, 197, 198, 199, 209, 212 n.3
mission education 15
Mkulesi, Nombule 133
Mosoeka, Ronnie 153 n.12
Mothopeng, Zeph 31, 60 n.1
Mozambique 199
Mphahlele, Es'kia 31, 60 n.1
Mpowane, Pinkie 197
Mseleku, Thami 198
Mtshali, Lionel 129
Mufamadi, Sydney 72

Naicker, Poobie 127
Naidoo, Jay 70, 216
Natal African Teachers' Union (NATU) 152 n.3
Natal Indian Teachers' Society (NITS) 30
National Council of Trade Unions (NACTU) 71
National Curriculum Assessment Task Team 107

National Democratic Revolution
  (NDR) 77
National Education and Training
  Forum (NETF) 54, 139, 196
National Education Collaboration
  Trust (NECT) 5, 6, 175
National Education Consultative
  Conference (1985) 32
National Education Crisis/
  Coordinating Committee
  (NECC) 31-2, 34, 37, 38, 69, 72,
  86, 91, 92, 95, 184, 189, 218
National Education Policy Act (1996)
  288
National Education Policy Initiative
  (NEPI) 92, 113 n.1, 196
National Educational and Training
  Council (NETC) 228
National Educational Union of South
  Africa (NEUSA) 29, 32, 34, 38,
  119
National Labour and Economic
  Development Institute
  (NALEDI) 140
National Professional Teachers'
  Organisation of South Africa
  (NAPTOSA) 11, 41-2, 46,
  62 n.31, 76, 86, 91, 97, 99-101,
  102, 105, 108, 120, 127, 130,
  140, 150, 152 n.3, 168, 220, 222
National Teacher Unity Forum
  (NTUF) 20, 39-40, 48-9, 51, 52,
  69, 70, 71-2, 76, 117, 131,
  212 n.16, 216
National Teachers' Union (NATU)
  108, 113 n.13, 168
National Union of Teachers (NUT,
  UK) 160
Native Educational Association 27, 30
Ndaba, Papa 153 n.13
Ndelu, Brenda 144, 152 n.2
Nene, Samora 128
nepotism see SADTU, and cadre
  deployment and nepotism

New Teacher 145
Nkondo, Curtis 188
Nkosi, Mxolisi 96
Norms and Standards for Educators
  (2000) 8, 98
Northern Transvaal Teachers' Union
  (NOTU) 33
Ntola, Thobile 134, 135, 201, 202, 229
Nxesi, Thulas 113 n.10, 133, 188, 197
Nzimande, Blade 95, 98, 103

outcomes-based education (OBE)
  101-3, 163

pandemics 112, 192, 241
patronage 49, 230
people's education 32, 34, 35, 38, 86
people's power 33, 34-5, 38, 43
performance management *see* teachers,
  performance management
Policy Framework for Education and
  Training (ANC, Yellow Book,
  1994) 92, 196, 226
Primary School Reading Improvement
  Project (PSRIP, National
  Education Collaboration Trust)
  241-2
principals 166, 171, 174, 177
private schools *see* independent schools
professional capital 17
Professional Educators' Union (PEU)
  108, 113 n.13
professional learning communities
  (PLCs) 175-6
professional unionism 21, 89, 123,
  144, 158, 176-7, 236; *see also*
  SADTU, and professional
  unionism
Progressive Teachers' League (PTL) 38
Progressive Teachers' Union (PTU)
  33, 38
public schools *see* government schools

reading 5, 23, 241
Reconstruction and Development
 Programme (RDP) 196
Revised National Curriculum
 Statement (RNCS) 103

SADTU (South African Democratic
 Teachers' Union)
 2030 Vision 118, 121-2, 137
 and ANC *see* and Tripartite Alliance
 and Bantustans 128-9
 and business unionism *see*
  corruption
 and cadre deployment and
  nepotism 166, 167-8, 170
 Code of Professional Conduct 224
 constitution and structure 40, 57,
  74-5, 92-3, 101, 117, 124-6,
  130-1, 138, 140-1, 144, 147,
  152 n.8, 190-1, 192, 193, 206-7,
  235-6, 239-40
 and corruption 166-7, 170, 201,
  202, 208, 225-6, 230
 and COSATU *see* and Tripartite
  Alliance
 and democratic centralism 134-5,
  144
 disciplining of members 172-3, 226
 disruption and violence of members
  165-6, 203, 208-9, 210-11, 216
 Eastern Cape 134-5, 141
 and education departments 170,
  171-2, 173, 229-30
 factional battles 134-5, 141, 151,
  200, 201, 202, 229
 finance 127, 146, 151, 153 n.18
 formation and development 1,
  9-10, 27, 28-9, 30, 40-1, 42,
  43, 58-60, 69, 76, 81-2, 91, 117,
  123-30, 132, 168-9, 184-5,
  188-91, 193-4, 195, 197, 198-9,
  215-16, 218, 221, 238-9
 Gauteng 141
 and gender 147-9, 191-2, 197,
  212 n.7
 history *see* formation and
  development
 lack of professional ethos 109
 leadership and leaders 40-1, 57-8,
  80, 120, 124-5, 132-4, 144, 148,
  151, 183-5, 186, 188, 190-1,
  192, 193-4, 195, 197-8, 199-
  200, 201-4, 205, 206-8, 209-10,
  211, 216, 218, 231-2
 and learner assessment 106, 107,
  111, 170
 membership 10, 41, 45, 62 n.31, 74,
  120, 130, 140-1, 144, 145, 150,
  204, 222
 national congresses 46, 48, 50, 52,
  55-6, 118, 121, 124, 131, 134,
  135-6, 137, 205, 215-16, 221-2
 and negotiations 158, 159, 194
 and non-racialism 44-5, 47-8, 74
 North West province 141
 organisational history *see*
  constitution and structure
 and planning and policy 53-4,
  85-6, 87, 88, 90, 92-3, 94-104,
  106-7, 110, 111-12, 131, 133,
  135-6, 137-40, 142-4, 195,
  196-8, 205, 218, 226-8
 and professional unionism 28, 47,
  51-3, 75-6, 82, 87, 89-90, 96,
  98, 101, 106, 108, 110, 112, 117,
  118-19, 122-3, 125, 127, 136-7,
  142, 144-5, 149-52, 157-8,
  164-5, 169, 174, 176-7, 185, 201,
  216, 217, 218, 220, 221-4, 236-7
 public perception of 1, 6, 157, 164,
  165, 168, 169-70, 176, 185, 186,
  203, 206, 208, 210, 216-17, 222,
  223, 227
 recognition of 41, 45-6, 47, 56, 93,
  117, 119, 146, 222
 and SACE 172, 203, 226
 and SACP *see* and Tripartite
  Alliance

and salaries and conditions 54-6, 80, 100, 112, 136, 195-6
as social movement 9, 10, 219-20, 231-2, 235, 237-8
and state 2-3, 6-7, 9, 12, 15, 118, 119, 135-6; *see also* and planning and policy
and strikes and protest 54-5, 56-7, 64 n.82, 109, 137, 141, 150, 158, 159, 165, 173-4, 185, 194, 203, 209, 216, 222, 223
and teacher accountability, appraisal and evaluation 48-51, 104-6, 111, 112, 135, 164, 169-70, 171, 173, 223, 227, 240-1
and technology 145, 150, 152
and transformation 42-4, 48-9, 53, 81, 82, 96-8
and Tripartite Alliance 2, 9, 11, 40, 51-2, 57, 69, 70, 71, 73, 74-5, 76-81, 86-7, 90, 93-4, 111, 112, 119, 120, 131-2, 141, 142, 150, 157, 172, 174, 193, 198, 205-6, 211, 217, 218, 222, 228-9, 230-1, 232, 237-8
SADTU Curtis Nkondo Professional Development Institute (SCNPDI) 107-8, 109, 137, 144, 174-5, 203, 224
SADTU Investment Holding (SIHOLD) 146, 151
SADTU Village (Kempton Park) 146
school governing bodies (SGBs) 96, 97-8, 164
schools *see* government schools; independent schools
science (in school curriculum) 175
Section27 174, 219, 238
Senior Certificate 163
Seoposengwe, Chris 70
Sifuba, Zanele 153 n.12
Sithole, Salome 133
social movements 33, 34-5, 57-8, 186-7, 215, 238

Soobrayan, Bobby 104
South African Communist Party (SACP) 2, 71
South African Congress of Trade Unions (SACTU) 37
South African Council of Educators (SACE) 98, 108, 132, 172, 224
South African Democratic Teachers' Union *see* SADTU
South African Schools Act (1996) 11, 96, 97, 99, 101, 103, 111, 135, 227
South African Workers' Union (SAWU) 71
Southern African Development Community (SADC) 220
Soweto uprising (1976) 31, 188
Suid-Afrikaanse Onderwysers Unie (SAOU) 102, 108, 113 n.9, 130, 140, 152 n.7
Swartz, Ronald 124, 152 n.9, 188, 212 n.3

teacher associations 31, 32, 36, 37, 39, 40, 41, 44, 45, 46, 52, 70, 72, 73, 74, 75-6, 81, 86, 91, 152 n.6, 189, 220, 230, 237
Teacher Union Collaboration (TUC) programmes 108-9, 174, 236
teacher unions
  banning of 36
  history of 27, 30-4, 35, 36-40, 61 n.20, 160
  perception and support of 1, 2, 6, 217
  and professionalism 23, 88-9, 159-61, 220-1, 236, 237
  and state 2, 6-7, 9, 10-12, 85, 88-9, 110-11, 112, 136, 226
teachers
  and accountability 1-2, 162-3, 173, 175, 176, 177, 241
  apartheid-era 90-1, 164, 189

appointment of 164
in the community 189
and GEAR 200-1
Grade R 107
performance management 8, 15, 89, 91, 104
as professionals 157-8, 159, 161-2, 163, 172
radicalised 35
salaries and conditions 8, 27, 30, 36, 61 n.16, 78, 94, 165
training of 169, 174-5
unity 72
women 147-8
as workers 15-16, 158, 161, 162
see also teaching profession
Teachers' Action Committee (TAC) 33
Teachers' Association of South Africa (TASA) 31, 38, 62 n.28, 62 n.31, 75, 90, 125, 126, 127, 152 n.3
Teachers' Code of Conduct 46, 47
Teachers' Federal Council (TFC) 30, 31, 38, 41, 72, 152 n.3
Teachers' Journal (SADTU) 107, 109-10, 145, 224
Teachers' League of South Africa 30
teaching profession
  attributes and identity 12-13, 14-15, 16-18
  class position 78, 122
  democratised 17-18, 216
  as essential service 208-9, 223
  and ethics 224-5
  history of 8, 13-14
  see also teachers
theory without passion 10
trade unions *see* labour movement
transformational leadership *see* leadership
Transkei Teachers' Association (TTA) 126
Transvaal African Teachers' Association (TATA) 30, 31

Transvaal United African Teachers' Association (TUASA) 40, 152 n.3
Tripartite Alliance 71, 80, 82 n.1; *see also* SADTU, and Tripartite Alliance
Tsajwa, Lawrence 153 n.13

Uganda Teachers' Association 11
Umalusi 23 n.2
Union of Teachers' Associations of South Africa (UTASA) 31, 38, 46, 62 n.28, 90, 125, 126, 127, 152 n.3
United Democratic Front (UDF) 27, 31, 32, 37, 70-1, 184
United Kingdom 159, 160, 177
United States 159, 160, 177

Vadi, Ismael 197, 198
Van den Heever, Randall 133, 196, 197, 198
Vavi, Zwelinzima 201

Western Cape Teachers' Union (WECTU) 29, 32-3, 38, 188-9
Whole School Evaluation (WSE) 105
World Confederation of Organizations of the Teaching Profession (WCOTP) 37, 39, 42, 127, 152 n.6; *see also* Education International

xenophobia 4, 23, 219, 241

Yellow Book *see* Policy Framework for Education and Training

Zimbabwe Teachers' Association (ZIMTA) 37
Zuma, Jacob 200, 201

Printed and bound by CPI Group (UK) Ltd, Croydon, CR0 4YY
22/04/2026

14866397-0004